INTERPRETATIONS OF AMERICAN HISTORY

ANTE-BELLUM REFORM

INTERPRETATIONS OF AMERICAN HISTORY

★ ★ ★ JOHN HIGHAM AND BRADFORD PERKINS, EDITORS

ANTE-BELLUM REFORM

EDITED BY
DAVID BRION DAVIS
Cornell University

HARPER & ROW, PUBLISHERS
NEW YORK, EVANSTON, AND LONDON

CONTENTS

EDITORS' INTRODUCTION

This volume—and companions in the series, "Interpretations of American History"—makes a special effort to cope with one of the basic dilemmas confronting every student of history. On the one hand, historical knowledge shares a characteristic common to all appraisals of human affairs. It is partial and selective. It picks out some features and facts of a situation while ignoring others that may be equally pertinent. The more selective an interpretation is, the more memorable and widely applicable it can be. On the other hand, history has to provide what nothing else does: a total estimate, a multifaceted synthesis, of man's experience in particular times and places. To study history, therefore, is to strive simultaneously for a clear, selective focus and for an integrated, over-all view.

In that spirit, each volume of the series aims to resolve the varied literature on a major topic or event into a meaningful whole. One interpretation, we believe, does not deserve as much of a student's attention as another simply because they are in conflict. Instead of contriving a balance between opposing views, or choosing polemical material simply to create an appearance of controversy, Professor Davis has exercised his own judgment on the relative importance of different aspects or interpretations of a problem. We have asked him to select some of what he considers the best, most persuasive writings bearing on ante-bellum reform, indicating in the introductory essay and headnotes his reasons for considering these accounts convincing or significant. When appropriate, he has also brought out the relation between older and more recent approaches to the subject. The editor's own competence and experience in the field enable him to provide a sense of order and to indicate the evolution and complexity of interpretations. He is, then, like other editors in this series, an informed participant rather than a mere observer, a student sharing with other students the results of his own investigations of the literature on a crucial phase of American development.

JOHN HIGHAM
BRADFORD PERKINS

ANTE-BELLUM REFORM

ANTI-BELLUM REFORM

INTRODUCTION

Although American historians have generally subscribed to a liberal ideology and have shown a favorable attitude toward change, material improvement, and the extension of human rights, they have long displayed a certain uneasiness and awkwardness in their treatment of ante-bellum reform. Like Ralph Waldo Emerson, in the first selection of this book, they have usually applauded the *goals* of the early reformers; yet, they have been put off by the same reformers' extremism, fanaticism, eccentricity, and contentiousness. As a result, even in our best textbooks and general histories of the period, discussions of reform seem curiously equivocal and disjointed. And while we profit from an increasing number of excellent studies of individual reforms and reformers, we still lack a satisfactory overall treatment of the subject.

There are a number of reasons why ante-bellum reform has been uncongenial to twentieth-century scholars. Most of the early reformers were devout Protestants whose public expressions of piety have appeared sanctimonious to an age that, at least until the 1960s, has equated social progress with secular, rational thought. If the distinctive traits of ante-bellum reform were its moral fundamentalism and radical comprehensiveness, as Henry Steele Commager has observed, then it has been all the more alien to a society which is inclined to dismiss ethical arguments as subjective "value judgments," and which places a high premium on pragmatic solutions to limited and concrete problems. Then, too, the sentimental romanticism and tender sensitivity to human suffering, which permeated the writings of early reformers, have been unpalatable to men suspicious of emotion and hardened to human atrocity. Since the antislavery movement came to dominate all other reforms, and was inextricably linked with the coming of the Civil War, the subject of reform has unavoidably been tied to questions of guilt and responsibility for our greatest national trauma. The failure of the Eighteenth Amendment and a resulting consensus that alcoholism is an individual problem have created still another barrier to understanding the host of ante-bellum reformers who saw temperance as the grand route to national virtue and happiness. We still live in the wake of the great rebellion against the Genteel Tradition, which reflected the full flush of early New England idealism only as a sickly afterglow. We are still repulsed by the sour and cramped spirit of latter-day "reformers" who have sought to outlaw sex, art, and liquor. And if these more recent censors and moralists have differed markedly from their spiritual ancestors of the 1830s and 1840s, they have shared a sense of irrepressible outrage over personal sin. To a society at once permissive and tough-minded, no traits appear more offensive and dangerous than sentimental piety and moral self-righteousness.

Yet it is difficult to deny the importance of the social ferment and agitation, the utopian hopes and profound dissatisfaction that swept over America in the decades before the Civil War. The main issues raised by the reformers are still very much alive. We have by no means solved the problems of racial and sexual discrimination. We still dream of extending the intimate love of the private family to a wider circle of social relationships, and yet debate, as did the ante-bellum reformers, the justifications for monogamous marriage, the proper role of woman, and the best methods of child-rearing. We are still perplexed by the discrepancy between our penal institutions and our ideal of reforming and rehabilitating criminals. We argue endlessly over the most effective methods for redeeming what Theodore Parker called "the dangerous classes of society" and what we now term "the culturally deprived." If we are usually more cynical than the ante-bellum reformers, we have not abandoned their dream of a world without war. Indeed, the radical protest movements of the 1960s have hauntingly echoed the ante-bellum ideal of nonresistance, the "come-outer" spirit of disengagement from a sinful society, and the reliance on individual conscience as opposed to all forms of corporate and bureaucratic power.

In short, we continue to believe that without social criticism a nation is doomed to complacency, stultification, and hardening injustice. We like to think that American history is something more than a record of diverse groups and interests struggling for power. And if we are to find in our heritage some trace of the unfolding of an ideal, some evidence, however imperfect, of a continuing tradition of discontent, of repudiating the status quo, of insisting that things can and should be better, then we must see the ante-bellum reformers in part as they saw themselves: as the legitimate heirs of the American Revolution, as champions of the ideals of the Declaration of Independence.

This was the dominant view of the abolitionists, at least, among the nineteenth-century nationalistic historians who sought to justify the North's victory in the Civil War. But these same historians made the abolitionists appear as the mere vehicles of inevitable progress, which was identified with the broad forces of nationalism and increasing liberty. This not only obscured the reformers' role as social critics, but tended to associate them with the new status quo and its conservative defenders, and made them appear as the precursors of Grantism and the betrayers of Jeffersonian democracy. It is true that the temperance and feminist movements, which gained renewed vigor in the early twentieth century, stimulated a certain interest in the first leaders of such reforms. But as reform itself became more pragmatic and institutional in approach, it was often necessary to repudiate the supposedly naïve and visionary methods of the past.

Serious study of early reform movements required a degree of detachment that could come only with the passage of time. It also required a broadened view of the proper subject matter of history, which until the 1920s was largely conceived in terms of political, economic, and constitutional development. It was in the 1920s and 1930s that such scholars as Arthur M. Schlesinger, Merle Curti, Carl Russell Fish, Gilbert H. Barnes, and John Allen Krout wrote their pioneering accounts of social movements, and elevated social history to a high level of academic respectability. By and large their studies were objective and, if negative toward what Allan Nevins has termed the "extravagances" of many reformers, were sympathetic in their general evaluations.

In these same decades the image of ante-bellum reform was darkened by an intensifying debate over the causes and implications of the Civil War. This is not the place to review the vast controversial literature on this subject. It is sufficient to note that a group of extremely able and persuasive historians, many of whom were of Southern origin, developed the thesis that the Civil War had not been an inevitable conflict between two incompatible civilizations, that it had not been desired by the people in either the North or South, that it had nothing to do with slavery, which was a benign and dying institution, and that it had solved no problems. This view of the Civil War as an unmitigated and avoidable tragedy had great appeal to a generation that had come to see the First World War as a similar tragedy caused by malicious propaganda, mass hysteria, and the plotting of politicians and munitions makers. And in the eyes of Frank L. Owsley, Charles W. Ramsdell, Arthur Y. Lloyd, James G. Randall, and Avery Craven, the abolitionists were irresponsible fanatics who, along with the Southern "fire-eaters," helped to drive the nation to madness.

This so-called "revisionist" picture of abolitionist agitators drew much support from Gilbert H. Barnes's *The Antislavery Impulse, 1830–1844* (1933), one of the first studies to explore both the psychology of ante-bellum reform and its basis in revivalistic religion. Barnes himself was by no means an apologist for the South or its peculiar institution, and his pioneering book contributed some of our most prevalent ideas concerning the antislavery movement. It was Barnes (who oddly enough was an economist himself) who helped to divert historians' attention from economic interest to the effects of religious revivalism, who established a dichotomy between New England and Midwestern abolitionism, and who popularized a distinction between supposedly practical and conscientious abolitionists such as Theodore D. Weld and James G. Birney, and the irresponsible fanatics such as Garrison.

The first modern attempt to relate all the ante-bellum reform movements to the social and religious developments of the age was Alice Felt Tyler's *Freedom's Ferment* (1944). In Mrs. Tyler's view, religious revivalism, Transcendentalism, Jeffersonian rationalism, and frontier democracy all merged to create an era of ferment, of restlessness, and of exuberant confidence in man's ability to perfect human institutions. Unfortunately, these concepts acquired little precision as Mrs. Tyler applied them to specific movements, and for the most part she was content with a textbookish survey of popular cults, utopias, and reform movements. A more successful integration of reform movements with the economic and social history of a limited region was Whitney Cross's *The Burned-Over District* (1950), which related the religious revivals of Charles Grandison Finney and the subsequent social fervor to economic dislocations and denominational competition in upstate New York.

By the 1940s and 1950s ante-bellum reform began attracting the attention of some of America's most eminent historians, such as Allan Nevins, Merle Curti, and Arthur M. Schlesinger, who sought to find common themes and characteristics in the seemingly diverse movements. Their interpretations have helped to crystallize the image of early reform as it is found in standard textbooks and survey courses in American history. However successful these new syntheses were in listing common traits of the various movements, they were distressingly ambiguous on a number of crucial matters such as the sources of reform ideology, the motives of reformers, the relative radicalism or conservatism of the movements, and their ultimate effect on public opinion and legislation. It is well to give brief consideration to each of these questions.

In his *The American as Reformer* (1950), Arthur M. Schlesinger pictured all American reform as part of a liberal tradition derived from the philosophy of the Enlightenment and from the Protestant concern for public welfare and individual moral responsibility. According to Merle Curti, in *The Growth of American Thought* (1943), the main "roots" of American reform were to be found first in the Enlightenment's faith in the goodness of man and his capacity for progressing through the use of reason toward a heavenly city on earth; and second, in a liberal, humanitarian religion which also preached the goodness of man and his capacity for perfection by following the example of Christ. In an effort to show how ideas interacted with changing social conditions, Curti suggested that the new faith in change and improvement was related to the needs of a rising middle class seeking release from commercial and political restraints. The ideas of progress and perfectibility were instruments well-adapted to the fluid conditions of American life. There was a natural fit between the needs of America in an era of westward expansion and urban growth and the newer currents of imported doctrine, such as romanticism, Transcendentalism, and utilitarianism.

As plausible as this functionalist approach might seem, especially to a generation that thought of ideas as instruments or weapons tooled to the needs of particular classes, it left much unexplained. To describe all reform as part of the widening spirit of democracy leads to a blurring of important distinctions and makes it extremely difficult to account for the large number of reformers who believed in man's inherent depravity, or for radical abolitionists who repudiated majority rule, or for anti-slavery champions like Beriah Green who called for "Heaven-anointed" leaders who would rule by "divine right." Obviously reformers drew on ideas and beliefs that we associate with the Enlightenment or with evangelical revivalism; but why did these "streams" or "roots" converge when they did? Charles and Mary Beard, in their *The Rise of American Civilization* (rev. ed., 1940), pointed out that the abolitionists had no monopoly on evangelical religion or the Declaration of Independence. Not only were there thousands of Americans who never supported a reform movement but who drew moral and intellectual nourishment from the supposed "roots" of reform; there were also deeply conservative elements to both the Enlightenment and the revivals. In fact, the great object of American revivalists from Jonathan Edwards to Billy Graham has not been to perfect society but to save men's souls by arousing them to a full awareness of their involvement in sin. Insofar as the Enlightenment encouraged respect for balance, order, and rational moderation, it led to a frame of mind that could only be repelled by the uncompromising moralism of most reformers of the ante-bellum period. Moreover, traditional institutions could be defended as well as condemned by the principle of utility or the philosophy of natural rights. If one agreed with some eighteenth-century thinkers that men were governed by self-interest and that maximum wealth and harmony depended on minimum interference with individual desires and actions, it would appear that most reformers were upsetting the balance of nature and working to extinguish basic liberties. The harshest critics of reform were frequently devout Christians or good disciples of the Enlightenment.

Since the moral and intellectual sources seem inadequate to explain the emergence of reform at a particular time, it is reasonable to look at the motives of the reformers themselves. But here historians have faced a formidable problem. By and large the ante-bellum reformers could not be likened to an oppressed group struggling for economic security; they seldom had vested material interests in their causes. The Beards, who usually emphasized the economic basis of historical change, were frank in admitting their bafflement. In two massive volumes by Edward Westermarck on the history of moral ideas they could find no clue to the inspiration of such a crusade as abolitionism. They stressed the context of sectional struggle and the fact that the North had no slaves to lose, and yet finally concluded that devotion to the abolitionist creed arose from "sentiments of a moral nature." Merle Curti suggested that receptivity to reform ideas was related to social structure; because of its own mobility, the middle class was prepared to think in terms of social improvement. But Curti did not show that reformers came from more mobile groups than did nonreformers, and he ultimately stated that historians could not really know the motives behind reforms.

Nevertheless, as early as 1906 Frank T. Carlton tried to find a more precise relationship between the motives of reformers and a specific social situation. In an article on "Humanitarianism, Past and Present," in the *International Journal of Ethics,* Carlton proposed the theory that ante-bellum reform was essentially the protest of a declining ruling class against the ruthless, competitive world of business. As the old leaders and old families lost power and became isolated from the dynamic social and business currents of the 1820s and 1830s, they struck out desperately against the evil consequences of profit-seeking and laissez-faire capitalism. Carlton did not imply that humanitarianism was a mere screen concealing ignoble motives, nor, apparently, did he think of reform as the attempt of displaced leaders to regain social status. Indeed, it was the remoteness and isolation of the old ruling class which provided a relatively objective view of social problems: ". . . no golden stream was flowing into their pockets to obscure and blur their vision as to past and present conditions." Their value as social critics arose from their independence of economic pressures and their commitment to values and ideals of the past.

More recently several imaginative historians have refined these concepts with respect to radical antislavery. The thesis that abolitionists were responding not so much to slavery as to social and economic dislocations in their own society has been skillfully employed by revisionist historians like Avery Craven, who is represented in this volume. David Donald, in an influential essay in *Lincoln Reconsidered* (1956), maintained that the abolitionists were so violently aggressive and uncompromising that they must have been affected by some profound social or psychological dislocation, and consequently seized upon antislavery as an outlet for irrational needs and fears. After carefully analyzing the social and economic background of 106 key abolitionists, and finding that their families had been linked with the rural social order which began to disintegrate in the 1820s and 1830s, Donald concluded that the antislavery crusade was the protest of "a displaced social elite" against the new industrial world. Abolitionists found self-fulfillment in a cause that offered a chance for moral leadership and a reassertion of traditional values. A somewhat similar approach was taken by Stanley M. Elkins in his seminal work, *Slavery: A Problem in American Institutional and Intellectual Life* (1959). Though less interested in motives than in why ante-bellum Americans were incapable of dealing with slavery in a flexible and realistic manner, Elkins was struck by the abolitionists' excessive individualism, their hostility toward all institutions, their rigidity and abstractness of thought, and their inclination to reduce complex problems to simple, moral absolutes. These traits, he argued, were the product of America's amorphous social structure. Because of the lack of tradition and of truly national institutions, intellectuals and reformers were cut off from sources of power and thus from a sense of responsibility. There were no established channels through which reform could flow. There were no moderating influences which would make protest more flexible, concrete, and effective.

Future studies of American reform will be heavily indebted to the new approaches taken by Donald and Elkins. Nevertheless, in recent years the ante-bellum reformers have appeared in a somewhat different light as modern radicals have grown increasingly skeptical about flexible, pragmatic methods and about working within the framework of established institutions. It has also become apparent that we have little evidence of how ante-bellum reformers differed from other segments of the population. As we shall see in the selection by Martin Duberman, there is reason to doubt broad generalizations about the motives and psychology of such groups as the abolitionists when our knowledge is limited to a few leaders who were perhaps unrepresentative, and when psychological theory is itself in a state of flux.

When we turn to the question of the relative conservatism or radicalism of reform, we again encounter considerable confusion. In 1950 Arthur M. Schlesinger drew a bland picture of American reform. Because American society lacked the "impediments" of an aristocracy or established church, and was continually stimulated by the arrival of restless immigrants, the desire for improvement could flow freely in safe, middle class channels, without challenging private property or other basic institutions. It should be noted that Stanley Elkins derived almost opposite conclusions from America's lack of institutional restraints. On the other hand, Allan Nevins, in his *Ordeal of the Union* (1947), affirmed that American reform was distinctive not in its fanaticism or eccentricity but in the fact that it was a "pragmatic growth in a pragmatic society." The practicality of American reformers was especially evident in such causes as the amelioration of prisons and asylums, and the abolition of flogging in the Navy. Although Nevins considered men like Garrison narrow-minded fanatics, he applauded the practicality and entrepreneurial skill of the Midwestern abolitionists and spoke of the "conservative wisdom" of James G. Birney. He was bothered by the irresponsibility of many social critics and by a frequent failure to penetrate to the roots of social ills. Nevertheless, he found ante-bellum reform "an inspiring force and a powerful agency" in shaping America's future.

Merle Curti presented a sharper dichotomy between liberal and conservative factions. In the decades after the Revolution, American history was essentially a struggle between forces which on one side represented patrician privilege, reactionary religion, and the East; and on the other, the heritage of the Enlightenment, science, "democratic" religion, and the West. This dualism, though frequently adopted in genetal texts, has raised increasing problems. The division between democratic and undemocratic religion makes it difficult to account for abolitionists who believed in original sin and eternal damnation, or for pro-slavery theorists who embraced scientific rationalism. The evangelical crusade to save the West for Protestant Christianity, which Curti classes as part of the patrician reaction, was in reality the seedbed of later reforms. It is clear that ante-bellum reform spanned a wide spectrum from utopian anarchism to an obsessive quest for social order. But the subject is so complex that the conventional meanings of "conservative," "liberal," and "radical" have proved inadequate as modes of classification. Few subjects in American history are in such need of rigorous analysis as the interrelationship of specific reform movements and the transition from an evangelical drive for social control to a romantic and humanitarian crusade for liberty, uplift, and social justice.

Perhaps the vaguest of all answers concerning ante-bellum reform pertains to its ultimate effects. According to Curti, the reformers served an important function, though they had, in the last analysis, little popular appeal. The Beards tell us that the influence of abolitionists outran their poor showing at the polls. Nevins seems to credit the reformers with a more positive effect in shaping opinion both at home and abroad. Alice Felt Tyler affirms that the movements flowed into the mainstream of American life and contributed to our later democratic philosophy. To the revisionist historians the abolitionists bear much of the blame for the Civil War. According to Stanley Elkins, the abolitionists contributed to America's failure to deal imaginatively and realistically with the problem of slavery and race relationships. Few questions are so difficult to answer as those of influence and responsibility. Hopefully we will acquire more precise criteria for measuring the impact of ante-bellum reformers, but as our own experience changes our perspective on the problems they faced and the methods they adopted, it seems probable that we will continue to alter our views of their significance and accomplishment.

The selections in this book are largely taken from recent studies which build upon the research, the hypotheses, and the controversies just described. They reflect a growing interest in motivation, social structure, and intellectual history, and succeed in moving beyond many of the clichés and conventional labels of earlier histories. If the emerging picture is rather smudged and lacking in clear and simple shapes, the student should be reassured by knowing that we have gone beyond the superficial level of categorizing people as progressives and reactionaries, as puritans and liberals, as crackpots and saints. Though few questions have yet been answered, at least many of the right questions have been asked. It should be noted that the second chapter focuses on the motives and personality of reformers, and indicates how changing views of individual commitment may influence our attitude toward reform. In the third chapter we turn to the place of reform movements within the broader context of evangelical revivalism and Jacksonian democracy.

The selection by Frank Thistlethwaite not only emphasizes the wide Anglo-American basis of ante-bellum reform, but points to the liberating and secular tendencies that emerged from the religious revivals. The following essays by Clifford S. Griffin, William G. McLoughlin, and Lee Benson explore the complex relations between reform and religious and political interests. They show how difficult it is to apply the conventional stereotypes of religious reactionaries or secular liberals to ante-bellum reformers and anti-reformers. In the fourth chapter we move from more general theories and concepts to analyses of two specific reform movements which illustrate some of the diverse themes of the earlier selections. In the last essay, John L. Thomas portrays the evolution of ante-bellum reform movements in a way that reconciles and synthesizes many of the conflicting generalizations of previous historians.

We should not conclude without briefly noting some of the blankest areas in our present knowledge of reform. In addition to the need for more detailed information on the psychology of reformers, there is an almost total lack of evidence on the differences between what might be called the verbalizers—the lecturers, journalists, and pamphleteers—and the activists or organizers. Little is known of the rank and file members, to say nothing of the passive supporters, of a single reform movement. Yet there is presumably important evidence in petitions, memorials, records of contributions, and membership lists, which might be subject to reasonably sophisticated quantification. It seems futile to talk about the social composition of reform movements until such data has been rigorously analyzed. We are virtually ignorant of the dynamics of reform organizations, of the relations between leaders and followers. Although sociologists and social psychologists have learned much about the workings of small groups, their generalizations have not been applied or tested by historians of reform. We also need to know much more about the relation of secular reform to the sectarian and perfectionist traditions. Despite the strong anarchistic and primitivistic strains within ante-bellum reform, these aspects of the subject have not been systematically studied. The whole relationship of reform propaganda to popular literature has been surprisingly neglected. Finally, we must ultimately ask whether the Civil War represents an abrupt terminus to an entire cycle of reform. Is it valid, in other words, to speak of ante-bellum reform as a self-contained phenomenon, or have we overlooked significant continuities between the first so-called "age of reform" and the later emergence of Reform Darwinism, the Social Gospel, and Progressivism?

MOTIVATION AND THE PSYCHOLOGY OF COMMITMENT

New England Reformers

RALPH WALDO EMERSON

This essay was originally delivered as a lecture on March 3, 1844. As a former minister who had himself cast off the faith of his fathers, Ralph Waldo Emerson (1803–1882) could perceive that the reform movements of his age were basically of religious origin, but represented "a falling from the church nominal." Like the antinomian fanatics who had outraged Emerson's Puritan forebears, the reformers repudiated custom, law, and civil authority in the interest of individual perfectibility. Emerson had a deep appreciation for individual discontent and rebellion, and he was sympathetic toward the reformers' quest for a better world. But Emerson was so much of an antinomian himself, so much opposed to creeds and covenants, that he was suspicious of

Ralph Waldo Emerson, *Essays, Second Series* (Boston: Ticknor and Fields, 1867), pp. 243–249, 251–258.

any attempts to socialize the individual reformer's vision. From a Transcendentalist point of view, the reform impulse was pure, but was inevitably corrupted by association and implementation. Emerson can thus applaud the reformers' idealism while fearing that commitment to a social cause must lead to partiality, narrowness, and hypocrisy. He can endorse a questioning, critical spirit, and yet arrive at the conservative conclusion that social evils can be ameliorated only by individual self-regeneration. This ambivalent attitude has been of profound importance in both the history and interpretation of American reform.

WHOEVER HAS HAD OPPORTUNITY OF ACQUAINTANCE WITH SOciety in New England, during the last twenty-five years, with those middle and with those leading sections that may constitute any just representation of the character and aim of the community, will have been struck with the great activity of thought and experimenting. His attention must be commanded by the signs that the Church, or religious party, is falling from the church nominal, and is appearing in temperance and non-resistant societies, in movements of abolitionists and of socialists, and in very significant assemblies, called Sabbath and Bible Conventions,—composed of ultraists, of seekers, of all the soul of the soldiery of dissent, and meeting to call in question the authority of the Sabbath, of the priesthood, and of the church. In these movements, nothing was more remarkable than the discontent they begot in the movers. The spirit of protest and of detachment, drove the members of these Conventions to bear testimony against the church, and immediately afterward, to declare their discontent with these Conventions, their independence of their colleagues, and their impatience of the methods whereby they were working. They defied each other, like a congress of kings, each of whom had a realm to rule, and a way of his own that made concert unprofitable. What a fertility of projects for the salvation of the world! One apostle thought all men should go to farming; and another, that no man should buy or sell; that the use of money was the cardinal evil; another, that the mischief was in our diet, that we eat and drink damnation. These made unleavened bread, and were foes to the death to fermentation. It was in vain urged by the housewife, that God made yeast, as well as dough, and loves fermentation just as dearly as he loves vegetation; that fermentation develops that saccharine element in the grain, and makes it more palatable and more digestible. No; they wish the pure wheat, and will die but it shall not ferment. Stop, dear nature, these incessant advances of thine; let us scotch these ever-rolling wheels! Others attacked the system of agriculture, the use of animal manures in farming; and the tyranny of man over brute nature; these abuses polluted his food. The ox must be taken from the plough, and the horse from the cart, the hundred acres of the farm must be spaded, and the man must walk wherever boats and locomotives will not carry him. Even the insect world was to be defended,—that had been too long neglected, and a society for the protection of ground-worms, slugs, and mosquitos was to be incorporated without delay. With these appeared the adepts of homœopathy, of hydropathy, of mesmerism, of phrenology, and their wonderful theories of the Christian miracles! Others assailed particular vocations, as that of the lawyer, that of the merchant, of the manufacturer, of the clergyman, of the scholar. Others attacked the institution of marriage, as the fountain of social evils. Others devoted themselves to the worrying of churches and meetings for public worship; and the fertile forms of antinomianism among the elder puritans, seemed to have their match in the plenty of the new harvest of reform.

With this din of opinion and debate, there was a keener scrutiny of institutions and domestic life than any we had known, there was sincere protesting against existing evils, and there were changes of employment dictated by conscience. No doubt, there was plentiful vaporing, and cases of backsliding might occur. But in each of these movements emerged a good result, a tendency to the adoption of simpler methods, and an assertion of the sufficiency of the private man. Thus it was directly in the spirit and genius of the age, what happened in one instance, when a church censured and threatened to excommunicate one of its members, on account of the somewhat hostile part to the church, which his conscience led him to take in the anti-slavery business; the threatened individual immediately excommunicated the church in a public and formal process. This has been several times repeated: it was excellent when it was done the first time, but, of course, loses all value when it is copied. Every project in the history of reform, no matter how violent and surprising, is good, when it is the dictate of a man's genius and constitution, but very dull and suspicious when adopted from another. It is right and beautiful in any man to say, 'I will take this coat, or this book, or this measure of corn of yours,'—in whom we see the act to be original, and to flow from the whole spirit and faith of him; for then that taking will have a giving as free and divine: but we are very easily disposed to resist the same generosity of speech, when we miss originality and truth to character in it.

There was in all the practical activities of New England, for the last quarter of a century, a gradual withdrawal of tender consciences from the social organizations. There is observable throughout the contest between mechanical and spiritual methods, but with a steady tendency of the thoughtful and virtuous to a deeper belief and reliance on spiritual facts.

In politics, for example, it is easy to see the progress of dissent. The country is full of rebellion; the country is full of kings. Hands off! let there be no control and no interference in the administration of the affairs of this kingdom of me. Hence the growth of the doctrine and of the party of Free Trade, and the willingness to try that experiment, in the face of what appear incontestable facts. I confess, the motto of the Globe newspaper is so attractive to me, that I can seldom find much appetite to read what is below it in its columns, "The world is governed too much." So the country is frequently affording solitary examples of resistance to the government, solitary nullifiers, who throw themselves on their reserved rights; nay, who have reserved all their rights; who reply to the assessor, and to the clerk of court, that they do not know the State; and embarrass the courts of law, by non-juring, and the commander-in-chief of the militia, by non-resistance.

The same disposition to scrutiny and dissent appeared in civil, festive, neighborly, and domestic society. A restless, prying, conscientious criticism broke out in unexpected quarters. Who gave me the money with which I bought my coat? Why should professional labor and that of the countinghouse be paid so disproportionately to the labor of the porter, and woodsawyer? This whole business of Trade gives me to pause and think, as it constitutes false relations between men; inasmuch as I am prone to count myself relieved of any responsibility to behave well and nobly to that person whom I pay with money, whereas if I had not that commodity, I should be put on my good behavior in all companies, and man would be a benefactor to man, as being himself his only certificate that he had a right to those aids and services which each asked of the other. Am I not too protected a person? is there not a wide disparity between the lot of me and the lot of thee, my poor brother, my poor sister? Am I not defrauded of my best culture in the loss of those gymnastics which manual labor and the emergencies of poverty constitute? I find nothing healthful or exalting in the smooth conventions of society; I do not like the close air of salons. I begin to suspect myself to be a prisoner, though treated with all this courtesy and luxury. I pay a destructive tax in my conformity.

The same insatiable criticism may be traced in the efforts for the reform of Education. The popular education has been taxed with a want of truth and nature. It was complained that an education to things was not given. We are students of words: we are shut up in schools, and colleges and recitation-rooms, for ten or fifteen years, and come out at last with a bag of wind, a memory of words, and do not know a thing. We cannot use our hands, or our legs, or our eyes, or our arms. We do not know an edible root in the woods, we cannot tell our course by the stars, nor the hour of the day by the sun. It is well if we can swim and skate. We are afraid of a horse, of a cow, of a dog, of a snake, of a spider. The Roman rule was, to teach a boy nothing that he could not learn standing. The old English rule was, 'All summer in the field, and all winter in the study.' And it seems as if a man should learn to plant, or to fish or to hunt, that he might secure his subsistence at all events, and not be painful to his friends and fellowmen. The lessons of science should be experimental also. The sight of the planet through a telescope, is worth all the course on astronomy: the shock of the electric spark in the elbow, outvalues all the theories; the taste of the nitrous oxide, the firing of an artificial volcano, are better than volumes of chemistry. . . .

One tendency appears alike in the philosophical speculation, and in the rudest democratical movements, through all the petulance and all the puerility, the wish, namely, to cast aside the superfluous, and arrive at short methods, urged, as I suppose, by an intuition that the human spirit is equal to all emergencies, alone, and that man is more often injured than helped by the means he uses.

I conceive this gradual casting off of material aids, and the indication of growing trust in the private, self-supplied powers of the individual, to be the affirmative principle of the recent philosophy: and that it is feeling its own profound truth, and is reaching forward at this very hour to the happiest conclusions. I readily concede that in this, as in every period of intellectual activity, there has been a noise of denial and protest; much was to be resisted, much was to be got rid of by those who were reared in the old, before they could begin to affirm and to construct. Many a reformer perishes in his removal of rubbish,—and that makes the offensiveness of the class. They are partial; they are not equal to the work they pretend. They lose their way; in the assault on the kingdom of darkness, they expend all their energy on some accidental evil, and lose their sanity and power of benefit. It is of little moment that one or two, or twenty errors of our social system be corrected, but of much that the man be in his senses.

The criticism and attack on institutions which we have witnessed, has made one thing plain, that society gains nothing whilst a man, not himself renovated, attempts to renovate things around him: he has become tediously good in some particular, but negligent or narrow in the rest; and hypocrisy and vanity are often the disgusting result.

It is handsomer to remain in the establishment better than the establishment, and conduct that in the best manner, than to make a sally against evil by some single improvement, without supporting it by a total regeneration. Do not be so vain of your one objection. Do you think there is only one? Alas! my good friend, there is no part of society or of life better than any other part. All our things are right and wrong together. The wave of evil washes all our institutions alike. Do you complain of our Marriage? Our marriage is no worse than our education, our diet, our trade, our social customs. Do you complain of the laws of Property? It is a pedantry to give such importance to them. Can we not play the game of life with these counters, as well as with those; in the institution of property, as well as out of it. Let into it the new and renewing principle of love, and property will be universality. No one gives the impression of superiority to the institution, which he must give who will reform it. It makes no difference what you say: you must make me feel that you are aloof from it; by your natural and supernatural advantages, do easily see to the end of it,—do see how man can do without it. Now all men are on one side. No man deserves to be heard against property. Only Love, only an Idea, is against property, as we hold it.

I cannot afford to be irritable and captious, nor to waste all my time in attacks. If I should go out of church whenever I hear a false sentiment, I could never stay there five minutes. But why come out? the street is as false as the church, and when I get to my house, or to my manners, or to my speech, I have not got away from the lie. When we see an eager assailant of one of these wrongs, a special reformer, we feel like asking him, What right have you, sir, to your one virtue? Is virtue piecemeal? This is a jewel amidst the rags of a beggar.

In another way the right will be vindicated. In the midst of abuses, in the heart of cities, in the aisles of false churches, alike in one place and in another,—wherever, namely, a just and heroic soul finds itself, there it will do what is next at hand, and by the new quality of character it shall put forth, it shall abrogate that old condition, law or school in which it stands, before the law of its own mind.

If partiality was one fault of the movement party, the other defect was their reliance on Association. Doubts such as those I have intimated, drove many good persons to agitate the questions of social reform. But the revolt against the spirit of commerce, the spirit of aristocracy, and the inveterate abuses of cities, did not appear possible to individuals; and to do battle against numbers, they armed themselves with numbers, and against concert, they relied on new concert.

Following, or advancing beyond the ideas of St. Simon, of Fourier, and of Owen,[1] three communities have already been formed in Massachu-

[1] EDITOR'S NOTE: Claude Henri de Rouvroy, Comte de Saint-Simon (1760–1825), one of the founders of modern socialism, fought on the American side in the War of Independence and later had both a direct and indirect influence on American utopian and communitarian thought. François Marie Charles Fourier (1772–1837)

setts on kindred plans, and many more in the country at large. They aim to give every member a share in the manual labor, to give an equal reward to labor and to talent, and to unite a liberal culture with an education to labor. The scheme offers, by the economies of associated labor and expense, to make every member rich, on the same amount of property, that, in separate families, would leave every member poor. These new associations are composed of men and women of superior talents and sentiments: yet it may easily be questioned, whether such a community will draw, except in its beginnings, the able and the good; whether those who have energy, will not prefer their chance of superiority and power in the world, to the humble certainties of the association; whether such a retreat does not promise to become an asylum to those who have tried and failed, rather than a field to the strong; and whether the members will not necessarily be fractions of men, because each finds that he cannot enter it, without some compromise. Friendship and association are very fine things, and a grand phalanx of the best of the human race, banded for some catholic object: yes, excellent; but remember that no society can ever be so large as one man. He in his friendship, in his natural and momentary associations, doubles or multiplies himself; but in the hour in which he mortgages himself to two or ten or twenty, he dwarfs himself below the stature of one.

But the men of less faith could not thus believe, and to such, concert appears the sole specific of strength. I have failed, and you have failed, but perhaps together we shall not fail. Our housekeeping is not satisfactory to us, but perhaps a phalanx, a community, might be. Many of us have differed in opinion, and we could find no man who could make the truth plain, but possibly a college, or an ecclesiastical council might. I have not been able either to persuade my brother or to prevail on myself, to disuse the traffic or the potation of brandy, but perhaps a pledge of total abstinence might effectually restrain us. The candidate my party votes for is not to be trusted with a dollar, but he will be honest in the Senate, for we can bring public opinion to bear on him. Thus concert was the specific in all cases. But concert is neither better nor worse, neither more nor less potent than individual force. All the men in the world cannot make a statue walk and speak, cannot make a drop of blood, or a blade of grass, any more than one man can. But let there be

---

was a French social philosopher whose theories of harmonizing private property with social and economic planning inspired many American communitarian experiments in the 1840s and 1850s, including the famous one at Brook Farm. Robert Owen (1771–1858) was a British industrialist, philanthropist, and socialistic reformer. Although his utopian community at New Harmony, Indiana lasted only from 1825 to 1828, it stimulated considerable interest in socialism and reform in general.

one man, let there be truth in two men, in ten men, then is concert for the first time possible, because the force which moves the world is a new quality, and can never be furnished by adding whatever quantities of a different kind. What is the use of the concert of the false and the disunited? There can be no concert in two, where there is no concert in one. When the individual is not *individual,* but is dual; when his thoughts look one way, and his actions another; when his faith is traversed by his habits; when his will, enlightened by reason, is warped by his sense; when with one hand he rows, and with the other backs water, what concert can be?

I do not wonder at the interest these projects inspire. The world is awaking to the idea of union, and these experiments show what it is thinking of. It is and will be magic. Men will live and communicate, and plough, and reap, and govern, as by added ethereal power, when once they are united; as in a celebrated experiment, by expiration and respiration exactly together, four persons lift a heavy man from the ground by the little finger only, and without sense of weight. But this union must be inward, and not one of covenants, and is to be reached by a reverse of the methods they use. The union is only perfect, when all the uniters are isolated. It is the union of friends who live in different streets or towns. Each man, if he attempts to join himself to others, is on all sides cramped and diminished of his proportion; and the stricter the union, the smaller and the more pitiful he is. But leave him alone, to recognize in every hour and place the secret soul, he will go up and down doing the works of a true member, and, to the astonishment of all, the work will be done with concert, though no man spoke. Government will be adamantine without any governor. The union must be ideal in actual individualism.

The Northern Attack on Slavery

AVERY CRAVEN

Americans have often been inclined to ask Emerson's question: "When we see an eager assailant of one of these wrongs, a special reformer, we feel like asking him, What right have you, sir, to your one virtue?" This is essentially the point from which Avery Craven begins his analysis of the psychological, sociological, and political functions of reform. Professor Craven (1886–   ), who taught history for many years at the University of Chicago, was a pioneer in using such psychological concepts as frustration, compensation, displacement, and projection in an interpretation of ante-bellum reform. Assuming that Negro slavery was not in actuality a great moral problem, and therefore not a sufficient reason for the abolitionists' extreme attacks, Professor Craven explains the reformers' behavior in terms of social and economic dislocations, unconscious needs and motives, and growing sectional rivalry. His view of the diverse reform movements as an interrelated phenomenon, intimately connected with economic upheaval and social fluidity, has been accepted by historians who have little sympathy for his pro-Southern "revisionism" or for his obvious hostility toward the abolitionists.

REMOVING MOTES FROM A BROTHER'S EYE IS AN ANCIENT PRACTICE. The urge to make over other individuals and to correct real or fancied evils in society operates with unusual force in certain individuals. This used to be ascribed to a peculiar sensitiveness to wrongdoing —a willingness to sacrifice personal comfort for a larger good. Perpetual reformers, though resented as meddlers by those they disturbed, have been hailed as pioneers and martyrs who have unselfishly helped to usher in new eras and a better world.

The modern psychologist is somewhat skeptical of such explanations.

Avery Craven, *The Coming of the Civil War,* 2nd ed., pp. 117–118, 122–140, 142, 144–150. Reprinted without footnotes and with minor deletions by permission of the University of Chicago Press. Copyright © 1942 by Charles Scribner's Sons; Second edition © 1957 by Avery Craven.

He talks of youthful experiences, maladjustments, inferiority complexes, and repressed desires. He is not so sure about the sources of the reform impulse or the unselfish character of the reformer. The student of social affairs is likewise less inclined to grant unstinted praise to the fanatic and is not certain about the value of the contribution. He views him as a normal product of social phenomena acting on certain types of personality. He sees the triumph of emotion over reason in the extremist's course and sometimes wonders if the developments of history might not have been more sound without him. He talks with less assurance about "progress" in human affairs.

At all events, recent historians have been inclined to reconsider the part played by the abolitionists in the coming of the War Between the States. They have judged the reformer and his efforts to be open fields for new study. The old assumptions that the movements against slavery arose entirely from a disinterested hatred of injustice and that their results were good beyond question can no longer be accepted without reservations. Those who force the settlement of human problems by war can expect only an unsympathetic hearing from the future. Mere desire to do "right" is no defense at the bar of history.

. . . .

The first indication that slavery might become a sectional issue appeared in the Congressional debates over the Missouri Compromise. Livermore of New Hampshire asked:

How will the desire for wealth render us blind to sin of holding both the bodies and souls of our fellow men in chains. . . . Do not, for the sake of cotton and tobacco, let it be told to future ages that, while pretending to love liberty, we have purchased an extensive country to disgrace it with the foulest reproach to nations!

Senator King of New York went so far as to insist that "no human law, compact, or compromise can establish or continue slavery. . . . There is no such thing as a slave." His assault was so vicious that one senator alleged that King would not dare publish it "in the naked ugliness of its original deformity."

Southern men in turn defended their institution. Most of them could have said with Reid of Georgia: "Believe me, sir, I am not a panegyrist of slavery. It is an unnatural state: a dark cloud which obscures half the lustre of our free institutions." All agreed with Barbour of Virginia that the opponents of slavery exaggerated the evils in the system and knew all too little about it. "He has shaded it too deeply, with the coloring of his own imagination," Barbour said of one speaker. But a few men, like

William Smith of South Carolina, "justified slavery on the broadest principles, without qualification or reserve." Smith declared that it was right and viewed it as a benefit which should be perpetuated.

Thomas Jefferson, from the seclusion of his mountain, viewed the controversy as "a fire-bell in the night." The use to which politicians in sectional conflict could put slavery had been clearly revealed. A grave national crisis had been averted only because the public mind was not as yet inflamed on the subject and complete sectional cleavage did not yet exist. It was perfectly clear, however, that back of the attack on slavery lay Northern resentment of Southern strength in national affairs. The three-fifths rule gave the South an advantage and the steady addition of new states from Jefferson's Louisiana Purchase added to it. The Virginia dynasty held on to its control while the Federal Party steadily crumbled. The panic of 1819 bore heavily on commerce and industry, while slave-manned plantations, seen from a distance, seemed to continue prosperous. Tariff legislation, designed to remedy such disparity, met increasing opposition from the South. Reprisal was in order. When Missouri asked for the right to join the opposition as a state, the opportunity was presented to strike back, and that opportunity could not be overlooked. Well might the Fathers view the future with alarm.

The politicians, however, were not destined to be the leaders in the great fight against slavery about to be launched in the North. Nor were the forces behind the Missouri struggle those which were to lift an abolition crusade to national importance and ultimately to precipitate a civil war. The new abolition movement was to born out of an entirely different set of conditions, and expressed a far more profound set of attitudes. To understand it, a whole series of fundamental changes going on in the northeastern corner of the United States must be considered.

In the decades immediately after 1800 parts of New England and neighboring states underwent profound alteration under the impact of the Industrial Revolution. Up to that time the region had been made up of coastal towns, inhabited by venturous merchants and hardy fishermen, and self-sufficing farms, whose owners tilled the rugged hillsides and the more fertile hinterland. They supplemented agriculture with domestic manufacturing. Now the factory made its appearance. The making of cloth, and later of shoes and implements, passed gradually out of the home and into the hastily built towns which sprang up wherever water power could be found. Here and there industry invaded old urban centers, but people and capital tended to shift as needed to the places more favorable to new types of economic effort. The early New England factories centered about Providence, Rhode Island, but the center of industry soon shifted northward into Massachusetts, where Lowell and

Lawrence and Waltham rose to compete with Salem and Newburyport, and where Boston took her place in the minds of New Englanders as the Hub of the Universe.

In 1810, less than seven per cent of the people in this section lived in cities of 10,000 and over; by 1860, more than thirty-six per cent lived in such cities and the region could be described as one in which most people through investments, labor and consumption were linked to industry. Improved transportation and banking facilities, necessary for the production and distribution of goods in mass, helped give numbers and power to the urban centers. A new group of businessmen found opportunities in these new enterprises to reap fortunes soon large enough to permit them to intermarry with the aristocracy which trade in wines and slaves and other very commonplace things had earlier created.

The growth of finance-industrial cities, largely dependent on the outside for food and raw materials, opened markets for the farmers who in earlier days had had little incentive for improved methods and surplus production. An agricultural revolution followed. Farmers of enterprise and capital began to specialize their crops. Near the factory towns they produced increasing quantities of vegetables, fruits, and dairy produce. Travelers noted a greater beauty of farms and a higher state of cultivation in such neighborhoods. Improved breeds of stock were introduced and better farm machinery came into use.

On the hillsides, farther away, beef cattle were fattened and driven to the Brighton market in such numbers as to excite the protest of clergymen whose services on the once quiet Sabbath were interrupted by the constant passing of great "phalanxes of horned cattle." The sheep industry flourished in parts of the hill country less favorably situated. Men of capital bought the lands of the unfortunate and enclosed them for their flocks. By 1835 Vermont boasted more than a million head of sheep; half her people had turned shepherd. Western Massachusetts was not far behind. In some places there the farmers had so completely gone over to sheep raising that they were dependent on other states for their bread and pork. With these changes, the agricultural society prospered and the agricultural periodical made its appearance. The factory had remade New England's agriculture.

These revolutionary developments, however, did not come without suffering. Many were crowded aside; others were crushed. The shift of activity centers and the increased use of capital in both industry and agriculture left old towns and isolated rural communities outside the benefits of the new developments. Even where old levels were maintained, people once influential found themselves overshadowed by the greater men and institutions produced by the new day. Thousands turned their faces westward toward upper New York, Ohio, and Michigan where lands were cheap and old crops and methods would still yield sufficient returns. Thousands entered the new urban centers where opportunity for energy and talent was equally great. Young people went first; their elders followed. Boston not only lured the ambitious youth, but soon drew the old aristocratic families of Salem, Beverly, and Newburyport as well. The West took few of wealth and fewer of high social standing, but it did, in some cases, persuade whole communities to abandon their native section. Parent towns suffered heavily and their bitterness and resentment kept pace with their losses. The coming of industry was not an unmixed blessing.

Nor was all permanently satisfactory in the factory or on the new type of farm. Opportunity in textile manufacture led to overexpansion, and the panic of 1837 brought ruin to the weaker units. The reorganization and consolidation which followed, placed control in the hands of a relatively few capitalists. Favored communities outstripped their rivals. Labor everywhere lost ground. Wages were lowered, and when labor troubles followed, foreigners in large numbers found their way into the factories. The Lowell girl, who had excited the admiration of many a traveller, was replaced by the Irish woman or by an inferior type of native worker. Strikes and lockouts were of frequent occurrence. Paternalism passed. Capital and labor began to assume their modern attitudes and relationships. The politicians, meanwhile, both at the state capitals and in Washington, looked after the interests of the favored few and glorified the political policies which favored industry and urban development.

Agricultural expansion brought even greater disappointments. Canals and railroads, which in the beginning promised only wider access to expanding markets, soon reached out into the rich, cheap lands of New York, Ohio, and Michigan. At first they brought back supplies of wheat and flour to help complete the agricultural specialization in New England. But the pioneer, carrying wheat, the first great frontier crop, ever farther west, was constantly forcing those immediately behind him into other lines of production. Before long the New York farmer had turned to beef cattle, sheep, hogs, and dairy products. He poured his surplus back upon the Atlantic coast in quantity great enough to satisfy all demands and at prices below those at which the stingy soils of New England could compete. Step by step the New England farmer yielded ground. He shifted crops. He tried new methods. He mortgaged his lands to the Boston insurance companies to get new capital. But his fight was a losing one. Only those unusually well situated as to markets for perishable supplies could hold out against the constant changes required by the continued spread of wheat into the farther West. A new restlessness developed. Writers spoke of the "moving, nomadic character of our population"; one of them insisted that "you will not find one in twenty who lives where his fathers lived or does as his fathers have done." The *New England Farmer* declared that it was "perfectly evident that farmers, with moderate means, must go down under this burden. They do go down by the thousands. And what is infinitely the most to be regretted, they go down in poverty. . . ." The city and the West enlisted new recruits. The abandoned farm became a permanent part of the New England countryside.

Those who moved west to form a Greater New England in upper New York and along the Great Lakes also met conditions less than satisfactory. The frontier was harsh and exacting. Tasks were arduous; rewards not always in proportion to efforts. The restless pioneer, filled with hopes and dreams which he expected to realize by the exploitation of fresh resources and the development of a new society, found himself forced to return to a more or less primitive way of living and to fight his way slowly back to comfort and security. Legislation framed to give easy access to lands and to profitable markets met opposition from the older sections. New Wests, forming constantly out ahead in the wilderness, quickly threw their first surpluses back eastward, forcing agricultural readjustments upon those who had only just begun to prosper. Then the panic of 1837 struck. In regions where overexpansion had taken place the suffering was acute and long continued. In the late 1830's and early 1840's New York experienced all the ills of Western competition and production shifts which New England had known earlier. Prosperity came only at infrequent intervals. After 1845 Ohio and Michigan were in the same plight.

Such were the economic conditions which combined with a stern and forbidding Calvinism to interfere with the pursuit of happiness in both the New Englands. Together these factors constituted a somber background against which sharp reactions now developed. These sometimes took the form of violent protest against existing conditions; sometimes of fantastic schemes by which perfection of society might be achieved. It was a day of ideals in every camp, of high-flying souls, of keener scrutiny of institutions and domestic life. Lowell humorously described the situation as one in which

> every possible form of intellectual and physical dyspepsia brought forth its gospel. Bran had its prophets. . . . Plainness of speech was carried to a pitch that would have taken away the breath of George Fox. . . . Everybody had a mission (with a capital M) to attend to everybody-else's business. No brain but had its private maggot. . . . Not a few impecunious zealots abjured the use of money . . . professing to live on the internal revenues of the spirit. Some had an assurance of instant millennium so soon as hooks and eyes should

be substituted for buttons. Communities were established where everything
was to be common but common sense. . . .

These stirrings were, no doubt, partly the result of spiritual forces;
they could not have been unrelated to the great economic and social
changes which were so fundamentally altering the lives and thwarting the
purposes of this people. Filtering in from the Old World, transcendental
thinking and humanitarian impulses furnished forms of expression to
American spokesmen, but they did not supply the motives which made
them speak. The injustice and inequality against which these men reacted
existed in their own immediate environment. A reactionary Federalism
and a repressive theocracy had long held the stream of New England
thought within safe and accepted banks. The dawn of the new economic
day, however, thawed out the frozen social-intellectual landscape. Every
phase of life became more fluid. People moved about, ideas changed,
forms altered. Old impediments and new ones felt the pressure of flood
waters which left their banks and spread out into every lowland. Both
destruction and new life were the result.

Reactions and reform efforts varied sharply according to the regions in
which they developed. Near Boston, where the Unitarian revolt had
already made liberals out of conservatives, the tone was decidedly philosophical. The emphasis was on man's innate goodness and his capacity
for improvement. Sometimes the movement took the form of revolt
against reason and asserted that truth is known by intuition and intro-
spection, not by contact with material things. Sometimes it was highly
individualistic, becoming anti-social and anti-governmental. At other
times, it expressed itself in bitter hatred of the injustices and restrictions
which increasingly plagued the individual. It set earnest men and women
at the tasks of ending war, achieving temperance, winning women's
rights, and building new communities where greater opportunities for
self-expression and social justice might be found. Emerson, Channing,
Parker, Garrison, Ladd, Thoreau, Alcott, and their kind were the leaders.
A social order, sane and just enough to permit men to realize their
potentialities, was the end sought by them all.

A second type of expression developed in the rural sections and ran
back from New England into the farther West where many lesser persons, carrying the imprint of Puritan training, had settled in the wilderness and had met there the streams of emigrants from other sections. In
line with frontier ways of thinking, the purpose here was the practical
one of bolstering up and restoring a faltering American Democracy. This
included the destruction of all special privileges and a restoration of
prosperity. It implied an acceptance of the Declaration of Independence

as an integral part of the American political system and a recognition of the teachings of Christianity as binding on the government. Because it operated in frontier and rural surroundings, it moved much of the time through religious channels. It was closely associated with the spread of the Methodist and Baptist denominations in New England, where the revival meetings lingered on in the regions in which Jonathan Edwards had labored, and in New York and Ohio where Charles Grandison Finney had given Calvinism a warmer and more practical social turn.

For the same reason it became tangled with politics. Western men, especially, believed in the efficacy of governmental action for the achievement of social and moral ends. Both Church and State ought to serve democracy. Democracy was one with the will of God and the natural law. It guaranteed a moral order and when men or the misinterpretation of constitutions violated that order appeal to the higher law might be made. Reform movements in such an atmosphere became crusades. Even material problems had their moral aspects.

Variations in regional and group expression, however, should not obscure the larger fact of unity in the whole great reform impulse, nor hide the fact that it arose out of apprehension engendered by changes going on in the immediate environment of the reformers. The underlying idea, common to all moves and found in all places, was that something hoped for in American life was not being realized; that democracy—meaning everything from the Holy Commonwealth and men free from all kinds of unpleasant restraints to a high degree of material prosperity for all Americans—was being threatened by the rise of new and greater aristocrats and the imposition of new and harsher restraints. The Industrial Revolution was creating a new rich group and reducing labor to a new degree of dependence. The spread of cotton was bringing into existence a new and overshadowing power in a rival section. The urban center, differing from the farm in material standards and moral codes, lured the rural youth and exercised an increasing influence in legislative halls. The Southern plantation seemed even more extravagant and foreign. The acquisitive drive was growing stronger, and the world and the flesh more enticing. Inequality was becoming everywhere more apparent. The purposes of God and of the Founding Fathers were in grave danger.

Men took part in a half dozen different crusades at the same time. It is sometimes difficult to tell whether Garrison was more interested in the abolition of slavery, or in peace, or in women's rights. The appeal made by a single crusade might be at once moral, social, and material. Gerrit Smith insisted that no man's religion was better than his politics. The course of development in different movements and the technique of propaganda employed by different groups were strikingly similar. The possibility of the fusion of them all into one great drive which fully expressed the determination to rescue American democracy from some all-embracing evil was present from the beginning.

The thoroughly local and immediate character of early resentments and reform efforts and their relation to democratic appeal needs further emphasis. As has been said, the aristocracy which was threatening American freedom and equality had been produced largely by the new economic shifts in the Northeast itself. The cotton planter was much more a symbol than a reality to most of them. The New England farmer saw, as the "only legitimate and fruitful parent of [his] ruinous debts and mortgages," "the excessive accumulations of property in the hands of a limited number of individuals." He bitterly complained that life in his own section was made up of "industry on the part of the farmer and pleasure on the part of the aristocracy." He rejected utterly the suggestion that his daughters helped relieve the strain by turning to domestic service and declared that he would "sooner, infinitely sooner, follow [his] daughters to the grave than see them go out to service in the kitchens of those who by successful industry, by good luck, or possibly fraud, were in a situation to make hewers of wood and drawers of water out of their less fortunate sisters and brethren." A thoughtful observer in a neighboring state sensed a feeling of "envy and even hatred . . . in persons [against merchants] as strong as those of serfs in Europe against the privileged classes."

Professor Darling, discussing Massachusetts politics from 1824 to 1848, says that:

> Jacksonian Democracy was essentially a rural party in rebellion against the domination of urban wealth and social position. . . .
> Antagonism toward the city of Boston had existed from colonial times, but as manufacturing developed and the wealth of such financiers as the Lawrences and Appletons increased, hostility between country and city heightened. As these capitalists acquired commanding positions in the conservative party, rural elements which were irked by such accumulations of wealth gathered in the opposition and protested against "corporations" and exclusive privileges.

He also says that the Workingmen's Movement in Massachusetts was almost exclusively a farmers' effort—"a protest against the 'accumulations' in Boston society, the assault of 'country folk' on the exclusive privileges of the wealthy." Even in New York and Philadelphia the labor movements were class struggles—the poor against the rich. When the Journeymen Mechanics of Philadelphia organized, it was to ward off "from ourselves and families those numerous evils which result from an unequal and very excessive accumulation of wealth and power into the hands of a few. . . ." A New York group resolved that "the greatest knaves, imposters, and paupers of the age, are our bankers. . . ."

The locofoco movement, which found its support among New York farmers and mechanics, was even more deeply concerned about inequality and privilege. Philip Hone once said that this group waged its fight entirely "upon . . . the grounds of the poor against the rich" and that its cry was: Down with the aristocracy. A locofoco convention, held in Utica, New York, in 1836, condemned the Banking System because it was a "plan by which the idle few live by the labor of the many"; because it was an effort to "fill the coffers of the already wealthy" at the expense of the poor. It denounced the practices of the courts of law as aristocratic and declared, in a form consciously modelled after the Declaration of Independence, that "the foundations of Republican Government are in the equal rights of every citizen in his person and property, and in their management." The following year a locofoco committee declared that "at present, although we may live under the *cloak* of republicanism, we are in reality subjected to the worst of all tyrannies— an aristocracy of wealth. Our actual government, our real regulator of social rights and social intercourse, is *money*—the greater heaps ruling the less. . . ."

Close association of democratic ends with morality and religion also characterized locofocoism. One contemporary called its devotees "these Methodists of Democracy" and insisted that they had "introduced no new doctrines . . . into the true creed" but had "only revived these heaven-born principles which had been so long trodden under the foot of Monopoly. . . ." The historian of the movement dedicated his volume "To a Believer who has rejoiced in the light of Locofocoism, as an outward sign of the inward light of Christianity." The *Democratic Review* declared that "democracy is the cause of Humanity. . . . It is essentially involved in Christianity, of which it has been well said that its pervading spirit of democratic equality among men is its highest fact." Gerrit Smith's congregation at Peterboro in December, 1840, resolved, among other things, that:

Whereas there is, even amongst professors of religion, a prevailing opinion that it is wrong to preach politics on the Sabbath. *Resolved,* That the correctness of this opinion turns wholly on the character of the politics which are preached: for whilst it is clearly wrong to preach anti-Bible or unrighteous politics on the Sabbath or any other day, nothing can be clearer than that no day is too holy to be used in preaching the politics which are inculcated in the Bible.

Smith himself believed that sound government depended on "the prevalence of [a] Christianity" which kept from office "anti-abolitionists, and land-monopolists and other enemies of human rights." To leave God out of a moral reformation was like enacting the play of Othello and leaving out the part of Othello. To Smith civil government was of God.

In the farther West this temper was revealed most clearly in the condemnation of speculators in public lands. A Missouri Assembly voiced a common opinion when it said that "Our Country is peculiarly the asylum of the oppressed and emphatically the poor man's home." One of its resolutions declared that "Every law . . . which opens to the poor man the way to independence . . . not only subserves the cause of Humanity but advances and maintains the fundamental principles of our Government." Another Western spokesman assailed the speculators who were establishing a petty aristocracy and choking the "tree of Liberty . . . so that her sons [could] no more recline under her balmy shadows, but [were forced to] . . . endure the scorching rays and blasting influences of the slavery making idol of money tyrants." Yet another compared them to the flies which came "upon the borders of Egypt." Senator Lewis Cass of Michigan added the moral note by declaring that Americans should forget the profits to be made from lands and "look to our duty as a Christian people." One of Cass's colleagues in the House argued that the public lands should go, as "God intended, and as good government and good men desire they should go, into the hands of the people."

. . .

The abolition movement was part and parcel of this whole great stirring. It was closely related in origins, leadership, and expression to the peace movement, the temperance crusade, the struggles for women's rights, prison and Sabbath reform, and the improvement of education. It was not unrelated to the efforts to establish communities where social-economic justice and high thinking might prevail. It was part of the drive to unseat aristocrats and re-establish American democracy according to the Declaration of Independence. It was a clear-cut effort to apply Christianity to the American social order.

The anti-slavery effort was at first merely one among many. It rose to dominance only gradually. Fortunate from the beginning in leadership, it was always more fortunate in appeal. Human slavery more obviously violated democratic institutions than any other evil of the day; it was close enough to irritate and to inflame sensitive minds, yet far enough removed that reformers need have few personal relations with those whose interests were affected. It rasped most severely upon the moral senses of a people whose ideas of sin were comprehended largely in terms of self-indulgence and whose religious doctrines laid emphasis on social usefulness as the proper manifestation of salvation. And, what was more important, slavery was now confined to a section whose economic interests, and hence political attitudes, conflicted sharply with those of the Northeast and upper Northwest.

Almost from the beginning of the new anti-slavery movement, two distinct centers of action appeared, each with its distinct and individual approach to the problem. One developed in the industrial areas of New England. Its most important spokesman was William Lloyd Garrison, founder and editor of a Boston abolition paper called the *Liberator*. Garrison at first accepted the old idea that slavery was an *evil* to be pointed out and gradually eradicated by those among whom it existed, but he shifted his position in the early 1830's and denounced slavery as a damning crime to be unremittingly assailed and immediately destroyed. The first issue of his paper announced a program from which he never deviated: *". . . I do not wish to think or speak or write with moderation. I will not retreat a single inch, and I will be heard."* The problem, as Garrison saw it, was one of abstract right and wrong. The Scriptures and the Declaration of Independence had already settled the issue. Slavery could have no legal status in a Christian democracy. If the Constitution recognized it, then the Constitution should be destroyed. Slaveholders were both sinners and criminals. They could lay no claim to immunity from any mode of attack. . . .

The extreme and impractical nature of the Garrison anti-slavery drive served to attract attention and arouse antagonism rather than to solve the problem. It did, however, show how profoundly the conditions of the time had stirred the reform spirit and how wide the door had been opened to the professional reformers—men to whom the question was not so much "how shall we abolish slavery, as how shall we best discharge our duty . . . to ourselves." Garrison may be taken as typical of the group. His temperament and experiences had combined to set him in most relationships against the accepted order of things. His life would probably have been spent in protesting even if slavery had never existed. From childhood he had waged a bitter fight *against* obstacles and *for* a due recognition of his abilities. A drunken father had abandoned the family to extreme poverty before William was three years old, and the boy, denied all but the rudiments of an education, had first been placed under the care of Deacon Bartlett, and then apprenticed for seven years to one Ephraim Allen to learn the printing trade. His first venture after his apprenticeship was over failed. His second gave him the opportunity to strike back at an unfair world. He became an editor of the *National Philanthropist*, a paper devoted to the suppression of "intemperance and its Kindred vices." This publication served also as a medium through which to attack lotteries, Sabbath-breaking, and war. A new Garrison began to emerge. His personality, given opportunity for expression, asserted itself. Attending a nominating caucus in Boston, he made bold to speak, and, being resented as an upstart, he replied to his critic in a letter to the Boston *Courier:*

It is true my acquaintance in this city is limited. . . . Let me assure him, however, that if my life be spared, my name shall one day be known to the world—at least to such an extent that common inquiry shall be unnecessary.

To another critic he reiterated this statement, adding these significant words: "I speak in the spirit of prophecy, not of vainglory—with a strong pulse, a flashing eye, and a glow of the heart. The task may be yours to write my biography. . . ."

The second center of anti-slavery effort was in upper New York and the farther Northwest. Influences from this center included in their sweep, however, much of rural New England and the Middle States and the movement found liberal financial help in New York City. Benjamin Lundy and other Quaker leaders started the crusade, but it did not come to full and wide expression until Theodore Weld, already the ablest temperance orator in the Northwest, set about cultivating the great field prepared for social reform by the Finney revivals.

Weld was, like Garrison, unusual both in abilities and in personal characteristics. He was much given to "anti-meat, -butter, -tea, and -coffee, etc. -ism [s]." He indulged in excessive self-effacement and in extravagant confessions of selfishness, pride, impatience of contradiction, personal recklessness, and "a bad, unlovely temper." Of his pride, "the great besetment of my soul," he wrote:

I am too proud to be ambitious, too proud to seek applause, too proud to tolerate it when lavished upon me, proud as Lucifer that I can and do scorn applause and spurn flattery, and indignantly dash down and shiver to atoms the censer in which others would burn incense to me; too proud to betray emotions, too proud ever for an instant to lose my self possession whatever the peril, too proud to ever move a hair for personal interest, too proud ever to defend my character when assailed or my motives when impeached, too proud ever to wince when the hot iron enters my soul and passes thro it.

He wrote also of his contempt of opponents—"one of the *trade* winds of my nature [which] very often . . . *blows a hurricane,*" and he listed by name those "who strangely and stupidly idolize me . . . and yield themselves to my sway in all confidence and love." He boasted of his daring and told of how as a child a tremendous thunderstorm would send him whooping and hallooing through the field like a wild Indian. He had the Puritan's love of enduring; the saint's "right" to intolerance. He was, in fact, always a revivalist—a man with a mission to perform in the great West—"the battlefield of the World."

The campaign which he launched was but an expansion of the benevolence crusade already a part of the Western revival effort. As W. C. Preston said: "Weld's agents made the antislavery cause 'identical with religion,' and urged men, by all they esteem[ed] holy, by all the high and exciting obligations of duty to man and God . . . to join the pious work of purging the sin of slavery from the land." The movement, as it developed, was generally temperate in tone, and tended to function through the existing agencies of religion and politics. Lane Theological Seminary, founded in Cincinnati to train leaders in the Finney tradition, became the center from which Weld worked. Here, in a series of debates, he shaped the doctrine of gradual immediatism which by insisting that *gradual emancipation* begin *at once,* saved the movement from Garrison's extremes; from here he went out to win a group of converts which included James G. Birney, Joshua Giddings, Edwin M. Stanton, Elizur Wright, and Beriah Green; and here he adapted the revival technique to the abolition crusade and prepared the way for his loyal band of Seventy to carry that crusade throughout the whole Northwest.

There was, however, another aspect to the movement in this region—a very hard-headed practical aspect. Its leaders believed in action as well as agitation. And action here meant political action. Western men had a way of viewing evil as something there ought to be a law against. They thought it was the business of government to secure morality as well as prosperity. They were even inclined to regard the absence of prosperity as the result of the existence of evil. Naturally, therefore, in spite of the revival-meeting procedure used to spread the gospel of abolition, action against slavery followed political precedent. This action began with petitions to Congress for such a practical end as the abolition of slavery in the District of Columbia. When Southern resentment of such a measure brought the adoption of gag rule methods, the contest was broadened into a fight on the floors of Congress for the constitutional rights of petition and free speech. This proved to be an excellent way to keep the slavery question before the public and to force slaveholders to reveal their undemocratic attitudes. Petitions arrived in such quantities as to clog the work of Congress. A Washington organization for agitation and lobbying became necessary. Weld himself went to Washington to advise with John Quincy Adams and his fellow workers. Slavery thus again entered national politics, this time by way of the Northwest. Anti-slavery politicians, such as Joshua Giddings and Salmon P. Chase of Ohio, quickly proved the value of the cause as a stepping-stone to public office. . . .

As economic rivalry between North and South increased, the anti-slavery movement gained strength and began to emerge as the dominant reform effort of the period. The motives underlying this development are partly revealed by a letter written by Joshua Leavitt to his friend Joshua Giddings in October, 1841. Leavitt spoke of Giddings' belief that the best policy for action was to aim "at specific points . . . which you deem beneficial to free labor or rather to the North, as a bank, tariff, etc." and then declared that his own purpose was to make opposition to slavery the *leading object* of public policy. "We must have a leading object," he continued,

> in which we can all harmonize, and to which we shall agree to defer all other favorite objects. It is vain to think of harmonizing the North in favor of a restrictive policy or an artificial credit system. . . . There is no object but slavery that can serve our turn . . . it is the greatest of evils and the prime cause of other evils. . . .

With the new growth and new importance of the movement, the technique of its propaganda also reached new efficiency. Never before or since has a cause been urged upon the American people with such consummate skill and such lasting effects. Every agency possible in that day was brought into use; even now the predominating opinions of most of the American people regarding the ante-bellum South and its ways are the product of that campaign of education. . . .

Juvenile story books, with some parts written in verse and printed in large and bold type and the rest written in prose and set in smaller type, were issued with the explanation that the verses were adapted to the capacity of the youngest reader, while the prose was well suited for being read aloud in the family circle. "It is presumed," said the preface, "that [with the prose] our younger friends will claim the assistance of their older brothers and sisters, or appeal to the ready aid of their mamma." Such volumes might contain pictures and stories from *Uncle Tom's Cabin* or they might consist of equally appealing tales of slave children cruelly torn from their parents or tortured by ingenious methods.

For adults the appeal was widened. No approach was neglected. Hymn books offered abolition songs set to familiar tunes. To the strains of "Old Hundred" eager voices invited "ye Yeomen brave" to rescue "the bleeding slave," or, to the "Missionary Hymn," asked them to consider

> The frantic mother
> Lamenting for her child,
> Till falling lashes smother
> Her cries of anguish wild!

Almanacs, carrying the usual information about weather and crops, filled their other pages with abolition propaganda. In one of these, readers found the story of Liburn Lewis, who, for a trifling offense, bound his slave, George, to a meat block and then, while all the other slaves looked on, proceeded slowly to chop him to pieces with a broad ax, and to cast the parts into a fire. Local, state, and national societies were organized for more efficient action in petitioning, presenting public speakers, distributing tracts, and publishing anti-slavery periodicals. The American Anti-Slavery Society "in the year 1837-38, published 7,877 bound volumes, 47,256 tracts and pamphlets, 4,100 circulars, and 10,490 prints. Its quarterly *Anti-Slavery Magazine* had an annual circulation of 9,000; the *Slave Friend,* for children, had 131,050; the monthly *Human Rights,* 189,400, and the weekly *Emancipator,* 217,000." From 1854 to 1858 it spent $3281 on a series of tracts discussing every phase of slavery, under such suggestive titles as "Disunion, our Wisdom and our Duty," "Relations of Anti-Slavery to Religion," and "To Mothers in the Free States." Its "several corps of lecturers of the highest ability and worth . . . occupied the field" every year in different states. Its Annual Reports, with their stories of atrocities and their biased discussion of issues, constituted a veritable arsenal from which weapons of attack could be drawn. Like other anti-slavery societies, it maintained an official organ, issued weekly, and held its regular conventions for the generation of greater force.

Where argument and appeal to reason failed, the abolitionists tried entertainment and appeal to emotion. *Uncle Tom's Cabin* was written because its author, "as a woman, as a mother," was "oppressed and broken hearted, with the sorrows & injustice" seen, and "because as a Christian" she "felt the dishonor to Christianity—because as a lover of [her] country, she trembled at the coming day of wrath." It became a best seller in the most complete sense. Only the Bible exceeded it in numbers sold and in the thoroughness with which it was read in England and America. Editions were adapted to every pocketbook, and translations carried it throughout the world. Dramatized and put on the stage, it did more to make the theatre respectable in rural America than any other single influence. The fictitious Uncle Tom became the stereotype of all American Negro slaves; Simon Legree became the typical slaveholder. A generation and more formed its ideas of Southern life and labor from the pages of this novel. A romantic South, of planter-gentlemen and poor whites, of chivalry and dissipation, of "sweet but worthless" women, was given an imaginative reality so wide and so gripping that no amount of patient research and sane history writing could alter it. Other novels, such as *Our World: or the Slaveholder's Daughter,* built their plots about the love affairs of Southern planters with their Negro slaves.

Jealousies between wives and mistresses, struggles between brothers for the possession of some particularly desirable wench, or the inner conflict of a master over his obligation to his mulatto bastards, constituted the main appeal in such works. The object was always the same: to reveal the licentious character of Southern men, the unhappy status of Southern homes, and the horrible violation of Negro chastity everywhere existing under slavery.

Reformed slaveholders and escaped slaves were especially valuable in the crusade. Under the warming influence of sympathetic audiences their stories of cruelty and depravity grew apace. Persecution and contempt from old friends increased their zeal. Birney, the Grimké sisters, Frederick Douglass, and many others influenced the movement and were influenced by it in a way comparable only to the relation of reformed drunkards to the temperance cause.

By means of such agencies and methods a well-defined picture of the South and slavery became slowly fixed in Northern minds. The Southern people were divided into two distinct classes—slaveholders and poor whites. The former constituted an aristocracy, living in great white-pillared houses on extended plantations. The latter, ignorant and impotent, made up a rural slum which clung hopelessly to the pine barrens or the worn-out acres on the fringes of the plantations. Planters, who lived by the theft of Negro labor, completely dominated the section. They alone were educated; they alone held office. Non-slaveholders were too poor to "buy an education for themselves and their children," and the planters, not wishing to "endanger their supremacy," refused to establish public schools. Few poor whites could either read or write. They gained their opinions and their principles from "stump speeches and tavern conversations." They were "absolutely in the slaveholder's power." He sent "them to the polls to vote him into office and in so doing to vote down their own rights and interests. . . ." They knew "no more what they [were] about, than so many children or so many Russian serfs. . . ."

Social-economic condtitions in the South were described as tumble-down and backward. The slave, lacking the incentive of personal gain, was inefficient. The master, ruined by power, self-indulgence, and laziness, was incapable of sound management. James Birney described the section as one

whose Agriculture is desolation—whose Commerce is mainly confined to a crazy wagon and half fed team of oxen or mules as a means of carrying it on —whose manufacturing "Machinery" is limited to the bones and sinews of reluctant slaves—whose currency is individual notes always to *be* paid (it may be at some broken bank) and mortgages on men and women and children who may run away or die, and on land, which without them is of little value. . . .

Others went so far as to charge the panic of 1837 to Southern profligacy. "The existence of Slavery," resolved the American Anti-Slavery Society in 1844, "is the grand cause of the pecuniary embarrassments of the country; and . . . no real or permanent relief is to be expected . . . until the total abolition of that execrable system." Joshua Leavitt called the slave system "a bottomless gulf of extravagance and thirftlessness." Another explained its "withering and impoverishing effect by the fact that it was the "rule of violence and arbitrary will. . . . It would be quite in character with its theory and practice," he said, "if slave-drivers should refuse to pay their debts and meet the sheriff with dirk and pistol." Leavitt estimated that the South had "taken from the North, within five years, more than $100,000,000, by notes which will never be paid," and quoted an English writer to the effect that "planters are always in debt. The system of society in a slaveholding community is such as to lead to the contraction of debt, which the system itself does not furnish the means of paying. . . ."

Nor did the Southern shortcomings, according to the antislavery view, end with things material. Moral weaknesses were even more offensive. Sexual virtue was scarcely known. "The Slave States," wrote an abolitionist, "are Sodoms, and almost every village family is a brothel." Another writer declared that "in the slaveholding settlements of Middle and Southern Mississippi . . . there [was] not a virtuous young man of twenty years of age." "To send a lad to a male academy in Mississippi," he said, "is moral murder." An anti-slavery pamphlet told of "a million and half of slave women, some of them without even the tinge of African blood . . . given up a lawful prey to the unbridled lusts of their masters." Another widely circulated tract described a slave market in which one dealer "devoted himself exclusively to the sale of young mulatto women." The author pictured the sale of "the most beautiful woman I ever saw," without *"a single trace of the African about her features"* and with "a pair of eyes that pierced one through and through" to "one of the most lecherous-looking old brutes" that he had every seen. The narrative closed with the shrieking appeal: "God shield the helpless victim of that bad man's power—it may be, ere now, that bad man's lust!" The conclusion was inescapable. Slavery and unrestrained sexual indulgence at Negro expense were inseparable.

In such a section and in the hands of such men, abolitionists assumed that slavery realized its most vicious possibilities. Anti-slavery men early set themselves to the task of collecting stories of cruelty. These were passed about from one to another, often gaining in ferocity as they travelled. Weld gathered them together in a volume entitled *American Slavery As It Is* and scattered them broadcast over the North. The annual reports of the anti-slavery societies, their tracts and periodicals, also revelled in atrocities, asking no more proof of their absolute truth than the word of a fellow fanatic.

The attempt to picture slavery "as it was," therefore, came to consist almost entirely of a recital of brutalities. Now and then a kind master and seemingly contented slaves were introduced for the purpose of contrast—as a device to deepen shadows. But, as a rule, Southerners, according to these tracts, spent their time in idleness broken only by brutal cock-fights, gander pullings, and horse races so barbarous that "the blood of the tortured animal drips from the lash and flies at every leap from the stroke of the rowel." Slavery was one continual round of abuse. The killing of a slave was a matter of no consequence. Even respectable ladies might cause "several to be *whipped to death.*" Brandings, ear cropping, and body-maiming were the rule. David L. Child honestly declared: "From all that I have read and heard upon the subject of whipping done by masters and overseers to slaves . . . I have come to the conclusion that some hundreds of *cart whips* and cowskin instruments, which I am told make the skin fly like feathers, and cut frequently to the bone, are in *perpetual daily motion* in the slave states." John Rankin told of Negroes stripped, hung up and stretched and then "whipped until their bodies [were] covered with blood and mangled flesh," some dying "under the lash, others linger[ing] about for a time, and at length die[ing] of their *wounds. . . .*" The recital was indeed one of *"groans, tears, and blood."*

To abuse was added other great wrongs. Everywhere slaves were overworked, underfed, and insufficiently clothed and sheltered. Family ties were cut without the slightest regard for Negro feelings—infants were torn from the mother's breast, husbands separated from their wives and families. Marriage was unknown among slaves, and the right to worship God generally denied. Strangely enough, little was said of slave-breeding for market. That charge was largely left to the politicians of the next decades and to the historians of a later day.

Two principal assumptions stood out in this anti-slavery indictment of the slaveholder. He was, in the first place, the arch-aristocrat. He was the great enemy of democracy. He was un-American, the oppressor of his fellow men, the exploiter of a weaker brother. Against him could be directed all the complaints and fears engendered by industrial captains and land speculators. He, more than any other aristocrat, threatened to destroy the American democratic dream.

In the second place, he was a flagrant sinner. His self-indulgence was unmatched. His licentious conduct with Negro women, his intemperance in the use of intoxicating liquors, his mad dueling, and his passion for war against the weak were enough to mark him as the nation's moral enemy number one! The time for dealing moderately had passed. Immediate reform was imperative.

Thus it was that the slaveholder began to do scapegoat service for all aristocrats and all sinners. To him were transferred resentments and fears born out of local conditions. Because it combined in itself both the moral and the democratic appeal, and because it coincided with sectional rivalry, the abolition movement gradually swallowed up all other reforms. The South became the great object of all efforts to remake American society. Against early indifference and later persecution, a handful of deadly-in-earnest men and women slowly built into a section's consciousness the belief in a Slave Power. To the normal strength of sectional ignorance and distrust they added all the force of Calvinistic morality and American democracy and thereby surrounded every Northern interest and contention with holy sanction and reduced all opposition to abject depravity. When the politician, playing his risky game, linked expansion and slavery, Christian common folk by the thousands, with no great personal urge for reforming, accepted the Abolition attitudes toward both the South and slavery. Civil war was then in the making.

The Abolitionists and Psychology

MARTIN B. DUBERMAN

Revisionist historians sometimes used psychology to discredit as well as to explain the motives of reformers. There has long been controversy over the use of psychological theory in historical interpretation, but in recent years a number of historians have been particularly concerned over the implications of "explaining" idealism, social commitment, and altruistic behavior as the products of inner tensions and disguised needs. Martin B. Duberman (1930-   ),

Martin B. Duberman, "The Abolitionists and Psychology," *The Journal of Negro History*, XLVII (July 1962), pp. 183–191. Reprinted without footnotes and with minor deletions by permission of the author and The Association for the Study of Negro Life and History, Inc., Washington, D.C.

the biographer of Charles Francis Adams and James Russell Lowell, the author of the play, "In White America," and an associate professor of history at Princeton, has restored a note of intellectual humility and critical common sense to discussions of the psychology of reform.

O
UT OF THEIR HEIGHTENED CONCERN WITH THE PRESSING QUESTION of Negro rights, a number of historians, especially the younger ones, have begun to take a new look at the abolitionists, men who in their own day were involved in a similar movement of social change. About both them and ourselves we are asking anew such questions as the proper role of agitation, the underlying motives of both reformers and resistants, and the useful limits of outside interference. From this questioning a general tendency has developed to view the abolitionists in a more favorable light than previously. As yet, however, it is a tendency only, and hostility to the abolitionists continues to be strong among historians.

Perhaps one reason why no fuller reevaluation has taken place is that historians have been made cautious by the fate of previous "revisionist" scholarship. We have seen how current preoccupations can prompt dubious historical reevaluations. But this need not always be the case. Contemporary pressures, if recognized and contained, can prove fruitful in stimulating the historical imagination. They may lead us to uncover (not invent) aspects of the past to which we were previously blind.

If historians need more courage in their re-consideration of the abolitionists, they also need more information. Particularly do they need to employ some of the insights and raise some of the questions which developments in related fields of knowledge have made possible. Recent trends in psychology seem especially pertinent, though historians have not paid them sufficient attention. It is my hope in this paper to make some beginning in that direction.

It might be well to start by referring to one of psychology's older principles, the uniqueness of personality. Each individual, with his own genetic composition and his own life experience, will develop into a distinctive organism. There are, of course, certain universal processes common to the species—that cluster of basic drives and reflexes which are more or less "instinctive." There are also a variety of common responses conditioned by our membership in a particular group, be it family, class, church or nation. These similarities among human beings make possible such disciplines as sociology, anthropology and social psychology, which concern themselves with patterns of behavior, and demonstrate that no man is *sui generis*. But it does not follow that the qualities which are uniquely individual are mere irrelevancies. As Gordon Allport has said, ". . . all of the animals in the world are psychologically less distinct from one another than one man is from other men."

This is not to question, of course, the validity of attempts, whether they be by sociologists, psychologists or historians, to find meaningful similarities in the behavioral patterns of various human groups. The point is to make certain that such similarities genuinely exist, and further, to be aware that in describing them, we do not pretend to be saying *everything* about the idividuals involved. Historians, it seems, are prone to ignore both cautions—their treatment of the abolitionists being the immediate case in point.

With barely a redeeming hint of uncertainty, many historians list a group of "similar traits" which are said to characterize all abolitionists: "impractical," "self-righteous," "fanatical," "humorless," "vituperative," and,—if they are very modern in their terminology—"disturbed." The list varies, but usually only to include adjectives equally hostile and denunciatory. The stereotype of the "abolitionist personality," though fluid in details, is clear enough in its general outlines.

But did most abolitionists really share these personality traits? The fact is, we know much less about the individuals involved in the movement than has been implied. Some of the major figures, such as Joshua Leavitt, have never received biographical treatment; others—the Tappans, Edmund Quincy, and Benjamin Lundy, for example—badly need modern appraisal. And the careers and personalities of the vast majority of significant secondary figures—people like Lydia Maria Child, Sidney Gay, Maria Weston Chapman, Henry B. Stanton, and Abby Kelley Foster—have been almost totally unexplored. Whence comes the confidence, then, that allows historians to talk of "the abolitionist personality," as if this had been microscopically examined and painstakingly reconstructed?

Certainly the evidence which we do have, does not support such confident theorizing. In order to adhere to this conceptual strait-jacket, it is necessary to ignore or discount much that conflicts with it—the modesty of Theodore Weld, the wit of James Russell Lowell, the tender humanity of Whittier, the worldly charm of Edmund Quincy. This does not mean that we need leap to the opposite extreme and claim all abolitionists were saints and seraphs. But if some of them were disagreeable or disturbed, we want, instead of a blanket indictment, to know which ones and in what ways; we want some recognition of the variety of human beings who entered the movement.

It seems to me that what too many historians have done is to take William Lloyd Garrison as a personality symbol for the entire movement (at the same time, ironically, that they deny him the commanding leadership which he was once assumed to have had). Fixing on some of the undeniably "neurotic" aspects of his personality (and bolstered, it should be said, by the eccentric psychographs of other abolitionists—a Gerrit Smith say, or a Stephen Foster), they equate these with the personality structures of all the abolitionists, and conclude that the movement was composed solely of "quacks." In doing so, they fail to do justice to the wide spectrum of personality involved; in fact, they do not even do justice to Garrison, for to speak exclusively of *his* oracular and abusive qualities is to ignore the considerable evidence of personal warmth and kindliness.

It may be that when we know more of other abolitionists, we may with equal certainty be able to single out qualities in them which seem palpable symptoms of "disturbance." But let the evidence at least precede the judgment. And let us also show a decent timidity in applying the label "neurotic." Psychiatrists, dealing with a multitude of evidence and bringing to it professional insights, demonstrate more caution in this regard than do untrained historians working with mere traces of personality. If the disposition to be hostile exists, "neurosis" can almost always be established. Under the Freudian microscope, it would be a rare man indeed whose life showed no evidence of pathological behavior. (Think, for one, of the admirable William James, who, as his devoted biographer, Ralph Barton Perry, has shown, was subject to hypochondria, hallucinations, and intense oscillations of mood.) I am not suggesting that all men's lives, if sufficiently investigated, would show equally severe evidence of disturbance. I mean only to warn that, given the double jeopardy of a hostile commentator and the weight of a hostile historical tradition, we must take special precaution not to be too easily convinced by the "evidence" of neurosis in the abolitionists.

And even were we to establish the neurotic component of behavior, the story would certainly not be complete. To know the pathological elements in an individual's behavior is not to know everything about his behavior. To say that Garrison, in his fantasy world, longed to be punished and thus deliberately courted martyrdom, or that Wendell Phillips, alienated from the "new order," sought to work out his private grievances against the industrial system by indirectly attacking it through slavery, is hardly to exhaust the range of their possible motives. We know far too little about why men do anything—let alone why they do something as specific as joining a reform movement—to assert as confidently as historians have, the motives of whole groups of men. We may never know enough about the human psyche to achieve a comprehensive analysis of motivation; how much greater the difficulty when the subject is dead and we are attempting the analysis on the basis of partial and fragmentary remains.

Our best hope for increased understanding in this area—aside from the artist's tool of intuition—is in the researches of psychology. But at present there is no agreed-upon theory of motivation among psychologists. Gordon Allport, however, summarizing current opinion, suggests that behavior does not result solely from the need to reduce tension, but may also aim (especially in a "healthy" person) at distant goals, the achievement of which can be gained only by maintaining tension. Allport does not press his views, realizing the complexity of the problems at issue. But his hypotheses are at least suggestive as regards the abolitionists, for their motives, rather than being solely the primitive ones of eliminating personal tension (under the guise of ethical commitment), may also have included a healthy willingness to bear tension (in the form of ostracism, personal danger and material sacrifice) in order to persevere in the pursuit of longrange ideals.

Acceptance of these suggestions runs into the massive resistance of neo-Freudian cynicism. How old-fashioned, it will be said, to talk in terms of "ideals" or "conscience," since these are only unconscious rationalizations for "darker" drives which we are unable to face. How old-fashioned, too, to talk as if men could exercise choice in their conduct, since all our behavior is determined by our antecedents.

But the surprising fact is that such views are not old-fashioned. On the contrary, they have recently returned to favor in psychoanalytical circles. Increasing dissatisfaction with the ability of behaviorist theory fully to explain human action, has led to a re-consideration of the role of reason and the possibilities of purposive, deliberate behavior. The result is the influential new school of "ego psychology," which views man as endowed with a considerable margin of freedom and responsibility, and which has restored to the vocabulary such "old-fashioned" terminology as character, will-power and conscience. Moral earnestness, moreover, is no longer equated with self-deception. As Allport has said, the very mark of maturity "seems to be the range and extent of one's feeling of self-involvement in abstract ideals." Some of these new emphases had been prefigured in the work of such philosophers as Sartre, who have long stressed social action as a sign of "authenticity" in man.

But although all of this makes a re-evaluation of the abolitionists possible, it does not make one necessary. Men may now be thought capable of impersonal devotion to ideals, but this does not mean that the abolitionists were such men. Maturity may now be defined as the ability to commit ourselves objectively to ethical values, but it does not follow that every man who makes such a commitment does so out of mature motives.

Yet at least some doubts should be raised in our minds as to whether we have been fair in regarding the abolitionists as psychologically homogeneous, and at that, homogeneous in the sense of being self-deceived. My own feeling goes beyond doubt, into conviction. I do not claim, to repeat, that because the abolitionists fought in a noble cause, their motives were necessarily noble—i.e., "pure" and "unselfish," unrelated in any way to their own inner turmoil or conflicts. A connection between inner problems and outer convictions probably always exists to some degree. But an individual's public involvement is never completely explained by discussing his private pathology. Yet it is just this that historians have frequently done, and to that degree, they have distorted and devaluated the abolitionist commitment.

To provide a concrete example, by way of summary, consider the case of James Russell Lowell, whose biography I am writing, and about whom I can talk with more assurance than I might some other figure.

His history seems to me convincing proof that at least *some* people became abolitionists not primarily out of an unconscious need to escape from personal problems, but out of a deliberate, rational commitment to certain ethical values—recognizing, as I have said, that the two are never wholly unrelated. Lowell's active life as a reformer came during the period of his greatest contentment—secure in a supremely happy marriage, and confident of his talents and his future. His contemporaries agree in describing him as a gay, witty, warm man, without serious tensions or disabling anxieties. I have come across so little evidence of "pathology" in the Lowell of these years that when the standard picture of the abolitionist as a warped eccentric is applied to him, it becomes absurd.

And he *was* an abolitionist, though various arguments have been used to deny this. Lowell, it has been said, came to the movement late—and only at the instigation of his bride, Maria White, who was a confirmed reformer, never fully committed himself to abolition, and finally left the ranks in the early 1850s. There may be some justice to these charges, but on the whole the argument is not persuasive. Given Lowell's youth (he was born in 1819) he could not have joined the movement much earlier than he did (which was around 1840), and there is evidence that he was involved in the cause before he met Maria White. The important point is that for roughly ten years he was unquestionably a serious abolitionist, both as an active member of the Massachusetts Anti-Slavery Society, and as a frequent contributor to abolitionist periodicals. The reasons for his drifting out of the movement are complex, but turn largely on the fact that his wife's death in 1853 destroyed the structure of his life and left him apathetic to public issues. (Might not this give added weight to the argument that it takes a reasonably contented man to interest himself in the problems of others?)

Even when it is admitted that Lowell was an abolitionist, he is dismissed as not having been a "typical" one. But who was the typical abolitionist? Is the standard of measurement meant to be some outstanding individual—Garrison, say, or Theodore Weld—and is everyone else to be considered more or less of an abolitionist depending on how closely he approximated the personality structure of the model? But a man may be prominent in a movement without necessarily typifying it. And which of several leading—and very different—figures should be chosen as the model? The decision is likely to be arbitrary (and unconscious), varying with each historian.

Or is the standard of measurement meant to be some composite group of traits which accurately describe the large number of abolitionists, so that when any single individual fails to exhibit these traits, he may justifiably be dismissed as "the exception which proves the rule?" This approach is more reasonable, but here again we run up against the old difficulty of drawing a genuinely valid group portrait. We know so little about the individual personalities and careers of the majority of abolitionists that it seems like putting the cart before the horse to even talk about a composite portrait. Certainly the one which is now commonly accepted ("impractical"; "self-righteous," etc.) fails adequately to describe many of the abolitionists about whom we do have information. I mean here not only Lowell, but a number of others. What I have seen in my researches into the papers of people like Edmund Quincy, Lydia Maria Child or Maria Weston Chapman (to name only a few of the more prominent), has created the strong suspicion in my mind that if their personalities were to be investigated in depth, they too would be found to deviate from the accepted portrait in so many significant ways as further to undermine its reliability.

A conceptual scheme may yet be devised which adequately describes the motives and actions of most of the abolitionists. But if so, it will not be of the primitive kind thus far suggested. There is no reason why historians cannot legitimately investigate group patterns, but to do so meaningfully, they must become skilled in the techniques of sociology and other related disciplines. This takes time and inclination, and the historian, busy with his special interests and orientated towards the particular, rarely has either. Unfortunately this does not always prevent him from trying his hand, though the result has too often been the elementary kind of categorizing used to describe the abolitionists.

. . .

Opinions will continue to differ as to the best way of achieving desired social change. Our own generation's confrontation with segregation has made this clear. Many of us feel as strongly about the evil of that practice as the abolitionists did about the institution of slavery. Like them, too, we have scant faith in Southern voluntarism or the benevolent workings of time; patience and inactivity have not done their work. Naturally we would like to believe that our sense of urgency comes from concern for the Negro rather than from a need to escape from some private torment of our own. Because of this we are admittedly prone to credit our historical counterparts with the kind of "good" motives we would like to impute to ourselves. Our wish to think well of these people may account for our doing so. But as Erich Fromm has said, "the fact that an idea satisfies a wish does not mean necessarily that the idea is false." There is much in the new psychology to encourage the belief that the idea is not false. At any rate, if we are to find out, we need less dogma, more research, and a chastening sense of wonder at the complexities of human nature.

The Psychology of Commitment: The Constructive Role of Violence and Suffering for the Individual and for his Society

SILVAN S. TOMKINS

In searching for fresh approaches to the psychology of reformers, Martin Duberman recently enlisted the cooperation of Silvan S. Tomkins (1911–   ), a specialist in personality theory, a professor of psychology at Princeton, and now Director of the Center for Research in Cognition and Affect, City University of New York. Professor Tomkins pursues three important questions which have been touched upon in the preceding selections: What types of personalities are predisposed toward reform? How do an individual's "affects," or feelings, become involved in a social cause? What are the social dynamics of commitment, and what effect do reformers have on society? Far from seeing the abolitionists as irresponsible fanatics whose neurotic strivings brought the nation to the brink of ruin, he portrays them as bold extroverts whose deepening commitment to social justice led to increasing risks, persecution, and violence. He suggests that by engaging the feelings, emotions, and finally the sympathy of the public, the abolitionists made it impossible to ignore or evade the problem of slavery.

THIS IS AN ESSAY IN THE PSYCHOLOGY OF COMMITMENT; WHY AND how individuals and societies become committed to ideologies and to social movements. We will examine four abolitionists—Garrison, Phillips, Weld, and Birney as committed reformers. Why and how did each become attached to abolitionism? How did they influence others to become

Silvan S. Tomkins, "The Psychology of Commitment: The Constructive Role of Violence and Suffering for the Individual and for His Society," in Martin B.

t to oppose the extension of
sychological dynamic underlies
e group. More particularly, we
critical in a democratic society,
of democratic values and in
ıch violations. A radical magni-
pressors and of positive feeling
mic which powers the commit-
then of increasing numbers who

quire a preliminary presentation
ıed that the primary motives of
feelings. These are the positive
prise, and the negative affects of
distress, anger, fear, shame, and ......pt. These are innate. One does
not learn to smile in enjoyment nor to cry in distress. However, the
objects of each affect are *both* innate and learned. A baby does not learn
the birth cry. It is an innate response to the excessive stimulation attend-
ant upon being born. He will later cry when he is hungry or tired or
exposed to too loud sounds. None of these are learned responses. But
eventually he *will* learn to cry about many things about which he was
initially unconcerned. He may learn to cry in sympathy when others are
in distress and cry. But if the crying of others may be learned to evoke
one's own distress cry, so may it also be learned to evoke contempt or
shame rather than sympathy. There is nothing under the sun which some
human beings have not learned to enjoy, to fear or hate, to be ashamed
of, or to respond to with excitement or contempt or anger. This innate
plasticity of the affect mechanism which permits the investment of any
type of affect in any type of activity or object, makes possible the great
varieties of human personalities and societies. Cultural diversity rests
upon the biological plasticity of the affect system in man. "Puritanism,"
or negative affect about pleasure, and masochism, or positive affect about
pain, are extreme examples of the possibilities of affect investment. The
variety of possible affect investments are without limit. I may be very
happy as a child and very sad as an adult, or conversely. I may be angry
for a moment, for an hour, for a day, or always, or never. I may be
frightened only occasionally or I may be anxious all my life. I may feel
mildly ashamed of myself or deeply humiliated. I may feel ashamed

Duberman (ed.), *The Antislavery Vanguard: New Essays on the Abolitionists*,
1965, pp. 270–298. Reprinted without footnotes and with minor deletions by permission of Princeton University Press. Copyright © 1965 by Princeton University
Press.

because I have shown my feelings too publicly or because I was unable to show my feelings at all. In short, the object, the duration, the frequency, and the intensity of affect arousal and investment are without limit.

We will now introduce a corollary—the "density" of feeling and thought. "Low density" refers to those experiences which generate little or no feeling (affect) and little or no thinking (ideation), or, if the feeling and thought are intense, they do not last long. "High density" occurs whenever the individual has intense feelings and thoughts which continue at a high level over long periods of time. In such a case there is a monopolistic capture of the individual's awareness and concern. Low and high densities represent two ends of a continuum of organization of motive, thought, and behavior which are critical for the understanding of commitment. For brevity, we will hereafter arbitrarily refer to "low and high density organizations of feeling and thought" as "weak and strong affects."

There are two weak affect types, transitory and recurrent. Consider first the positive transitory case. Such would be the laughter in response to a joke. The experience might be extremely enjoyable but nonetheless of very low density, because it recruited no continuing ideation or affect beyond the momentary experience. An example of the negative transitory case would be a cut while shaving which occasioned a brief stab of pain and distress, but no further thought or feeling beyond this isolated experience. Each individual's lifetime contains thousands of such relatively trivial encounters. Collectively they may amount to a not inconsiderable segment of the life span. Nonetheless they constitute an aggregate of isolated components without substantial impact on the personality of the individual.

Recurrent weak affects characteristically begin with considerable intensity of feeling and thought but end with minimal involvement. Consider first the negative recurrent case. Everyone learns to cross streets with minimal affect and ideation. We learn to act *as if* we were afraid, but we do not in fact experience any fear once we have learned how to cope successfully with such contingencies. Despite the fact that we know that there is real danger involved daily in walking across intersections and that some pedestrians are in fact killed, we exercise normal caution with minimal attention and no fear. Street-crossing remains weak in its affect despite daily repetition over a lifetime. This is not to say that it was always so. The earliest such experiences may well have been high adventures for the daring child or they may have been the occasion of severe punishment at the hands of an anxious parent terrified at the sight of his toddler walking in front of a speeding automobile. Both the excitement and the pain or distress which might have been suffered at the hands of a parent do not long continue. Quickly all children learn some caution in this matter and it ceases to claim much attention. Such attenuation of feeling and thought necessarily depends upon the success of problem solutions. Paradoxically, human beings are least involved in what they can do best—when problems, once solved, remain solved. Man as a successful problem solver ceases to think and to feel about successful performance and turns ideation and affect to continuing or new, unsolved challenges.

This is so whether the original affect which powered problem solving was negative or positive. Just as we experience no terror in confronting traffic at the curb, so too in the positive, low density case, we experience no significant enjoyment or excitement in the daily recurrent performances which once delighted. As I finish my daily shaving I rarely puff with pride and think, "There, I've done it again."

What then of the strong affects? By definition they can be neither transitory nor recurrent but must be enduring. Whether predominantly positive or negative in tone, they must seize the individual's feelings and thoughts to the exclusion of almost all else. Consider first, negative monopolism of thought and feeling. If successful and *continuing* problem solution is the necessary condition of the weak affect, *temporary* problem solution is the necessary condition of strong affect. Consider our man on the curb. He is normally cautious but not overly concerned because his solution to the problem has always worked. But suppose that one day a passing motorist loses control of his car and seriously injures our hero. After his return from the hospital he is a bit more apprehensive than before, and now stands back a little farther from the edge of the curb than he used to. He may continue his somewhat excessive caution for some time, and (as he notes a car approaching with what appears a little too much speed) may even begin to wonder with occasional fear, whether such an accident might ever happen again. But if all goes well this increase in density of ideation and affect will pass and before long he will be indistinguishable from any other casual pedestrian.

But in our tragedy all does not go well. Uncannily a drunken driver pursues our hero and he is hit again. This time it is more serious and we see the beginnings of a phobia. Our hero stations himself inside of a building peering up and down the street before he will venture out to dare negotiate the crossing. By now his preoccupation with and fear of the deadly vehicle has grown to invade his consciousness even when he is far from the scene of potential danger. In the last act of this drama it is a bulldozer which penetrates his apparent fortress. What next? Will he be safe in the hospital? His ideation and affect have now reached a point of no return. He will henceforth generate possibilities which no reasonable man would entertain and these phantasies will evoke affects proportional to their extremity. Such strong affect is capable of providing a lifetime of suffering and of resisting reduction through new evidence. This happens if, and only if, there has occurred a sequence of events of this type: threat, successful defense, breakdown of defense and re-emergence of threat, second successful new defense, second breakdown of defense and re-emergence of threat, third successful new defense, third breakdown of defense and re-emergence of threat and so on, until an expectation is generated that no matter how successful a defense against a dread contingency may seem, it will prove unavailing and require yet another new defense, ad infinitum. Not only is there generated the conviction that successful defense can be successful only temporarily, but also, as new and more effective defenses are generated, the magnitude of the danger is inflated in the imagination of the "victim." This same process, as we shall see, was involved in the polarization of North and South which culminated in the Civil War. . . .

Let us turn to the interpretation of abolitionism in the light of our theory. We will now also examine more closely just how such strong affects are formed as well as the numerous ways in which they may fail to be sustained.

The commitment of Garrison, Phillips, Weld, and Birney to abolitionism proceeded in a series of steps consistent with our general theory of commitment. The critical role of adult experience in gradually deepening commitment is underlined by the differing early careers of these men and the diverse paths each took toward a common ultimate commitment to abolitionism. No one could have predicted with any confidence that these four young men would eventually provide leadership for the abolitionist movement. Garrison was first attracted to writing and to politics as a way of life. Phillips led the life typical of the Boston Brahmin of his time: attendance at Harvard College, Harvard Law School and then the opening of a law practice. Weld first gave a series of lectures on mnemonics, the art of improving the memory. Birney was twice suspended from Princeton for drinking, though he was each time readmitted and finally graduated with honors. He, like Phillips, became a gentleman lawyer, priming himself for a political career. After an early failure in politics he became a planter and lived the life of the young Southern aristocrat, drinking and gambling to excess. Paradoxically, of the four, he was the earliest to interest himself in the slaves, but the last to commit himself to their emancipation as his way of life.

It is essential to recognize that one cannot account for the abolitionist reformer on the assumption that his was a commitment such as that of "falling in love at first sight." None of these men knew at first that they were to commit their lives to the emancipation of the slave; three of the four were first attracted to a career in politics. But if there is a perennial danger of exaggerating the continuity of human development, and especially the influence of the early years on the adult personality, there is also the opposite danger of exaggerating the impact of adult experience on crucial adult choices, and overlooking the contribution of the early years to choices which on the surface appear to represent novelty in the adult's experience. Our argument will stress both the continuity and the discontinuity in the development of Garrison, Phillips, Weld, and Birney in their growing commitment to abolitionism.

All were early prepared and destined for leadership of a special kind, for saving the self through saving others. Each might have become a crusading politician, writer, orator, or preacher. Indeed Birney did later run as a crusading candidate for the Presidency of the United States. Weld later, because of his failing speech, did become a writer for abolitionism instead of an orator. Phillips, after the Civil War, did continue crusading for labor, for temperance, for Ireland against England, for the American Indians, and for the abolition of capital punishment. Garrison, too, after the Civil War, maintained his interest in women's rights and in temperance reform, though with much less zeal than Phillips. Given the continuity of their concern with salvation, the interest of these men in abolitionism was not wholly novel. On the other hand, it would be a mistake to assume that their concern with salvation *necessitated* their becoming abolitionists.

Let us begin by examining the original "resonance" which first attracted these and other men to abolitionism. By resonance we mean the ability of any organized ideology or social movement to engage feeling and thought. The fit between the individual's own, often loosely organized feelings and ideas, and the more tightly organized ideology or social movement, need not be a very close one to induce resonance. Some men resonated to abolitionism because slavery violated their Christian faith, or because of a general sympathy for the underdog. Others resonated to the idea of abolition because of a belief in the perfectibility of man. Still others were attracted because of a belief in the democratic assertion of the equal rights of all men, or a belief in individualism. Some were originally attracted because their own salvation required that they save others. There were those who were attracted because they hated oppression and oppressors and some because they could not tolerate humiliation, even vicariously. The plight of the slave induced resonance for these and many other reasons.

The bases for the original resonance of Garrison, Phillips, Weld, and

Birney to abolitionism contained common elements and also differences. All four were deeply Christian. Three of the four had conversion experiences. For Garrison, Phillips, and Weld their Christianity required that they save others if they would save themselves. Each of these three had been impressed by strong, pious Christian mothers that to be good meant to do good. The fourth, Birney, had been left motherless at the age of three, and his strongest relationship was with his father who believed not only in Christian good works, but more specifically had, along with *his* father, fought to make Kentucky a free state: though they lost this fight they continued to be active against slavery. In all four parents, moral and Christian zeal for the salvation of their children (and other sinners) was combined with great affection for the children. These parents provided the appropriate models for future reformers. The children were taught how to combine concern and contempt for the sinner with love for those sinners who would reform.

Not only was there a strong Christian influence which predisposed these men to resonate to abolitionism, but in addition their parents had also shown a pervasive concern with public service. Garrison's mother, who was the sole provider, nursed the sick. Birney's father was politically active in favor of emancipation. Phillips' father was mayor of Boston. Weld's father was a minister. All were concerned with service to others and provided a model which predisposed their sons to resonate to any movement based on public service.

Third, all four appeared to have been physically very active and extroverted as children. They had abundant energy which they translated into vigorous play and into fighting with their peers. This, too, contributed to their resonance to a movement which called for direct action and face to face confrontation before large groups.

Fourth, all were exposed to, influenced by, and modeled themselves after, the great orators of their day. As Perry Miller has noted, one of the salient features of the puritan's reformation was the substitution of the sermon for the Mass. All four men were early exposed to the magic of the great orators of the day, both Christian and secular. All four as young men were fluent and articulate and gave evidence of being able to hold audiences by their speaking powers. The combination of great energy, extroversion, and the power to influence others by oratorical ability predisposed them to resonate to a movement which required those who could influence others in just such ways.

Fifth, all of them were physically courageous. They had all experienced and mastered the art of fighting with their peers, so that they had a zest for combat rather than a dread of it. No one who too much feared physical combat could afford to resonate to the defense of those held in

bondage by the ever present threat of force. The overly timid cannot entertain a rescue phantasy.

These are some of the characteristics which these four men shared and which originally attracted them to abolitionism. But there were also important differences between them. Phillips was first actively attracted to a defense of abolitionism by the murder of the abolitionist Lovejoy. As a patrician, he was outraged at the tyranny of the mob and its violation of civil liberties. He was also outraged that "gentlemen" of his own class, from his own beloved Boston, should form a mob and threaten the life of Garrison. He was attracted at first more by disgust at mob violence than by concern over slavery. In contrast, Garrison, Birney, and Weld were first attracted to the problem of slavery out of direct sympathy for the slave. Each resonated first not to abolitionism but to the program of the American Colonization Society of gradual emancipation with transportation of free American Negroes to Africa. Nor, for two of them, was even this interest salient from the outset. Although slavery interested Weld increasingly, temperance and manual labor education were his primary concerns for some time. Birney, due to his exposure to his father's and grandfather's political activity on behalf of emanicpation, was earliest interested in the problem of slavery, but it was some time before he committed himself wholeheartedly to even the program of the American Colonization Society. It was to be several more years, when he was over forty, that he committed himself to abolitionism.

Garrison and Weld were soon to change the nature of their relationship to the problem of slavery. Garrison led the way with a frontal attack on the slaveholder and those who trafficked in slavery, and with a denunciation of the American Colonization Society. In this he was radically to influence others, including Weld, Phillips, and finally Birney. Added to sympathy for the slave was now contempt and anger both for the Southern sinners and for those Northerners who either cooperated with or were indifferent to Southern tyranny. Birney held back because he was not yet convinced that the Southern slaveholder could not be reached by reason, because he was temperamentally allergic to enthusiasm, and because he was at that time more interested in improving and preserving his beloved South than in destorying the slaveholder. Only painfully and reluctantly was he forced to leave the South and become an abolitionist.

Garrison, in contrast, had the greatest enthusiasm for nailing the sinner to the cross, while Phillips, disgusted more with his own class than with the Southern slaveholder, also resonated, as we have seen, to somewhat different aspects of abolitionism. Weld, in contrast both to Phillips and Garrison, was a shy "backwoodsman" as he described himself. He was indifferent to the political action which Birney espoused, disliked politicians and all sophisticates, was suspicious of too great a reliance on "reason," was greatly troubled by exhibitionism (in contrast to Garrison who thrived on it) and was much concerned about the general problem of sin. The resonance to abolitionism on the part of these four was prompted, then, by both the similarities and the differences we have here examined.

So much for the first stage in the development of commitment, the resonance by which the individual is initially attracted to the new ideology. The second stage occurs when risk is first ventured following this initial resonance. Not all who are attracted to an ideology will venture any risk on its behalf. Garrison was perhaps the boldest risk-taker, in part because he wanted so much "to be heard," as he said. To be heard he had not only to write but to speak in public. Early in his career he had been invited by the Congregational Societies in Boston to give the Fourth of July address at the Park Street Church. Garrison, in a letter to Jacob Horton, tells of his knees shaking in anticipation of the lecture, and a newspaper account reported that at first his voice was almost too faint to be heard; but eventually he overcame his stage fright and made a strong plea for the gradual emancipation of the slaves. Soon after this speech, however, he was to decide that immediate emancipation was required. Then he became more bold and accused a Northern ship captain and ship owner of trafficking in slaves. For this he spent seven weeks in jail. It cannot be said that this was altogether painful to Garrison. He appeared to enjoy both his martyrdom and the notoriety he gained, writing to everyone and conducting interviews from his cell. Although Garrison suffered least of the four abolitionists, and indeed appeared to enjoy combat, it would be a mistake, as his "shaking knees" tell us, to overlook the fear he sometimes experienced. Indeed all four men continually exposed themselves to physical and verbal opposition, and sometimes violent opposition. Each reacted somewhat differently. Garrison, though sometimes frightened, was more often delighted to be the center of attention. Phillips responded primarily with patrician contempt. Birney became depressed at the unreasonableness of his opposition, and Weld regarded his trials as tests by God of his mettle and worthiness.

This third stage, suffering in consequence of risktaking, troubled each man in different ways. Phillips lost his status and former friends in Boston upper-class society. Weld was severely reprimanded by the Trustees and President of the Lane Seminary for his "monomania" in stirring the students to debate slavery. After joining the American Anti-Slavery Society he toured Ohio, converting thousands to the cause, but always facing angry mobs intent on attacking him and breaking up his meetings.

He was hurt on numerous occasions. Indeed, he came to consider riots to be a test not only of his own mettle but of all his converts. Birney, too, met violence in response to his pro-Negro activity. He reacted with disappointment at the intransigency of the South, depression at the turning away of former friends and his loss of status, chagrin and surprise at the inability of "reason" to exert influence, considerable regret at having to leave his homeland and settle in the North, and not least, depression over the increasing alienation between his father and himself. Garrison clearly had least to lose and most to gain from assuming the risks of abolitionism though he, too, despite his zest for the fight and his love of being the center of attention, could on occasion become frightened and distressed. It should be noted that the same characteristics which prompted the initial resonance were also critical in creating the ability to tolerate the violence of the opposition and such negative affect as this ordinarily provokes. It was the combination of the general wish to save and reform coupled with energetic, articulate extroversion which diminished the sting of fear, of disappointment, and of depression at the loss of status and friends and the threat of physical injury and possible loss of life.

As a consequence of suffering, the fourth stage in the development of their commitment set in—an increase in their resonance to the movement, an increased identification with the oppressed Negro, an increased hostility toward the oppressor and toward those who remained uncommitted. This stage blends into later stages: an increased willingness to take still greater risks and to tolerate still greater suffering, with a proportionate increase in the intensity and duration of positive affect, until finally an irreversible commitment is reached. Thus Phillips now began to see for the first time, he said, the nobility and generosity of the Negro and of the lower classes in general. He began to compare their nobility invidiously with the smugness and corruption of upper-class society. He now found for the first time, he insisted, real and true friends. "Who are we that we should presume to rank ourselves with those that are marshalled in such a host? What have we done? Where is the sacrifice we have made? Where is the luxury we have surrendered?"

In Weld's case, the continual violent opposition he faced while on his speaking tour served to deepen his commitment also: "God gird us to do all valiantly for the helpless and innocent. Blessed are they who die in the harness and are buried on the field or bleach there."

Birney's initial response to the violence of the opposition was loneliness and depression. In 1834 he wrote to Weld: "I have not one helper— not one from whom I can draw sympathy, or impart joy, on this topic! . . . My nearest friends . . . think it is very silly in me to run against the world in a matter that cannot in any way do me any good. . . . Even my own children . . . appear careless and indifferent—if anything rather disposed to look upon my views as chimerical and visionary. . . . My nearest friends here are of the sort that are always crying out 'take care of yourself—don't meddle with other people's affairs—do nothing, say nothing, get along quietly—make money.' " However, this seems to have increased Birney's determination again and again to confront both censure and the threat of physical violence, "believing that if ever there was a time, it is now come, when our republic, and with her the cause of universal freedom is in a strait, where everything that ought to be periled by the patriot should be freely hazarded for her relief." Men must "themselves die freemen [rather] than slaves, or our Country, glorious as has been her hope, is gone forever."

Garrison, too, responded to opposition with increased defiance and with an increased identification with the Negro. . . . In an address to an audience of Negroes he said: "It is the lowness of your estate, in the estimation of the world, which exalts you in my eyes. It is the distance that separates you from the blessings and privileges of society, which brings you so closely to my affections. It is the unmerited scorn, reproach and persecution of your persons, by those whose complexion is colored like my own, which command for you my sympathy and respect. It is the fewness of your friends—the multitude of your enemies—that induces me to stand forth in your defense."

It should not be assumed, however, that opposition did nothing but deepen early commitment. It also raised, at least temporarily, serious doubts and conflicts about the wisdom of such a commitment. As might have been expected it was Phillips and Birney, they who had most to lose in social position and privilege, who had the most serious and prolonged reservations before finally committing themselves. Phillips, almost thirty, traveled through Europe with his invalid wife. He knew that his mother and family expected that he would return from his year abroad cleansed of his youthful enthusiasm for the radical movement. By the end of the year 1841, he had made a firm decision. He wrote to Garrison: "I will recognize in some degree the truth of the assertion that associations tend to destroy individual independence; and I have found difficulty in answering others, however clear my own mind might be, when charged with taking steps which the sober judgement of age would regret, . . . with being hurried recklessly forward by the enthusiasm of the moment and the excitement, though not I hope of all enthusiasm . . . upon the course we have taken for the last few years; and . . . I am rejoiced to say that every hour of such thought convinces me more and more of the overwhelming claims our cause has in the lifelong devotion of each of us."

Birney's period of doubt and indecision, as we have seen, was prolonged. In 1828 he had written "It [is] is hard to tell what one's duty [is] toward the poor creatures; but I have made up my mind to one thing . . . I will not allow them to be treated brutally." He was always concerned lest he be seduced by feeling: "Fearing the reality as well as the imputation of enthusiasm . . . each ascent that my mind made to a higher and purer moral and intellectual region, I used as a standpoint to survey very deliberately all the tract that I had left. When I remember how calmly and dispassionately my mind has proceeded from truth to truth connected with this subject (i.e., slavery) to another still higher, I feel satisfied that my conclusions are not the fruits of enthusiasm."

Even after Birney had apparently firmly committed himself to abolitionism he wrote to Gerrit Smith: "I am at times greatly perplexed. To have alienated from us those with whom we [went] up from Sabbath to Sabbath to the house of God—many of our near connections and relations estranged from us, and the whole community with but here and there an exception, looking upon you as an enemy to its peace, is no small trial."

For Weld the only doubts which ever assailed him were doubts about his own worthiness, his ability to control himself and to tolerate trial by fire. To his beloved Angelina Grimké he had confessed: "You know something of my structure of mind—that I am *constitutionally,* as far as emotions are concerned, a quivering mass of intensities kept in subjection only by the *rod of iron* in the strong hand of conscience and reason and never laid aside for a moment with safety." Whereas Phillips was concerned with the wisdom of his choice and Birney with the nature and consequences of his choice, Weld was concerned with his ability to tolerate the inevitable consequences of the morally necessary choice.

Only Garrison suffered no serious doubts once he had embarked on his voyage "against wind and tide." As he had written in an editorial on his twenty-fifth birthday, "I am now sailing up a mighty bay with a fresh breeze and a pleasant hope—the waves are rippling merrily, and the heavens are serenely bright. I have encountered many a storm of adversity —rough, and cruel, and sudden—but not a sail has been lost, nor a single leak sprung." Later that year he was to spend seven weeks in jail. After this experience he wrote: "How do I bear up under my adversities? I answer—like the oak—like the Alps—unshaken, storm-proof. Opposition, and abuse, and slander, and prejudice, and judicial tyranny, are like oil to the flame of my zeal. I am not dismayed; but bolder and more confident than ever. I say to my persecutors, 'I bid you defiance.' Let the courts condemn me to fine and imprisonment for denouncing oppression: Am I to be frightened by dungeons and chains? can they humble my spirit? do I not remember that I am an American citizen? and, as a citizen, a freeman, and what is more, a being accountable to God? I will not hold my peace on the subject of African oppression. If need be, who would not die a martyr to such a cause?"

In the deepening commitment of all four men there was an increasing boldness in the risks they ventured and in the felt righteousness of their cause. None regretted having given his life to the struggle and each thought it was appropriate that they and others had been prepared to surrender their lives in defense of the struggle to free the slaves. The continuing alternation between opposition, violence, and suffering, and the partial victories with the deep, if brief, excitement and enjoyment they brought, gradually made it appear to all of them that this was what they had been born for.

The stages in the development of their commitment to abolitionism can now be summarized. First, there is a resonance to the general idea of the salvation of others; second, risk is ventured on behalf of those who need to be saved; third, as a consequence of the risk taken, there is punishment and suffering; fourth, as a consequence of such suffering resonance to the original idea of the necessity of salvation is deepened and identification with the oppressed is increased, as is hostility toward the oppressor; fifth, as a result of increased strength of affect and ideation, there will be an increased willingness to take even greater risks and more possible punishment and suffering; sixth, increased risk-taking does evoke still more punishment and more suffering; seventh, there is still greater willingness to tolerate suffering concomitant with a proportionate increase in intensity and duration of positive affect and ideation in identification with the oppressed and with fellow abolitionists, and an increase in negative affect toward the enemy, whose apparent power and undesirability is magnified as the density of affect and ideation increases. The alternation between resonance and risk-taking—suffering and punishment—and the increased density of positive feeling and thought resulting in increased risk-taking endlessly repeated, cumulatively deepens commitment until it reaches a point of no return—or irreversibility at which point no other way of life seems possible to the committed reformer. It should be noted that the pathway from early resonance to final commitment is not necessarily without internal conflict. In the four men studied, each suffered doubt at some point whether to give himself completely to abolitionism as a way of life, though Garrison little.

. . .

The same dynamic violence and suffering which gradually deepened the commitment of these four men was also responsible for engaging the commitment of others to abolitionism or at least to resistance against the extension of slavery to free soil. The violence inflicted on the early abolitionists and the suffering they endured led others to take up their cause; it is here that we see the collective influence of these men on their society.

The murder of the abolitionist Lovejoy, and the mob action against Garrison which had excited the sympathy and indignation of Phillips and drawn him into the struggle, also excited the sympathies and indignation of others at the time. Dr. Henry Ingersoll Bowditch, a prominent physician became an abolitionist in response to the Garrison mob: "Then it has come to this that a man cannot speak on slavery within sight of Faneuil Hall." Seeing Samuel A. Eliot, a member of the city government, Bowditch offered to help him suppress the rioters. "Instead of sustaining the idea of free speech . . . he rather intimated that the authorities, while not wishing for a mob, rather sympathized with its object which was to forcibly suppress the abolitionists. I was completely disgusted and I vowed in my heart as I left him with utter loathing, 'I am an abolitionist from this very moment.'"

Because the abolitionists were fearless, and again and again exposed themselves to the danger of physical violence, they evoked widespread sympathy and respect, and simultaneously indignation against those who hurt and threatened them.

The mob which destroyed Birney's press and threatened his life created widespread sympathy for both him and his cause. Salmon Chase, for one, was thenceforward ready to stand openly with the abolitionists; he was, in fact, to become the congressional representative of abolitionism. Chase later wrote that he "became an opponent of slavery and the slave Power while witnessing Birney's display of conviction and intelligence as he confronted the mobocrats."

William T. Allan's indecision between preaching Christianity or becoming an abolitionist was resolved by the Cincinnati mob. Even Birney's own son, William, was converted to the movement by virtue of having faced this mob when it came after his father. Following that episode, in fact, letters of encouragement came to Birney from all over the country. Not the least of these was from the influential and widely respected New England minister, Dr. William Ellery Channing, who had previously stood aloof from the abolitionist movement:

I earnestly desire, my dear Sir that you and your associates will hold fast the right of free discussion by speech and the press, and, at the same time, that you will exercise it as Christians, and as friends of your race. That you, Sir, will not fail in these duties, I rejoice to believe. Accept my humble tribute of respect and admiration for your disinterestedness, for your faithfulness to your convictions, under the peculiar sacrifices to which you have been called. . . . I look with scorn on the most gifted and prosperous in the struggle for office and power, but I look with reverence on the obscurest man, who suffers for the right, who is true to a good but persecuted cause.

Lewis Tappan expressed confidence that Birney would again publish his "Philanthropist." Daniel Henshaw, a Lynn, Massachusetts editor, called Birney "one of the noblest sons of the West" who had "dared to lift up his voice in favor of liberty when all around him seemed given over to corruption, to slavery, to moral destruction." Even Alva Woods, whom Birney had once hired as president of the University of Alabama, in his baccalaureate address expressed his deep indignation at this action by the mob.

But it was not only Garrison, Phillips, Weld, and Birney who evoked violence, sympathy, and indignation. There were hundreds of agents who were stoned, tarred and feathered, whipped, beaten, and, in some cases, killed. In Utica, New York, in 1835, delegates who had assembled to organize the New York State Anti-Slavery Society had been dispersed by a mob composed of "very respectable gentlemen." Gerrit Smith, the wealthy landowner who had been a colonizationist, was influenced by this demonstration to join the abolitionists; he invited the convention to meet at his estate at nearby Peterboro.

In addition to physical violence there was continual verbal abuse and threat of violence heaped publicly on every abolitionist. In Garrison's case, a price was actually placed on his head in the South. Indeed it seems clear that without the exaggeration of Garrison's reputation by the South, his influence could never have been as great as it was.

We have argued that violence and suffering played a central role in the commitment first of the abolitionist and then in influencing general public opinion. At this point I should clarify what I mean by violence and suffering. By violence I refer to any negative affect inflicted with intent to hurt. This negative affect may be an aggressive threat of physical violence or a verbal insult. By suffering, I refer to any negative affect produced in the victim as a result of violence, whether this be a feeling of humiliation, helpless rage, terror, or distress. It is my argument that such violence and suffering can, in a democratic society, arouse in outside observers equally intense feeling. In hierarchically organized societies identification with the upper classes and castes will radically attenuate empathy with the victims of oppression. But in a democratic society, based on belief in individualism and egalitarianism, it is possible to arouse vicarious distress, shame, fear, or sympathy for a victim and anger or contempt for an aggressor. As a by-product, the ideas of the victim will then tend to become more influential than before such an attack. Most men in a democratic society share its values to some extent and so even those who identify with the aggressor will feel a certain amount of guilt at the challenge to democratic values. Thus in th North, some of those who had identified with slaveholders and been most hostile to the abolitionists, joined in lionizing them after the Civil War had ended; it is as if they were atoning for having identified with the "antidemocratic" position. I would argue that guilt over slavery was experienced in the South, too, though there it was defended against by exaggerating the villainy of the abolitionists and the evils of Northern "wage slavery." . . .

Because of heightened identification with the victim there results an increased polarization between the aggressor and the victim which magnifies the conflict and draws into the struggle thousands who would otherwise not have become involved. Quite apart from which side of the conflict gains the most converts, such polarization has the critical consequence of increasing the confrontation of the problem by the otherwise apathetic. One half of the battle of radical social change is to increase the density of affect and thought about the problem. To look steadily and hard at a social condition which violates the shared basic values of a society produces as much suffering for the society as a whole as does the condition itself for the segment of society primarily affected.

The Northern American citizen of the mid-nineteenth century was essentially ambivalent about slavery. He neither could approve it nor steadily disapprove it. He would have preferred to forget it. This is precisely what the abolitionists made more and more difficult. They were responsible for forcing confrontation and thereby radically increased the density of affect and ideation about the issue. Not all Northerners became maximally committed, but it is certain that the abolitionists greatly magnified the awareness and level of feeling of enemy and sympathizer alike and thereby exerted an amplified influence. The abolitionists did not permit Americans to look away from the ugly violation of the democratic ethos. In part they achieved this by provoking opposition and by offering themselves as victims. Thereby they evoked sympathy for themselves and their cause, and provoked anger and contempt for those who supported slavery.

By the 1850's it appeared to many, for the first time, that the abolitionists had not really exaggerated the moral iniquity of the South. In Boston, for example, many who at one time had regarded the abolitionists as the "lunatic fringe" were to have second thoughts when, in 1854, a former slave had to be taken by force from the city and shipped back to slavery as, ashamed and helpless, thousands were forced to look on. Gradually more and more Northerners came to experience the suffering of violence, at first vicariously and then more directly, until the climax at Fort Sumter. War is a special case of commitment and I would defend the position that a democratic society can commit itself to war only if it feels it has suffered violence upon itself directly or vicariously. It has therefore always been necessary for America to be attacked, before sufficiently intense and prolonged commitment can be generated to permit a defensive counterattack. This attack and counterattack, I have argued, is the way in which commitment to anti-slavery was first generated in the abolitionists, and finally, in more and more of the Northern citizenry.

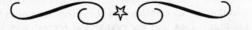

SOCIAL AND RELIGIOUS
FOUNDATIONS OF REFORM

The Anglo-American World of
Humanitarian Endeavor

FRANK THISTLETHWAITE

American historians have often been inclined to treat the ante-bellum reform movements as indigenous developments, even when acknowledging certain influences from abroad. We turn now from considering the motives and personality of reformers to a view of reform as a single Anglo-American movement. Frank Thistlethwaite (1915–), who is now Vice Chancellor of the University of East Anglia, gained insights into Anglo-American cooperation as a

Frank Thistlethwaite, *The Anglo-American Connection in the Early Nineteenth Century*, 1959, pp. 76–102. Reprinted without footnotes and with minor deletions by permission of University of Pennsylvania Press. Copyright © 1959 by the Trustees of the University of Pennsylvania.

member of the British War Cabinet Office in World War II. He has marshaled considerable evidence to show that in the pre-Civil War era there were important economic and philanthropic connections between British and American societies. In addition to his emphasis on the interaction of reform groups, one should note his suggestions that the evangelical revival was a potential source of secular agitation and radical protest, and that America, in the eyes of British reformers, was at once a model of republican justice and an underdeveloped nation in need of economic and moral support. While the Anglo-American character of reform will be touched upon again in the fourth chapter, the main emphasis of the third chapter will be on the relations between reform, religious revivalism, and democratic politics.

THE STARTING POINT OF THIS CHAPTER IS THE [BRITISH] DISSENTERS, the members of the great Non-conformist sects who, as a result of being shut away from the power and patronage of the established order had, by the close of the eighteenth century, created their own distinctive world, with its chapels, academies, journals, and its great interlocking family and mercantile connections. It was a world which had close relations with the United States. In 1793 an Anglican bishop was of the opinion that "the principles of a Nonconformist in religion and a republican in politics are inseparably united," and, in Southey's view "the American War made the Dissenters feel once more as a political party in the state. New England was more the country of their hearts than the England wherein they had been born and bred." The *Edinburgh Review* was more specific when in 1838 it reviewed Harriet Martineau's *Retrospect of Western Travel,* published after her return from the United States. Miss Martineau was, it will be remembered, a daughter of the great Norwich circle of Dissenting families which included the Gurneys, Smiths, Taylors, and Aldersons; and her brother James became the leading divine in the English Unitarian church.

She belongs to that party in England, religious and political, which, ever since the days of Priestley[1] has kept up a peculiar connection with one of the most important portions of American society. The very strongholds of that party in England—Liverpool and Manchester—are allied by close mercantile ties to Boston and New York; and the alliance of mind is closer still. The party of which we speak does not count a very numerous following in either country; but it is peculiarly distinguished by its high intellectual cultivation and by a certain degree of exclusive pride with which that cultivation is at-

---

[1] EDITOR'S NOTE: Joseph Priestley (1733–1804) was the English chemist, discoverer of oxygen, clergyman, and political radical who in 1794 emigrated to the United States.

tended. In England its tenets approach to a tempered republicanism; in America, it is looked upon as rather aristocratically inclined. But this is a difference which the opposite circumstances of the two countries naturally seem to produce; for, in England, intellectual superiority, wherever it does not bow in willing subjection to the existing oligarchy of birth and wealth, always has a tendency to train off from it and form a commonwealth apart; in America, a high degree of education is looked on as a sort of title of nobility, and regarded with some jealousy by the multitude. Affinity of opinion has produced between members of these parties on each side of the Atlantic, a sort of cousinship and similarity of manner and tone of thought, not to be met with between any other classes in the several countries. The slight peculiarities, both of habit and mind which appear to characterise well educated Americans of the Eastern States are more nearly to be matched among the higher classes of dissenters in the great provincial towns of England than anywhere else; and an English Unitarian, especially if connected by family and acquaintance with the select people of that sect in his own country, is pretty sure of meeting in America not only with the kind and hospitable reception which all travellers with good recommendations can procure, but with a sort of family greeting.

The Anglo-American connection to which the *Edinburgh Review* particularly referred consisted of those families, mercantile and professional, educated and often intermarried, who had come to Unitarianism, in England either as lapsed Anglicans or as descendants of the old Presbyterians, in America from the Congregational and Episcopal Churches. In the England of Priestley's generation the Unitarians were identified, not only with infidelity but with Jacobinism; and thenceforward the sect was coloured by those liberal attitudes towards faith and society, which were to appear in deeper shades in the career of Harriet Martineau herself. It is hardly surprising, therefore, that English Unitarians should have sympathized with the American revolutionaries and should look towards the United States for asylum during the reaction against the French Revolution, and thenceforward as an example of enlightened, republican institutions. The Priestley colony on the Susquehanna was not the only English Unitarian community-in-exile in the United States. The first permanent Unitarian Church in Philadelphia was founded in 1797 as a result of Priestley's lectures among a group of young English Unitarian emigrants; and the thinking of English Unitarians powerfully influenced Church congregations in New England and New York in their search for a more liberal creed and liturgy. The Rev. William Hazlitt, father of the essayist, visited Boston and gave decisive advice to Freeman and his flock at King's Chapel; the writings of Lindsey and Priestley provided the frame of reference within which American Episcopalians and Congregationalists followed their more advanced English brethren towards the full Unitarian position. Thenceforward, after the capture of

Harvard College and Boston, the New England Unitarians advanced independently and so rapidly that by the 1830's the writings of William Ellery Channing and Theodore Parker were setting the pace for James Martineau and his English Unitarian flock. Although advanced in theology, American Unitarians remained more conservative than their English co-religionists in social values; for these Boston merchant princes and their clerical allies had already achieved their revolution, and they did not have the same impulse towards social reform which continued to characterize some of the English Unitarians. But by and large English and American Unitarians shared a common set of values, powerfully influencing Atlantic opinion. Well-to-do and commercially connected, they habitually crossed the Atlantic in both directions, a traffic made easy by letters of introduction to Boston families and that informal consular service provided by the Rathbones and other Liverpool merchants in the American trade.

The *Edinburgh Review*'s description would equally have applied to the Society of Friends. The Quakers on both sides of the Atlantic formed a community, even more closely connected than the Unitarian, of intermarried, largely mercantile, families fenced off from the outer world by their particular beliefs and discipline. The American Revolution had disturbed the intimate relations between London and Philadelphia Yearly Meetings. Minutes were diligently exchanged; members were "released" for ministry in the other country; and important missions, like those of Stephen Grellet of Philadelphia to Britain and of Joseph Sturge, or J. J. Gurney to the United States, and the services of Quaker merchants often connected with the American trade, like the Thompsons in New York and James Cropper in Liverpool, were elements of a communications system as efficient, in its sphere, as the official diplomatic service. When the London Meeting for Sufferings wished to stop the import of rum into the South Sea Islands, Philadelphia Meeting duly passed on their minutes to Moses Brown, the Providence merchant, who had dealings in those parts. London Yearly Meeting contributed to the support of the poorer American meetings, to the establishment of new meetings in the West, to the building of schools and the provision of Bibles. When evangelicalism tinged English Quaker doctrine, it was London's representative, J. J. Gurney, who influenced orthodox American Quakerism in the same direction, and thereby helped to perpetuate the Hicksite schism; and when the Indiana Yearly Meeting revolted against orthodox policy towards the slavery controversy, a mission was sent from London in 1845 in vain to heal the breach. At the center of every aspect of humanitarian endeavor there was to be found a small body of Quaker philanthropists in England led by such men as William Allen and Joseph Sturge, providing organization and finance; and although in the United States Quaker influence was more diffuse and less dynamic, it was probably not less important.

But the Unitarians and the Friends, though probably the most influential sects, were small in numbers. Other, more popular denominations, although without the cohesion of Friends and Unitarians, preserved and strengthened their transatlantic links after the American Revolution. Presbyterians, Congregationalists, Methodists, Baptists, and Episcopalians, all established fraternal relations with their British co-religionists, corresponding on matters of doctrine and organization and exchanging delegates. Typical of such exchanges, for the years 1835–36 alone, were the visits to Britain of John Codman and Heman Humphrey from the New England Congregational Church and of the British Congregationalists Andrew Reed and James Matheson to the United States, the delegacy of Wilbur Fisk from the General Conference of the Methodist Episcopal Church of America to the Wesleyan Methodist Conference of Great Britain and that of F. A. Cox and J. Hoby from the British Baptists to the American Baptist General Convention. The American Methodists, who benefited greatly from the dis-establishment of the Church of England, and the Episcopalians, who suffered by it, re-defined their apostolic relations with their parent English bodies. The sects of the richer country contributed funds to their American denominationalists. Bishop Chase of Ohio, the Rev. Nathaniel Wheaton, and Bishop Hobart of New York, raised funds among prominent Anglicans like Admiral Gambier and Lord Kenyon to found the General Theological Seminary and the colleges of Kenyon, and Washington (later Trinity), Connecticut. Later, in 1844, this flow of funds was counter-balanced by funds raised among American Presbyterians for the endowment of the new Free Church of Scotland. Controversies like the Hicksite schism among Friends, the Free Church schism in Scotland, the quarrels over lay leadership involving the Methodist Protestant Church in America, and the Wesleyan Methodist Connection in England, and the conflict between evangelical and high church wings of the Episcopal Church, had repercussions and parallels in both countries. And as will be seen, the slavery controversy caused complex divisions in most denominations.

These sectarian connections were greatly strengthened and affected, at the opening of our period, by new winds of faith and doctrine which stirred most churches and deepened the transatlantic influence of religion. That "Protestant Counter-Reformation," the Evangelical Revival, set its stamp on a whole Anglo-American generation, and is of special importance to the Atlantic connection.

In the first place, as far as England was concerned, it particularly affected those classes which had the greatest affinity with the United States. It is true that its most powerful antecedent was the Wesleyan revival of sixty years before, that perhaps its most characteristic expression was the Methodism of the generation after John Wesley's death, and that the Wesleyan Methodists, having remained so long within the Established Church, supported an authoritarian church discipline and continued to claim intimate relations with the Church of England. However, although the Wesleyan Connection remained in a sense a bridge between the Established Church and Dissent, increasingly in the nineteenth century the spirit of Methodism, appealing as it did especially to the rising artisan and trading classes whose social connections were with Dissent, must be regarded as Non-conformist in character. It is also the case that at the outset evangelicalism's most powerful directing force was the group of aristocratic politicians, bankers and Anglican clerics of Clapham and Cambridge who burrowed from within the Church Establishment. But the Clapham sect[2] were denounced by High Anglican Tories as Methodists, only one remove from Jacobins, and the evangelical party remained a small, though highly influential body, within the Church of England. Though connected with what we have called "the establishment," evangelicalism was essentially rebellious and disruptive, and brought considerable strength to the mobilized forces of Dissent. For, in the words of an Anglican historian, the evangelicals "cared little for the Church or for the State as a Divine institution. Their business was with personal salvation," with individual as opposed to corporate religion. They thus encouraged a non-denominational temper, represented by the Evangelical Alliance of 1846 which united Anglicans and Non-conformists, and they were prepared to work with all Churches on both sides of the Atlantic in moral reform. In fact, the Evangelical Revival achieved its most notable successes among the commercial, manufacturing, and artisan classes, the growth of which, especially in the new industrial towns, was the chief phenomenon of the age; and its spirit probably exerted its widest social influence among the Non-conformist sects which, although representing a fifth of the population, in the opinion of Professor Halévy "equalled if they did not exceed the Anglicans who practiced their religion."

In the second place, the Evangelical Revival, though owing much to the pietistic writings of Germans like Arndt and Francke and the humanitarian practices of such centres as Halle and of the Moravians, may be

[2] EDITOR'S NOTE: Not a formal religious party but a group of evangelical philanthropists, all members of the Church of England, who frequently gathered at the home of the abolitionist leader, William Wilberforce, in Clapham, then a suburb of London.

treated in its later aspects, as an Anglo-American movement. It appeared about the same time in England and America and evangelists in each country powerfully affected each other. The movement may be said to have originated with the ministries of the two Englishmen John Wesley and George Whitefield. But the moment was propitious, for perhaps different reasons, on both sides of the Atlantic. Wesley reaped his most fruitful harvest in the English, and Whitefield in the American, vineyard; and if England produced the organizing genius, New England produced the movement's most formidable theologian. As a Congregationalist scholar has pointed out, its origins cannot be divorced from the Great Awakening which took place in Connecticut in the years 1736–40. "We have to go back," writes the Rev. E. A. Payne, "not to the Epworth Rectory where John Wesley was born on June 28th, 1703, but to a home in Connecticut, New England where, on October 5th of that same year, Jonathan Edwards saw the light." According to this authority, Edwards was "the decisive influence . . . on the new life which carried the Church out to distant continents." Edwards exerted a powerful hold over Whitefield, whose convictions were "cradled and strengthened" in America in 1740 and, through Whitefield and by his own writings and correspondence, Edwards influenced a number of important British divines, including John Erskine of Edinburgh, the Baptists Robert Hall, Andrew Fuller and William Carey, founders of the Baptist Missionary Society, and Thomas Chalmers, the founder of the Free Church of Scotland. For "classical Calvinism had within itself the essentially evangelistic impulse." It was significantly a New England divine who provided the most powerful argument pointing the way from total depravity and predestination to conversion and salvation. Jonathan Edwards and New England successors, like Emmons and Hopkins, provided British evangelicals with such useful ammunition that Newman complained of "American dissenting divinity" in English vicarages.

This interplay may be traced through the later course of the movement. The most powerful impulses which transformed orthodox religious habit in the Atlantic world radiated from Clapham and Cambridge, England. At the time when Britain was on the threshold of world maritime power, the outlook of her evangelicals, like that of her merchants, was expansive, all-embracing and oriented overseas—did not Charles Simeon claim India to be his diocese?—towards all continents including North America. By contrast, the American temper remained provincial and derivative, taking its lead from the ex-mother country, in spirit— William Wilberforce's *Practical View* ran through an edition a year in the United States from 1800 to 1826—and, as will be seen, in organization. Yet America contributed her own intense revivalistic practices.

Whitefield's early success had come during those long journeys through the American back-country from Georgia to Massachusetts at the time of the Great Awakening and the peculiar quality of the backwoods revival eventually touched the mean streets of England. Wesley may have started the practice of circuit riding and open-air preaching from farm wagons; the Welsh may have early had their own form of holy rolling and the jerks, but the techniques both of camp meeting and urban crusade were imported into England from the burnt-over district of western New York and the Broadway Tabernacle. After each of the great conflagrations of 1801, 1826, and 1857, the spiritual arsonists of America—Lorenzo Dow, Charles Finney, James Caughey, William Taylor, Phoebe Palmer, and others—crossed the Atlantic to kindle the dry tinder of English industrial towns. The camp meeting held by the Methodist Lorenzo Dow at Old Cop, Staffordshire, in 1806 prompted the potter William Clowes and the carpenter Hugh Bourne to break away from the Wesleyan Connection to found the Primitive Methodist Church. In 1844 Charles Finney inspired the young London shop assistant, George Williams, to start the Young Men's Christian Association which soon, in turn, found its way across the Atlantic to the United States; and it was from the Chicago YMCA that Dwight Moody began the evangelist mission which was to take him so often to Britain. That frontier phenomenon, the camp meeting, was not without influence in the metropolis.

Religious "enthusiasts" in Britain looked especially towards the United States. Some, like the Methodist William Arthur, crossed the Atlantic to evangelize America. Others, like the political radicals, went further. An exotic few, from Mother Ann Lee and her Manchester Shakers in the 1770's and the Mormon recruits from English towns and villages in the 1840's and fifties to the aristocratic Laurence Oliphant at the mystical community of Brocton in 1867, migrated to America in search of seclusion for spiritual experiment. American utopianism had a messianic strain, and "come-outers" on both sides of the Atlantic were convinced that the United States held out a special hope for spiritual progress.

Anxious Seat, Shaker dance, and Mormon trek were for ignorant and inarticulate folk; but they represent the exotic fringe of a religious movement which profoundly influenced Atlantic opinion. Highmindedness, piety, and zeal united the Churches of America with the interlocking connection of Dissent and evangelicalism in Britain in the common object of spiritual regeneration and moral reform. "Unite Britain and America in energetic and resolved co-operation for the world's salvation," wrote two Congregationalist delegates from Britain to the United States in 1836, "and the world is saved." They spoke for a generation of earnest souls whose brisk traffic across the Atlantic was concerned with nothing less than world salvation. And it was a generation which thought in extra-national terms; as Professor Spiller has written of the Americans among them who went to Britain:

[None] could be said to be either pro-British or anti-British. Their minds were coloured by religious rather than patriotic sympathies, they recognised the bonds of race and of human brotherhood to the exclusion of national antipathies and of political antagonism. They went to England to visit those who spoke and believed as they did and they were welcomed as brothers in the faith.

We are dealing with a genuine Atlantic community.

This co-operation quickly went further than Church doctrine and administration. Since the essence of evangelicalism was the saving of souls, it can hardly be conceived apart from the missionary movement which grew up within it. Here, as one would expect with a movement of world horizons, the initiative came from the metropolitan country. The missionary activities of the British evangelicals were minutely copied in New York, New Haven, and Hartford. Wilberforce's first preoccupation, the Society for the Suppression of Vice, was reproduced in New York by the society of the same name in 1802. Robert Raikes' Sunday School was copied by the Philadelphia First Day Society of 1790 and later by the American Sunday School Union, while, independently, Samuel Slater had carried in his head to Rhode Island the model not merely of his erstwhile employer's spinning frame, but of his Belper Sunday school. Hannah More's Religious Tract Society, founded in 1799 was followed within four years by the Massachusetts Society for the Promotion of Christian Knowledge, and later (1814) the New England, and then (1823) the American Tract Society. The great British overseas missionary societies, and especially the non-denominational London Missionary Society (1795) which was working in Canada before the end of the century, and the (Anglican) Church Missionary Society were quickly paralleled by American missions to the Indians and ultimately by the Board of Home Missions. In 1816 at the prompting of, and with funds from, the Church Missionary Society there was established the first American overseas mission, the Domestic and Foreign Missionary Society of the American Episcopal Church. In 1804 the concern of British evangelicals at the lack of Bibles, especially among the Welsh and the Canadian Indians, led to the formation of the British and Foreign Bible Society. Four years later the Philadelphia Bible Society was founded to remedy a similar dearth in the American back-country, and it was followed in the next few years by the formation of some sixty-two other

Bible societies in America, culminating in the American Bible Society of 1816. These were supplied by the British society with Bibles and stereotype plates and by funds which at the close of 1817 amounted to over three thousand pounds. A similar service was provided by English Quakers. The poverty of the world in the matter of the Holy Writ overrode all considerations of patriotism. During the War of 1812 the British and Foreign Bible Society supplied Bibles to American prisoners of war in Dartmoor and the American Bible societies subscribed to buy the cargoes of British Bibles captured by American privateers and sent them on their way to the Canadian Indians.

It was only a step from the souls of Indians and Africans to Christian souls maimed by physical and social circumstance. The acid of evangelicalism gave a sharp etching to the benevolence of the Enlightenment. Penal reform owed much to the legal and utilitarian outlook of Bentham and Romilly[3]; but it began in the 1770's with a Dissenting Sheriff of Bedford, Robert Howard, and caught public imagination in 1817 with the evangelical ministry to the prisoners of Newgate, by the Quakers Elizabeth Fry (sister of J. J. Gurney) and William Allen. This, too, was an Anglo-American as well as a French movement. Stephen Grellet, who had a Quakerly concern for prisoners in his native Philadelphia, is said to have been instrumental in arousing Elizabeth Fry's interest in London; and the penitentiaries at Philadelphia, Auburn, and Sing Sing, with their rival and so-called improved systems, were objects of earnest investigation in the 1830's by European reformers. The idea of visiting America was first suggested to Harriet Martineau by a philanthropist's saying: "Whatever else may be true about Americans, it is certain that they have got at principles of justice and mercy in the treatment of the least happy classes of society which we may be glad to learn from them. I wish you would go and see what they are." She made a point of visiting American prisons and it is symbolic that she crossed the Atlantic with Dr. Julius, the Prussian prison reformer, just as her fellow reporter, E. S. Abdy, had crossed a few months previously with William Crawford, investigating prisons for the British government, and both followed in the wake of a more famous pair, de Tocqueville and Beaumont, engaged on a similar errand. Reform in the treatment of the insane owed most to the example of the English Quaker, Samuel Tuke, whose description of his Retreat near York provided a text for the establishment of a Quaker retreat near Philadelphia in 1817 and other asylums in New York and Massachusetts

---

[3] EDITOR'S NOTE: Jeremy Bentham (1748–1832) was the great British philosopher of utilitarianism and of legal and constitutional reform. Sir Samuel Romilly (1757–1818), British lawyer and statesman, worked for a more humane and rational criminal law.

which, in turn, were the basis for Dorothea Dix's campaign of the 1840's.

These ardent and impatient men and women, in their war of the spirit, were not content with local successes. Only an eccentric fringe may have thought in terms of the Millennium; but many hoped for large, strategic victories in the Atlantic campaign of moral reform. Philanthropic radicals attacked simultaneously on several broad fronts. The first spate of activity, beginning in the last decade of the eighteenth century, was concerned with the saving of souls through the agency of Bibles, tracts and home and foreign missions; the second, beginning in the years of peace following on 1815, was concerned especially with three evils which appeared to that Anglo-American generation to be the most corrosive to the human spirit: drink, war, and slavery.

Before dealing with this three-pronged attack, a word must be said about the methods of organization. These campaigns were elaborately mounted. Doing good by modest example was not sufficient, especially in the cases of war and slavery. It was necessary to awaken the conscience of nations. New and ingenious techniques of agitation were invented which revolutionized the machinery for mobilizing public opinion and ultimately, as will be seen, the practice of politics itself. In America, agitation had broken the power of the British establishment at the Revolution, and now in England what might be properly called a public opinion was beginning to influence the narrowly-based politics of the landed gentry. In both countries the techniques for forming public opinion were powerfully influenced by the Evangelical Revival. The preacher who called sinners to repentence became the agitator who demanded immediate and sweeping moral reforms. The agitator was a characteristic early Victorian figure. As Daniel O'Connell[4] said, "I am a practiced agitator and I know that you can never succeed in the most just cause without agitating the public mind until you have a sufficient moral force by means of public opinion." The agitator was a new and important phenomenon: an orator, capable of moving vast audiences to laughter, tears, and moral indignation; a fundamentalist, concerned with ends, not means, with principle, not practice. We have already met the agitator among the political radicals; and in the gallery of Anglo-American agitators, alongside such figures as Frances Wright, Thomas Devyr, and John Cluer, must be placed philanthropic radicals like John Bartholomew Gough in temperance, William Lloyd Garrison, and George Thompson

---

[4] EDITOR'S NOTE: Daniel O'Connell (1775–1847), Irish national leader, founder of the Catholic Association, took seat in Parliament after Catholic emancipation (1829) and worked for the abolition of Negro slavery and also for the repeal of the union of Great Britain and Ireland.

in antislavery, Elihu Burritt in the peace movement and, above all, that past master of the art, Wendell Phillips, whose energies extended to antislavery, temperance, feminism, and labor reform. It is perhaps significant that most of these mentioned were Americans; for it was in that populistic democracy that the agitator's powers were most fully developed. As Phillips put it, "the agitator's purpose is to throw the gravest questions upon the conscience of the masses because they are the ultimate governors in a republic." However, the agitator became a powerful force in moral reform on both sides of the Atlantic.

If the Americans excelled as agitators, the British genius lay in organization. Agitation involved propaganda. It was only a step from riding the preacher's circuit and distributing Bibles and Cheap Repository Tracts to holding public meetings, raising funds, pamphleteering, and placarding; only another step and, behold, there had come into being that great force which has become the very stuff of Atlantic politics: the voluntary association, or, if you like, the pressure group, devoted to a single, urgent reform. The British antislavery leaders were pioneers in developing methods which were to become standard for other reforms in Britain and, to a modified extent, in the United States. Local, voluntary societies up and down the country organized processions, public meetings, and lectures, raised funds, distributed pamphlets, signed pledges, memorialized the Queen, the President, and State Governors, and petitioned Parliament and Congress. These local societies were linked together to support a national organization with "anniversaries" or conventions and a central office with salaried agitators and officials to promote new auxiliary societies, conduct campaigns and exert pressure on government. The British headquarters of philanthropic radicalism was Exeter Hall in the Strand, built in 1831; its American counterparts were the Marlboro Chapel, Boston, built in 1838, and the ill-fated Pennsylvania Hall, Philadelphia, built and burnt in the same year. Although these methods were peculiarly well adapted to mobilize the power of the politically underrepresented middle class in Britain, they were a major means of agitation in both countries; and if the men who directed the campaigns—in Britain such representative men as Joseph Sturge, Thomas Fowell Buxton, William Allen, J. J. Gurney, George Thompson, James Silk Buckingham, in America, the Tappan brothers, William Jay, Gerrit Smith, Samuel May, Henry C. Smith, W. L. Garrison, James Birney, Joshua Leavitt, Elihu Burritt, Frederick Douglass—if these men were something of a stage army, appearing in different uniforms in different scenes, their influence upon philanthropic opinion was profound. The finishing touches were given to this organization when, in the 1830's, not only were the British methods adopted in America but the two countries became linked in a single Atlantic communications system. Correspondence, pamphlets, journals, "Friendly Addresses," and memorials were exchanged and reprinted, delegates voyaged back and forth, and by 1840, the first of a series of "international," that is to say, largely Anglo-American, conventions trumpeted to the world the unison of philanthropic endeavor in the Atlantic world.

. . .

An early and logical extension of missionary work was the crusade against strong drink. The temperance movement was a peculiarly Anglo-American contribution to the reform of morals. The pervasiveness of evangelicalism is shown in the fact that efforts to combat drunkenness became manifest at about the same time in relation both to the urban masses of Britain and the largely rural population of the United States. However, its origins and chief leadership were American.

Cheap spirits and gruelling conditions in isolated settlements combined to make drunkenness a special problem of the frontier. The first temperance society was organized in 1808 among the lumberjacks of the little frontier town of Moreau, New York, and there came to be a strong concentration of such societies in that "burnt-over" district of western New York which Gilbert H. Barnes and Wilbur R. Cross have shown to have been a weather-breeder of the evangelical climate. But western New Yorkers were largely transplanted New Englanders and the leadership in the crusade to put down strong drink was provided by the east and especially by the evangelical empire of New England. The Massachusetts Society for the Suppression of Intemperance, founded in 1811, marks the start of twenty years of mushroom growth in temperance societies which, in 1831, were estimated at four thousand in number. The American Society for the Promotion of Temperance was founded in 1826 and in 1833 (the year of the American Anti-Slavery Society) a multitude of local societies were federated into an American Temperance Union.

This American example prompted a sister movement in Britain. John Dunlop of Glasgow was impressed by the temperate habits of the wine-drinking French; but he drew upon American facts and experience for lectures in 1828 which led to the formation of the first temperance societies in Scotland. This example together with the "Six Sermons" of Lyman Beecher of the Massachusetts society, spurred Henry Forbes, a Bradford merchant, to organize a society in his own city in 1830 which was quickly followed the same year by the formation of some thirty other societies in the industrial north with a reputed membership of ten thousand. This colonization was rapidly annexed, in a way which was becoming standard, to the evangelical empire; and it owed not a little to the experience of Bible, tract, and especially, antislavery, societies. In 1831 temperance leaders united at the new headquarters of philanthropy in Exeter Hall as the British and Foreign Temperance Society, and within a year fifty-five auxiliary societies had been affiliated and nearly one hundred thousand pamphlets issued.

Nathaniel Hewitt of the American Society for the Promotion of Temperance was present at the inaugural meeting, and from the start relations between the British and American societies were close. American delegates like Hewitt and E. C. Delaven took a lead in drafting policy. Vast quantities of American pamphlets were distributed, special attention being paid to warning intending emigrants of the special dangers of drink in the United States. American speakers, from E. C. Delaven in the thirties to the spellbinder John B. Gough in the fifties, commanded large, enthusiastic audiences. English visitors to the United States like Joseph Sturge concerned themselves with the progress of temperance in America and J. S. Buckingham earned large sums there as a temperance lecturer between 1837–39. This co-operation reached a climax in 1846 with the holding in London of a World Temperance Convention, along the lines of the Antislavery Conventions of 1840 and 1843. This Convention, with its twenty-five American delegates and with Lyman Beecher as vice-president, was an Anglo-American jamboree.

British and American crusades were rent by similar dissensions over policy. As will also be seen in the case of the peace movement, there was conflict between "gradualists" and radicals. Many of the earliest temperance advocates, concerned only with the evils of dram drinking, were averse from taking a stand on beer or wine. But evangelicals, impatient, dogmatic, and fundamentalist, and reformers with experience of drunkards, came to demand a pledge of total abstinence for all true believers. The term "teetotal" was probably coined in England in 1833 at a meeting of the society formed by the famous "Seven Men of Preston," led by Joseph Livesey; four years later the teetotalers withdrew from the national society to form a new British and Foreign Society for the Suppression of Intemperance on a basis of total abstinence. In the same year, E. C. Delaven and other root-and-branch men introduced a thoroughgoing teetotal pledge to the American Temperance Union which caused heated controversy throughout the movement in the United States. A similar conflict in the British society between "long" and "short" pledges, was eventually solved in 1839 by the adoption of the American pledge after a debate, in which Delaven and other Americans participated. The two movements had other common characteristics. The temperance hotels which Joseph Sturge so much admired in New England, were paralleled on a more modest scale in Britain; a concern for youth promoted Bands of Hope in England and Cold Water Armies in America; and although Britain developed no separate Washingtonian movement, there was also a shift from the prevention of drunkenness to the cure of the drunkard. As with the peace and antislavery movements, temperance moved from moral exortation to political action: and here again the Americans took the lead. The prohibition of the sale of intoxicants by law in the State of Maine in 1851 was a new spur to temperance efforts in Britain. Two years later the United Kingdom Alliance was formed in Manchester to lobby Parliament for a similar measure; and Neal Dow, the Quaker merchant of Portland who was responsible for the Maine Law, was brought over in 1857 to promote it. The contrast between the failure of British temperance enthusiasts to do more than impose gradually more stringent regulations on the sale of intoxicants, and the persistent, and ultimately triumphant prohibition movement in the United States illustrates a difference in national temperament. But within those limits the temperance movement must be regarded as Anglo-American in its inspiration. Although the earnest deliberations of the temperance crusaders make dreary reading now, their influence transcended its immediate object. In Britain especially, temperance, appealing as it did to the chapel-going, manufacturing middle class, became an important element in the moral force which was mid-Victorian radicalism.

.   .   .   .

During the World Temperance Convention in 1846 at a soirée held at the Freemason's Tavern, Joseph Sturge persuaded some sixty delegates to sign a new pledge, not to temperance, but to peace. The peace movement also had Anglo-American origins and drew strength from the Atlantic climate of reform. The English-speaking peoples seemed destined by Providence to lead the world on a crusade to eliminate war. Despite the serious diplomatic friction between the United States and Britain in the 1830's and forties, reformers and philanthropists came to see special possibilities for peace across the Atlantic. Here at least, between two countries with complementary interests and achievements in political and social reform, it should be possible to make progress with techniques for the peaceful settlement of international disputes. For the first time one hears the heartfelt belief, commonplace now, but novel then, that if the common people of the two countries could know each other there would be no war. Albert Prentice, the Anti-Corn Law Leaguer, voiced these popular sentiments in 1848. Speculating on the possibilities for Atlantic travel of a new paddle wheeler, he wrote:

. . . With a reduction of one half of the time and one half of the expense I do think that there could be no more wars between the two countries. The citizens of the United States do not dislike Englishmen individually; . . . Their dislike is to John Bull—the traditional, big, bullying, boroughmongering and monopolist John Bull . . . And *we* do not dislike the citizens of the United States. . . . Our dislike is to Jonathan—bragging, annexing and repudiating Jonathan. The individual likings will become the national in proportion to the greater intercourse of the individuals of both nations. Give us then the quick and cheap steamboat. The paddle wheel is the emblem of civilization and peace. Why may it not be regarded as one of the means, in the hand of God, to hasten that happy time when men shall beat their swords into [plowshares] and their spears into pruning hooks and shall learn the art of war no more.

It was thirty years before the peace pledge and these sentiments by a Manchester traveler that the Anglo-American peace movement had its origins. After the turmoils of Napoleonic and American Wars, a few evangelicals had been seized with the revolutionary desire to limit and, if possible, abolish war. They hoped by the new opinion-forming techniques to mobilize a national opinion strong enough to hold in check the warlike tendencies of what would now be called "power diplomacy." An English group, meeting at the London house of the Quaker, William Allen, had discussed the idea of forming a peace society as early as June 1814; but it was the news of the forming of such a society in Massachusetts in 1815, together with a telling tract by an American, Noah Worcester's *Solemn Review of the Custom of War,* which spurred them in June 1816 to organise the London Peace Society.

Co-operation between the London and the American societies which came together in 1828 as the American Peace Society, remained so close that it is impossible to think of the two organizations except as part of a single movement. The English peace men held special hopes for the cause of peace in the American Republic. An early report of the London Peace Society ran as follows:

Our transatlantic friends are moving forward in their most honourable course with unabated zeal and ardour; and removed as they are from the scenes of bloodshed, your Committee hope that peace will find a safe and serene asylum in the land which was peopled by our sires and which we would fain regard as possessed by our brethren.

And many radicals would have subscribed to the belief of an English peace advocate that there was something in American institutions "more favourable to the progress of pacific principles" than in British institutions. The Americans, for their part looked up to the London Society for its zeal, resources, and organizing capacity.

British and American peace advocates evolved common policies and experienced similar controversies. The London Peace Society, dominated by the Friends, took its stand on the principle that "all war whether offensive or defensive is upon Christian principles utterly indefensible." Such a thoroughgoing pacifism went far beyond the more limited objectives of "practical" advocates of international arbitration; but tact and forebearance, expecially on the part of such men as Henry Richard and Richard Cobden, and a tempermental preference for compromise, enabled the two groups to work together. In the United States, on the other hand, a more extreme conflict between conservatives who justified defensive war and out-and-out pacifists was only settled in 1837 when the American Peace Society adopted a formula in line with that of the London society. Even this was not enough for the *outré* temperaments of Henry C. Wright and William Lloyd Garrison who developed a doctrine of non-resistance, the logic of which implied the complete breakdown of civil government. These radicals hived off to form the New England Non-Resistance Society in 1838. There was another temperamental difference between British and Americans. The Americans favoured especially William Ladd's ambitious goal of a Court and Congress of Nations; on the other hand, although the London Peace Society had sent Thomas Clarkson to the Congress of Aix-La-Chapelle in 1818 to lobby for such a scheme, the more pragmatic and cautious British were on the whole sceptical of what they came to call "The American Plan," and preferred to concentrate upon the more limited objective of arbitration.

The crusade developed a crescendo of activity between 1837 and 1852. Meetings and lectures were held, auxiliaries formed, and funds raised; pamphlets were distributed by the hundred thousand, journals were published, like the *Herald of Peace* (English) and the *Advocate of Peace* (American), and there was a continual exchange of correspondence, literature, and visits across the Atlantic. In 1843 following the pattern set by the antislavery movement, the British and American societies came together in London in a World Peace Convention which, with Sturge, Lewis Tappan, and Amasa Walker as vice-presidents, was predominently an Anglo-American affair, and the model for the more truly international peace conventions of Brussels, Paris, Frankfort, and London which followed from it between 1848 and 1851.

This activity was quickened by diplomatic friction between the two Governments. The succession of crises from the *Caroline* and Aristook affairs of 1838 to the Oregon question of 1846 presented a direct challenge to this Anglo-American movement. During the Oregon crisis "Olive Leaves" were broadcast through the press in both countries, and there originated in Birmingham, England, a system of "Friendly Addresses" between pairs of British and American towns like Manchester and New York, Boston and Boston, and between British and American working men, manufacturers and merchants. This "People's Diplomacy" achieved spectacular publicity.

The organizing genius behind this propaganda was Elihu Burritt, "the learned blacksmith" of Worcester, Massachusetts, who left his native shores to promote the cause in Britain in 1846 at the height of the Oregon crisis. Walking with knapsack and staff on a country road towards Worcester, England, that summer, he conceived the idea of a great League of Universal Brotherhood, bound by a pledge of peace; and at the little village of Pershore he collected pledges from twenty country people, the first members of a rapidly growing association which by 1847 boasted thirty thousand pledged members in England and America. The League pursued a broad program. In addition to organizing Friendly Addresses between Britain and France and distributing Olive Leaves, it promoted an ocean penny post to encourage international understanding among common people, and, like the temperance movement, assisted emigrants bound for the United States. Its advocacy of an English boycott of American slave-grown cotton took the movement into antislavery territory and illustrates the tendency of all reform movements in the late 1840's to impinge on each other in a broadening objective of "universal reform."

The League of Universal Brotherhood, with its peace pledge, was the high point of moral insurgency against war. But like all such pledges of good intentions, there was danger of a relapse. Something more than moral exhortation was necessary if the public concern which the League had aroused was to be made effective. The peace movement, like the temperance and antislavery movements was drawn irresistibly from moral exhortation to political action.

"The American Plan" for a Congress of Nations did not get beyond pious resolutions at peace conventions; but the idea of writing arbitration clauses into treaties looked more promising. The original idea was the work of an American, Judge William Jay, son of the negotiator of Jay's Treaty and a president of the American Peace Society. His proposals were seen by Joseph Sturge during his visit to the United States in 1841; and on Sturge's initiative were adopted by the American and London Peace Societies and, in 1843, by the London Peace Convention. These arbitration proposals, along with resolutions dealing with the munitions trade, were subsequently reaffirmed at the international peace congresses, beginning with that at Brussels in 1848. In 1849, Richard Cobden, at the prompting of Joseph Sturge and after a barrage of agitation by the League of Universal Brotherhood and the Peace Society, introduced a resolution on compulsory arbitration into the House of Commons which, although rejected, led to a six-hour-debate and attracted respectable support. In the following year the American Peace Society succeeded in getting the Senate Foreign Relations Committee to report a resolution in favor of arbitration to the Senate.

With Richard Cobden, who threw his energies into the cause of peace after his triumph against the corn laws, the crusade moved beyond evangelism into the larger world of politics and foreign policy. . . . Suffice it to say here that in the fifties the peace crusade languished. In England, enthusiasm for Garibaldi brought a conflict of loyalties and the Crimean War was a blow to facile optimism; in America the slavery controversy, with its increasing preoccupation with the use of force, took precedence. Yet the crusade had made its mark. An Anglo-American public had been made conscious of the issue and its possibilities; permanent machinery for agitation had been established, and in the cause of arbitration, Judge Jay's thoughtful drafting, Joseph Sturge's organizing genius, Elihu Burritt's evangelistic fervor, and Richard Cobden's deft political lobbying combined to achieve the insertion of an aribtration clause in the Treaty of Paris after the Crimean War.

Religious Benevolence as Social Control, 1815-1860

CLIFFORD S. GRIFFIN

According to Frank Thistlethwaite, the evangelical revival was a rebellious, disruptive force that nourished agitation and led to new social perspectives; from distributing Bibles to save men's souls it was but a short step to improving the condition of prisons and calling for an end to war, intemperance, and

From the *Mississippi Valley Historical Review*, XLIV, December 1957, pp. 423–444. Reprinted without footnotes by permission of the Managing Editor of the *Journal of American History*. Copyright © 1957 by the Organization of American Historians.

slavery. Clifford S. Griffin (1929–   ), who teaches history at the University of Kansas, does not discuss the latter reforms in this article, but rather portrays the deeply conservative aspects of the benevolent societies which sought to evangelize the country. The leaders of these societies for social control often agreed with Emerson that reform must begin with the individual, not with institutional change. Their social and political conservatism raises perplexing problems about the relation between evangelical Protestantism and the kind of radical commitment described by Silvan Tomkins. Although no historian has yet provided an adequate explanation of this discrepancy—of how a concern for social control could lead to a desire to liberate the slave—it is significant that the men Griffin discusses were primarily worried over the effects of unmitigated self-interest and the more tyrannical implications of popular democracy.

IN THE YEARS BETWEEN 1815 AND THE CIVIL WAR THE UNITED STATES was in a ferment of great and fundamental social, economic, and political change. Thousands of families were rushing westward, occupying land, and creating cities and state from forests and prairies. Native-born and immigrant factory workers, laborers, shopkeepers, and artisans were crowding the new centers of industry and the older cities, and creating new economic and social problems. Western settlers and enterprising eastern business pioneers were repeatedly crossing new horizons only to find that beyond lay seemingly boundless areas for expansion. While Federalism declined and new political parties remained ill-defined, men were casting about for other alliances which would embrace the expanding frontier and the growing electorate. Some welcomed changes that seemed to promise greater heights in the "rise of the common man" and wider vistas for "Young America." Others feared new forces in American life, worried about political and social upheavals, and deplored new moral standards. To many of those who could not accept the changing America, evangelical Protestantism seemed an excellent means of keeping the nation under control.

Between 1815 and 1826 many Presbyterians and Congregationalists, aided by a smaller number of Methodists, Baptists, and Episcopalians, seeking to supply the religious needs of the expanding country, joined to form five great national interdenominational societies. The American Education Society, organized in Boston in 1815, subsidized future ministers in colleges and seminaries. From its offices in New York the American Home Missionary Society helped poor congregations pay their pastors and sent men to new settlements. Between 1816 and 1861 the American Bible Society distributed millions of copies of the Bible; and the American Tract Society supplemented and extended religious and moral reading by issuing before 1861 almost 200,000,000 books and tracts. From Philadelphia the American Sunday School Union sent missionaries to establish schools and then furnished the young scholars with lessons, religious volumes, and moral stories. Held together by the idea of benevolence toward man as the highest Christian virtue and united in promoting what they considered the fundamentals of evangelical Protestantism, these societies worked outside regular church organizations to convert the nation to God.

From the changing Calvinsim of an earlier age, the managers of the societies inherited a religion which retained elements of the Genevan master's theology, but altered his idea of a predestined elect of God. Presbyterians and Congregationalists, together with men of other churches who claimed to be propagating only the essence of Christianity, accepted the Calvinistic stress on the original and actual sins of man and his evil in God's sight. But the late eighteenth and early nineteenth centuries finally saw the modification of the idea that Christ had died only for God's elect; instead, heirs of Calvinism emphasized that Christ had died for all mankind. More than man's sins, the societies stressed Christ's atonement, the mercy which God offered, and the grace which God would grant to those who repented and believed. Although this general theology emphasized that only God could bestow sanctifying grace—that man could not win it for himself—the managers believed that in forsaking sin and believing in Christ man could put himself in an excellent position to merit mercy and forgiveness. The societies' aim was to get the people into this state.

In striving toward this goal, the managers believed themselves to be expressing in action the idea of benevolence to man which the societies held was the essence of all Protestantism. This idea was not new. Colonial Puritans, for example, had been familiar with Cotton Mather's *Essays to Do Good*. But in the late eighteenth century the Congregational minister Samuel Hopkins, who preached in Newport, Rhode Island, in his later years, gave the concept great currency. It quickly became popular in several denominations. As interpreted by the societies, benevolence —or, as it was often called, charity, or love for man—was the idea that certain persons, having received God's sanctifying grace, were obliged to extend to all men the means of obtaining that grace. The managers reasoned that God's mercy was the greatest gift anyone could receive, that love, which was the fulfilling of the Law, directed the sanctified to share this gift, and that the societies' activities were the best ways to help sinners. Believing that most of the people in the United States were living in original and actual sin and that many of them were not aware of it, the managers considered it their duty, as sanctified men, to make sinners realize their evil, to persuade them to repent, and thus to help God's saving work. Benevolence was an infinite concern for other people's souls.

These men who were vitally interested in their fellow citizens' salvation were heirs of more than a modified Calvinistic theology. Out of the colonial past came the concept, equally strong in political and social spheres, that the sanctified of God had the right and duty to govern. Nurtured by the Calvinistic theocrats, especially in New England, the idea had passed into the philosophy of Federalism which supplemented the heritage by adding to the elect of God the elect of men. Both Puritans and Federalists claimed that a minority of special attainments should supervise the majority. This assertion harmonized well with the concern which men of benevolence had for the souls of others, for the test of an individual's conversion from sin was his secular action. All of these ideas came together in the benevolent societies. Their leaders, at first Federalists and afterward those who continued the Federalist traditions, asserted the right not only to guide men along God's narrow path, but also to direct proper political and social conduct.

The effort to mold a nation attracted both laity and clergy. Ministerial representation was considerable and, as befitted religious societies, ministers frequently expressed the aims of the organizations. But most of the more than five hundred officers who served in the period from the organization of the societies until 1861 were laymen. All of the lay officers were of rising social and economic station. The industrialists Anson G. Phelps and William E. Dodge of the Bible Society; the merchants Moses Allen of the Tract Society, John Tappan of the Education Society, and Christopher R. Robert of the Home Missionary Society; the bankers Samuel Ward of the Bible Society and Benjamin B. Comegys of the Sunday School Union; the financier Jay Cooke, also of the Sunday School Union; and the lawyers Charles Butler of the Home Missionary Society and Samuel A. Foot of the Bible Society were the type of men who felt themselves best qualified to guide others.

In selecting their presidents, the societies' managers reflected their own political, social, and economic position. As Federalism, with its desired rule by men of wealth, station, and ability, died, members of the party perpetuated their ideas in the benevolent groups. The Bible Society, for example, chose as presidents such staunch Federalists as the wealthy Elias Boudinot of New Jersey, the New York City lawyer Richard Varick, and former United States Supreme Court Chief Justice John Jay. From 1832 until 1845 John Cotton Smith, an equally steadfast Federalist, headed the society. A loyal party member and former governor of Connecticut, Smith had supported the Hartford Convention of 1814, that ill-fated protest to "Mr. Madison's War," and had just as vigorously opposed the disestablishment of the Congregational church in his state. Although Alexander Henry, first president of the Sunday School Union, tried to keep out of politics, his conservative views and his merchant's fortune made him the choice of the managers. Federalists in other groups were Home Missionary Society president Stephen Van Rensselaer, "The Patroon"; the Boston merchant William Phillips and the Boston lawyer Samuel Hubbard of the Education Society; and the merchant and international financier Sampson Vryling Stoddard Wilder, first president of the Tract Society.

When these men died, long after the expiration of Federalism, the managers turned to those who continued the tradition of the direction of society and government by men thought particularly qualified to lead. Theodore Frelinghuysen, Whig politician and later president of Rutgers College, served from 1842 to 1848 as president of the Tract Society and from 1846 to 1862 as head of the Bible Society. Thomas S. Williams, who followed Frelinghuysen in the Tract Society, was former chief justice of Connecticut. United States Supreme Court Justice and Sunday School Union president John McLean passed through a political spectrum as Democrat, Whig, Know-Nothing, and Republican—whatever allegiance seemed to increase his chances for the national presidency. Through all of these shifts, however, McLean maintained his firm belief that morality and religion were the only bases for proper government. In 1846 he claimed that the country had been declining in moral virtue since the administration of President James Monroe. In the Home Missionary Society, Henry Dwight, wealthy upstate New York banker, followed Stephen Van Rensellaer; Dwight was succeeded by Aristarchus Champion, reputed to be the richest man in Rochester. The third president of the Education Society was Samuel T. Armstrong, a prosperous Boston publisher and a Whig governor of Massachusetts. Before 1861 only two clergymen led the societies: Theodore Dwight Woolsey, president of Yale College and the Home Missionary Society, and Heman Humphrey, president of the Education Society and Amherst College. But clerical or lay, the managers saw in the benevolent groups a hopeful means of keeping society godly and orderly, stable and quiet.

The rise of Andrew Jackson's popularity coincided with the founding and early years of all the societies. Thus at their start the managers and their supporters faced first a man and then an administration characterized, as they thought, by everything wrong in the politics of the period. With the success of the Jacksonians and the general continuance of the Democratic party in power after 1829, benevolent men began to deplore unchristian politics and to claim that the perpetuity of the republic depended on the maintenance of evangelical Christianity in the land.

Jackson's popularity after the War 1812 and his electioneering between 1824 and 1828 made the managers apprehensive even before he took office. In the early fall of 1824 the Reverend Benjamin H. Rice took a quick look at Old Hickory and told the Education Society that the country needed religious guidance. Without it, said Rice, the people would soon become the "slaves of a military despotism." After Jackson's inauguration and the startling presidential reception, many good men trembled. Addressing the Home Missionary Society in May, 1829, the Reverend Jacob Van Vechten claimed that only despotism could rule a people who had forgotten the fear of God. If, as seemed possible, "an excited populace of irreligious men" ruled the country, the nation could not last. In a vivid verbal picture, Van Vechten predicted that in such circumstances laws would be ineffective, justice lacking, churches demolished, thefts and murders rampant, and streets drenched with blood.

As Jackson's terms continued, managers raged and despaired. By 1832 Bible Society secretary John Pintard, a lifelong Federalist, had had three years too many of the General and hoped for his defeat in the coming election. "My very soul," said Pintard, "sickens at the name of Jackson." In 1837 William M. Evarts, then a youth of nineteen but later a prominent Republican and a Bible Society manager, thought that the Jacksonians continued the "Jeffersonian dominion" in politics. Mercenary government officials, a growing party spirit, and the type of men who supported the Democrats, Evarts lamented, made impossible the election of any man of "talent and great eminence" to the presidency.

Understandably, the most important society leader, Theodore Frelinghuysen, was an outstanding opponent of Jackson. Tall, rugged, bewhiskered, and impressive in appearance, Frelinghuysen was a resolute opponent of new social and political trends. A devoutly religious Presbyterian, but later a member of the Reverend Thomas De Witt's Dutch Collegiate Church in New York City, he served as a vice-president of the Education and Home Missionary societies and the Sunday School Union, and as president of the Bible and Tract societies. From 1829 to 1835 he was a United States senator from New Jersey; and as the Whig vice-presidential candidate in 1844 he undertook to join his Christian talents with the political ability of Henry Clay in the hope of gaining a victory for conservatism. When the Whig ticket met defeat he sought to console Clay with religion. "Vain is the help of man," he wrote, "and frail and fatal all that trust in the arm of flesh." If Clay would seek solace in the Gospel and would trust in the Lord, he would be like "Mount Zion itself, that can never be removed."

Frelinghuysen opposed both Jacksonian philosophy and the policies of the Jackson administration. In the midst of the attack on the United States Bank, he vigorously defended the bank's president, Nicholas Biddle. In discussing the reasons for Jackson's popularity and warning good citizens against the Democrats, Frelinghuysen claimed that Americans had become too proud of their country and their liberties. Speaking in 1835 before the annual meeting of the Sunday School Union, he declared that this pride had resulted in a spirit of independence almost too strong for law. The words "resistance," "liberty," "independence," and "the rights of man" had become so familiar that Americans were likely to forget that these terms, with "the glow of patriotism" and "the love of country," became, without sound principles, the "mere watchwords for licentiousness and all misrule."

The managers knew that from the religiously destitute West had come much of Jackson's support. As the West grew, the prospect of seeing the control of Congress by the Mississippi Valley, within their lifetimes, alarmed them. In 1826 the Bible Society's managers printed with concern part of a report of the Young Men's Bible Society of Baltimore. Areas formerly wilderness, the report said, were now states. Westward migration was swelling and soon these new states would have a population and resources equal to or greater than the Atlantic commonwealths. Political power was passing across the Appalachian Range. Two years later the Education Society predicted that by 1850 the West would have a majority in Congress. Agreeing, the Home Missionary Society frequently printed statistics to show how fast the western states were gaining in relative political power. Summing up the situation, William H. Bulkley, president of the Young Men's Tract Society of Louisville, Kentucky, told the national managers that the political voice of the West would speak out to the nation in *"thunder tones."* By spreading the news of God's mercy and supplying the means of conversion, benevolent men hoped to bring others to Christ and at the same time allay fears of how the growing West would vote.

A combination of reports from the West and their own imaginations gave eastern managers a low opinion of most westerners. In 1831 the Bible Society was told by one of its agents that the "lower classes" from several southern states and Ohio had occupied a large part of Indiana and that many of these people had left "civilized & religious society for the simple purpose of getting out of its restraints." The Reverend John Spaulding of Cincinnati told the Education Society that prejudice, fanaticism, or political ambition easily controlled the western mind: "Its rush is like that of the ocean wave." Similarly warning the Tract Society, the Reverend John M. Stevenson said that in crossing the mountains easterners often changed character. They lost their culture, polish, and rectitude. Their enjoyments became coarse and their *"passions* violent and barbaric." Law and civil order vanished, he said, and in their places lynch law and border ruffianism reigned.

Easterners responded warmly to such descriptions. In 1830 Theodore Frelinghuysen, deeply worried, told the managers of the Sunday School Union that the West was in danger of losing its public and private virtue and that there was grave danger that this people, "but yesterday born into political existence," would exhibit a "universal degeneracy of manners." With murders, corruption, and disobedience of the laws prevalent, Frelinghuysen said, the only means of checking violence was the "reformation of public sentiment" through religion. Alarmed by this description and by what the Reverend James W. Alexander called the "growing but unformed, chaotic, tumultuating society" in the country, the Union urged the extension of its work. Future judges, senators, and statesmen were now children in the West, said the managers, and should receive proper training in their youth. In 1845 the Home Missionary Society fearfully asserted that without evangelical Protestantism the country's future was dark indeed. Among other evils, "the state will be the synonym of anarchy—Law the refuge and charter of violence—Justice the incarnation of partiality and revenge. Then stations of power will be the prizes of an ambition instinct with outrage and crime."

Although western voting strength disturbed the societies most, their solution for making the Mississippi Valley safe for good government applied to the entire nation. If the voters could be converted to Christ, they would presumably elect to office religious men who would govern wisely. If the rule of the country by the rich, the well-born, and the able was ended, at least the United States might have the government of the moral, the virtuous, and the sanctified.

In 1827 the Reverend John J. Aikin argued before a Utica, New York, Sunday school convention that great political benefits would be conferred on the country by the establishment of Sunday schools among the poor. "Does not the vote of a poor man at your polls count as much as the vote of a rich man?" Aikin asked. "Is not his example in the sphere in which he moves, whether good or bad, contagious and influential? Dismiss, then, your Sunday-schools; withhold from this interesting and important class of citizens religious instruction—and in vain will you try to fill your halls of legislation with honest and intelligent men." The reins of government would be in the hands of an "unprincipled mob, who care neither for law nor religion." The Education Society claimed that immorality in the electorate begot immorality in officialdom, but that religiously enlightened people elected religiously enlightened rulers. In the middle of Andrew Jackson's second term the Reverend Absalom Peters, secretary of the Home Missionary Society, asserted that amid political fights and financial embarrassments the only safety was in religion: "This alone can restore the conscience of the nation & give efficacy even to human laws."

Managers often contended that the very existence of the republic depended on evangelical Protestantism. In 1843 the Tract Society's executive committee surveyed the country and concluded that the United States had reached the critical point in the experiment of popular government. American liberties had produced national evils. Freedom of the press had degenerated to "unbridled licentiousness and blind partizanship"; freedom of immigration and an easily obtained franchise for foreigners had brought millions of voters who were ignorant of American institutions and laws; freedom of conscience had aided the "spiritual despotism" of Catholicism. According to the Tract Society committee, the remedy for all these ills was not political action but the evangelization of the whole people. Only when there was "absolute dependence on the spirit of God" would the country be safe.

Other societies and their managers agreed. They made the Reformation responsible for America's civil liberty, asserted that without the Gospel the body politic would sicken and decline, and stressed as axiomatic the idea that "moral power"—which the societies promoted— was the only true foundation for a free government. Even after the Whig victory in the election of 1840 many managers were apprehensive. In 1841 the Home Missionary Society warned that still the only hope of the country was in religion. Referring first to the symbolic log cabin used by the Whigs in the election and then to western churches built of logs, the Reverend Leonard Bacon declared that the latter were the *"only log cabins that can save the nation!"*

The millions of immigrants who came to America before the Civil War intensified political problems. Although they looked upon all immigrants as potentially troublesome, the managers considered the Catholics especially dangerous. Opposing them on religious grounds, the societies also feared that the "Romanists" eventually might either control the entire country through the polls or form an alliance with the ungodly and thus make good government impossible. The Reverend Gardiner Spring, well-known Presbyterian divine and for several years a manager of the Bible, Tract, and Education societies, said that Catholics joyfully seized all the civil rights Americans provided, but used these rights only as representatives of the Holy See. Spring claimed that Catholics held the balance of power between American political parties and that in using the franchise these foreigners might decide almost every question on their own terms. In his view, only the Pope would benefit. To other managers, also, Catholicism was anathema; it was a religion essentially opposed to all American civil institutions.

While thousands of Catholics settled in eastern cities, other thousands went to the politically influential Mississippi Valley. Accounts of their voting strength were alarming. In Ohio, said a report, to curry favor with Catholic voters would-be politicians opposed the Bible, Tract, and Home Missionary societies and thus threatened to leave the people in darkness, a prey alike to demagogues and priests. The Reverend S. E. Miner reported from Madison, Wisconsin, in 1845 that Catholics were steadily becoming more influential and that already they had "crouching whining politicians" as servants. In 1852 the Reverend George Sheldon, Bible Society agent in Indiana, advised the national managers to urge upon both Whig and Democratic nominees for school superintendent the use of the Bible in common schools. But Sheldon thought that with their Catholic allies the Democrats, who did not favor the Bible in schools, would win. Democrats, Sheldon averred, did obeisance to "Romanists and Infidels. . . . The Romanists with the infidelity they carry with them, have the balance of power between democracy and Whigery [sic]." The Tract Society, by 1845, thought that the Irish alone constituted a serious threat to American institutions. Estimating their number at between 750,000 and 1,000,000, the managers saw Hibernians everywhere: "crowding our cities, lining our railroads and canals . . . and *electing our rulers.*"

While the societies were worrying about the political effects of western growth, they feared also the effect of social change in the East as well as in the West. Society managers trembled at the prospect of an unpacified urban population. In the jammed tenements and narrow streets of Atlantic coastal cities were crowded thousands of low-income workers and poor whom they held responsible for vice and crime, mobs and riots. Easterners had only to walk the streets of Boston, New York, and Philadelphia, or read their newspapers, the managers said, to learn of social unrest along the seaboard. Sunday School Union manager Joseph H. Dulles of Philadelphia looked at the rapidly growing ranks of youths between sixteen and twenty who were rioting in the cities and feared the "growing spirit of libertinism destructive of good order in Society & good morals in individuals" which he saw. The Reverend Charles Hall, secretary of the Home Missionary Society, woefully noted that men seemed to "rejoice in casting off restraints & unsettling the foundations of social order." Concerned over the recent riots in Philadelphia and the Dorr Rebellion in Rhode Island, the editors of the Presbyterian New York *Observer,* which had great influence among benevolent men, said in 1844 that such actions were a disgrace to the republic. Maintaining his original Federalist views in 1836, Frederick A. Packard, secretary of the Sunday School Union, was just as irate when he condemned a variety of evils: riotous assemblies, mobs, trade unions, and strikes.

In evangelical Christianity the managers saw a way to stop violence and disorder. Without religion among the people, said Packard, "law and lawful authority are trampled upon," and "riots and tumults" encouraged. By 1843 the Reverend Gardiner Spring was convinced that the American trait of insubordination was increasing in vigor. The characteristics of the age were fearful: "resistance to lawful authority," "clamor about the rights of man," "tumultuous conventions," "arraignment and abuse of the courts of justice, " "the bold assumption of the power of the law by an infuriated mob." A free government and the "absurd doctrine of liberty and equality" were responsible for such evils. God and Protestantism, according to Spring, were the only hopes of the American people. President John Cotton Smith of the Bible Society thought that the distribution and reading of the Scriptures would go far toward keeping social peace. The Education Society's managers firmly asserted that religion and religious institutions were sources of quiet in society and proclaimed that ministers should "exercise over the multitude . . . that power which is always the prerogative of superior attainments."

Allied with mobs and riots was crime. In 1841 the Home Missionary Society feared and deplored the great increase in the number of frauds, robberies, and murders. Although the laws forbade killing, said the managers, no statute ever reached the human heart. Only the precepts of religion could establish social tranquillity and "protect our persons from violence." The Sunday School Union, claimed its leaders, did much more than bring children to Christ. Religious training was an excellent way of keeping youths out of the ranks of crime and of bringing them into society as useful, worthy citizens. From the West came similar reports. In December, 1852, Z. M. Humphrey, secretary of the Racine County, Wisconsin, Bible Society, reported that his organization encouraged social order. The Bible was a guard over property and life, he said, for it had the same effect in rural areas that a police force had in cities in keeping down riots and crime.

Often including city immigrants with the poor, the societies ascribed to them a large part of these social sins. In an analysis in 1857 the Bible Society's managers said that poverty was in general the result of ignorance, vicious indulgences, or indolence. The poor forgot the moral virtues in a haste to be rich; they spent their money foolishly on worthless amusements; many of them had an aversion to honest work. Gripped by these evils, the city poor were "congregated in filth and bound together by the horrid ties of vicious and beastly appetites. In their sensual sty the man is transformed into the brute." There was no crime too base for these poor: "Amid these orgies, crimes against society are plotted, and the most savage passions stimulated to action." Viewing the immigrant horde of almost 5,500 foreigners who arrived in New York City on April 21, 1854, the Sunday School Union thought that among these new arrivals were at least 100 whose ideas made them "implacable foes to the best interests of society, if not to its peace and safety," and probably 1,000 private or public paupers.

The Bible Society's managers saw great social value in the Scriptures. They would show the poor their rights and duties and develop in them "whatsoever is honest, and pure, and of good report." The Bible tended to check the "rampant propensities to low and vicious indulgence" and to "enthrone reason and conscience over the depraved appetites of carnality." Further, it required and supplied motives for honest toil. The Reverend Franklin Y. Vail, city agent of the Tract Society, urged rich men to aid in bringing religion to the common people. Christianity would help to "bridge over the dangerous chasm between the rich and the poor; so that instead of . . . mobs and outbreaks destroying . . . life and property, there will be between these two great classes a reciprocation of confidence and good feeling, as there will be also a ready recognition of their mutual dependence, their harmonious interests, and their immortal brotherhood."

To keep the poor pacified, managers had a ready philosophy. There was nothing wrong with being poverty-stricken, the Sunday School Union told its children:

> And if we had riches, they could not procure
> A happy and peaceable mind;
> Rich people have troubles as well as the poor,
> Although of a different kind.

> It signifies not what our stations have been,
> Nor whether we're little or great;
> For happiness lies in the temper within,
> And not in the outward estate.

At the annual meeting of the Education Society in 1851 the Reverend Andrew L. Stone extolled the Christian poor and claimed that they had many advantages. Poverty produced piety, humility, and the spirit of self-sacrifice; it made people vigorous, hardy, and rugged, familiar with struggling, and inured to difficulty. For these reasons, Stone said, the best type of minister came from the poorer classes. In a similar but less complimentary vein the Reverend James Drummond told the Home Missionary Society that a man's worldly possessions showed his inherent energies. Those who succeeded in their earthly life had trod the right path; thus those who did not deserve to be rich remained poor.

The social philosophy of the managers provided means for the poor either to bear with their poverty or to improve their condition. Although it was benevolent to help the poor in material ways, said the directors of the Worcester County, Massachusetts, Bible Society, the Scriptures would help prevent extreme poverty, aid the poor in wisely enduring their lot, or enable them to rise to a new social rank. While the precepts of God would neither banish poverty nor end economic inequalities, the Gospel would bring "timely and greateful relief" to the poor and make the different classes more conscious of their mutual dependence. The Tract Society told poor children that the only way to the top of any profession was to start at the bottom, work up step by step and not try to rise too fast, and maintain a Christian character.

If hard work and faith in God were the only ways that people had to improve their condition, other means were wrong. Reports of socialistic communities and Fourierist societies caused great alarm. Managers heatedly condemned as godless all non-religious plans for saving society by changing its general structure. By supporting the Bible Society, said L. Q. C. Elmer, president of a New Jersey auxiliary, good citizens were protesting against "all that heartless deism, revolting socialism, blasphemous pantheism, and withering skepticism" which were the basis of those social reforms. Socialism, Fourierism, and similar ideas were considered anti-Christian and obviously against God's social plans. After receiving a report of socialistic communities in northern Indiana, the Home Missionary Society's managers said that no area needed "the conservative influence of an enlightened ministry" as much as the Mississippi Valley. A speaker before the Tract Society asserted that in their publications the managers had erected barriers against "Popery and Rationalism and Socialism, and every other wild ism and vile ism."

Benevolent men claimed that these schemes were radical and unchristian because they tried to reform society without first changing individuals. It was the original and actual sins of men, said the managers, that produced evils in society, rather than the reverse. God had set forth social principles; men had corrupted them. In 1849, noting an increasing popularity of plans to reform the whole of society at once, the Sunday School Union called these ideas ridiculous and the people who held them misguided and irreligious. The managers would reverse the principle: "Instead of making the invisible, intangible and irresponsible composition which we call society the scape-goat for the sins and sufferings of the visible, tangible and responsible individuals who compose it . . . we should . . . hold the individuals to answer for the burdens and griefs of society."

In the West were problems of more immediate concern to the benevolent societies than communal or socialistic villages. The failure of westerners to pay their debts brought losses to eastern creditors. By bringing religion to the Mississippi Valley, the managers hoped to insure economic stability and protect eastern investments. The Home Missionary Society was particularly interested in this problem. During the depression following the Panic of 1837 and at other times, the leaders remarked, western debtors had defrauded many eastern businessmen. By establishing a Christian sense of right in every man, the society would help to decrease in number or abolish these frauds: "Far better," agreed the managers with a missionary, "for the merchant to give his money, not to say his prayers, to make people good, where he intrusts millions of property, than to spend it upon bailiffs, to apprehend his runaway creditors, or to collect his debts among a dissolute people, without either responsibility or principle. *The Gospel is the most economical police on earth.*"

When the effects of the Panic of 1837 and overextended borrowing caused many western states to repudiate their debts, lay managers called this action fraudulent and enlisted ministers in the cause. Charles Butler, lawyer and manager of the Home Missionary Society, went west to Michigan and Indiana to represent the claims of bondholders. Back in the East men fumed against repudiation. The Reverend William R. Williams, a Tract Society manager, damned state legislatures for "repudiating their plighted word and bond. In the matter of good faith between man and man, as to pecuniary engagements, the wheels of the social machine groan ominously, as if they were . . . ready to tear asunder the fabric of society." From his pulpit the Reverend Gardiner Spring condemned repudiation. Had the forefathers of America been told that such a thing would happen, Spring said, they would have blushed with shame at "this horrid disgrace of their apostate descendants." Evangelical Protestantism and more abundant Christian literature were regarded as safeguards against such financial sinning.

Proper Christianity would also promote general economic stability. The Madison, Indiana, Bible Society, acting on the belief that where people read their Bibles good business conditions existed, argued that to get men of wealth and principle into Indiana the state must first have plenty of Bibles. "Intelligent capitalists," asserted the Reverend Daniel P. Noyes, Home Missionary Society secretary, knew that as essential to the growth of a new town as stores, buildings, and a dam were a church and minister. Moreover, religious institutions were cheaper. In giving money for the propagation of Sunday schools, said the Union's managers, businessmen added to the security and profits of all their other investments.

In May, 1847, Emory Washburn, prominent Massachusetts lawyer and later Bay State governor, spoke on the importance of the Bible Society to the preservation of good order in society. Every day, said Washburn, he saw new social schemes proposed, mobs trampling upon private rights and setting laws aside, and states repudiating their debts. New principles and new ideas contrary to all Christian truth were destroying the whole social structure. The only protection was the Bible. Far better than "every measure of secret espionage to which a Napoleon or a Nicholas may resort," he said, the Bible was a "moral police." If their spirit spread through every family and every school in the country, the Scriptures would cure America's social ills and insure a stable society.

If they were to change the ungodly poor into the Christian poor and make debtors pay by Christian means, these wealthy managers needed a rationale for their high economic position. If they could show that rich Christians had a right to their wealth, they reasoned that there would be no demand from the poor and debtor classes for a share of that wealth. Christians would certainly not rise against Christians; the poor would not desire the rich man's gold. Individuals might choose to feed the hungry, clothe the naked, and provide almshouses, hospitals, and asylums, said the Sunday School Union, but it was obviously no part of God's social plan that a common fund should exist to which the wealthy should contribute and from which the poor should draw. In trying to protect their property from verbal and physical assaults by the poor, the managers stressed the idea of the stewardship of wealth: that every man held what he had in trust from God and thus should always be willing to give some of this substance back to the Lord. Since the societies considered themselves God's agencies, a man could justify his wealth by turning over part of it to them.

In May, 1850, preaching in behalf of the Tract Society, the Reverend Gardiner Spring argued that those who became rich by their own toil and economy had superior intellectual faculties and strength of character. Both they and those who inherited wealth had influence in the community because they deserved to have influence. They were men of "mind," "forethought," "great practical wisdom," "energy." With few exceptions, Spring claimed, they were men of integrity and moral virtue. In thus justifying the rich, however, Spring added the important qualification of stewardship. Since money had tremendous influence for either good or evil and since God desired only good, rich men should contribute to Christian causes. Money hoarded was "accursed"; money squandered bought only "shame and a grave"; money used to corrupt others spoke of the "pageantry of vice . . . of the miserable victims of sin and perdition." Wealth meant either selfishness or benevolence and Spring emphasized that only the latter was proper. Similarly, Bradford Sumner told the Education Society that men should be "faithful stewards" of all they held. The greater the wealth, the greater was the accountability to God for its proper use. There was nothing wrong in holding money, houses, and land, according to the stewardship doctrine of the Reverend Heman Humphrey, but rich men had a duty to give away some of their possessions. Although no one should make his sole goal in life the acquisition of property, he could rightfully seek it if he would yield up a part of it.

In 1835 the Tract Society summed up the rules for a Christian merchant. The analysis was as important for what it omitted as for what in included. Stressed were such things as honesty, economy in expenses, accuracy in accounts, the moral and religious supervision of employees, and personal piety. But the managers made no mention of how far the merchant might expand his operations, what constituted a fair profit, and what constituted proper business ethics. Presumably, all these rules were overshadowed by the fourth: "I must pledge my purse, my time, and my influence, for the preservation of order, intelligence, morality and religion in the community." But the amount to be given was not stated; each merchant could salve his own conscience as he pleased.

As they justified, warned, and chastised, as they asserted that a safe future for America lay only in men's obeying God, the Gospel, and the tenets of evangelical Protestantism, the managers were both transmitting and enlarging the heritage of their forebears. From the colonial theocrats and Federalism, benevolent men received and continued the idea that only a small number of men of particular attainments were qualified to shape, govern, and lead society. As the theocracies vanished and the growing electorate made impossible Federalism's continuance, the managers believed that religion propagated by the benevolent societies could be made an effective means of controlling a seemingly chaotic society. Their fundamental tenet was that they should dictate right conduct to their fellow citizens. In so believing, benevolent men bequeathed a lasting legacy. Many of the societies' leaders gave to the Republican party much of its often voiced morality. They and others tried to Americanize and mold the immigrant. They and their descendants discouraged dissent from their idealized economic, political, and social order. In their era the societies perpetuated the religio-political tradition in American history which claimed that only those men who met their standards were responsible for establishing the rule of the righteous and the jurisdiction of the just.

Charles Grandison Finney

WILLIAM G. McLOUGHLIN

Although Clifford Griffin has demonstrated how the evangelical revival could lead to organized efforts to control society in the interest of conservative groups, William G. McLoughlin (1922–   ), a professor of history at Brown University and a leading authority on the history of religion in America, has found striking parallels between the principles of Jacksonian democracy and the beliefs of the most famous ante-bellum revivalist, Charles Grandison Finney. This is not to say that Finney was a supporter of Andrew Jackson or that he represented an abrupt departure from the economic and social philosophy which Griffin has described. Finney's main emphasis was on personal moral reform. Nevertheless, McLoughlin brings out the revivalist's dedication to democracy, perfection, and progress, and enables us to see how his optimistic faith could inspire far more radical reformers than himself.

CHARLES GRANDISON FINNEY, THE SON OF A REVOLUTIONARY VETeran and an heir of the Pilgrim tradition of seventeenth-century Massachusetts, was born in Warren, Connecticut, in 1792. He moved west with his family two years later, grew up in the "burnt-over district" of western New York, and in 1821, as the result of an intense religious experience, he gave up a promising career as a lawyer in order to become an itinerant evangelist. He was a tall, slim, handsome man with piercing blue eyes, sandy hair, and a burning conviction that he was "led by God" in his effort to convert and reform the nation. Because he was ordained as a Presbyterian minister and because orthodox Prebsyterianism at this time was Calvinistic, many who have not read his works erroneously

Charles Grandison Finney, edited by William G. McLoughlin, *Lectures on Revivals of Religion,* 1960, pp. vii–xi, xl–xlix. Reprinted without footnotes and with minor deletions by permission of The Belknap Press of Harvard University Press, Cambridge, Mass. Copyright © 1960 by the President and Fellows of Harvard College.

assume that Finney was a preacher of hellfire and damnation who excoriated the moral depravity of man and exalted the wrath of God. Because he ardently espoused such moral reforms as temperance, abolition, and Sabbatarianism, and because of his close association with such wealthy Whig merchants as Lewis and Arthur Tappan, David and William E. Dodge, and Anson G. Phelps, it has been commonly assumed that Finney was totally out of sympathy with the Jacksonian temper of his times. His famous revival meetings, conducted in towns and cities across the country in the second quarter of the nineteenth century, are mistaken for manifestations of a resurgent ecclesiasticism, a "Protestant Counter-Reformation" designed to put down the deistic radicalism of Tom Paine and Thomas Jefferson and to reassert Christian orthodoxy and clerical domination in the new nation. And despite the fact that in 1851 Finney became the President of Oberlin College, it is sometimes assumed that his evangelical theology brands him as anti-intellectual, antiscientific, and antiliberal.

Even a cursory reading of [Finney's] *Lectures on Revivals* [1835] will soon dispel these misconceptions. Unlike the majority of his clerical colleagues, Finney, was a child of his age, not an enemy of it. He had little use for Calvinism, and the basic philosophical and social principles underlying his thought were essentially the same as those associated with Jacksonian democracy. Like the Jacksonians, Finney had an ardent faith in progress, in the benevolence of God, and in the dignity and worth of the common man. Like the Jacksonians, he believed that the restrictive clerical and aristocratic traditions of the seventeenth and eighteenth centuries were out of date and that they must give way to a new and more liberal outlook if the nation was to continue to grow in peace, liberty, and prosperity under God. Finney was no backward-looking fundamentalist exhorter, longing for the good old days of Puritanism and inculcating a fear of hell to keep the wickedness of the common man in check. He was in fact just the opposite of a theocrat—he was a pietist. And that is why he spent his life at odds with the Calvinists of his day. He disliked man-made creeds; he saw no need for institutionalized denominational systems; he believed in the priesthood of all believers. His mission, as he saw it, was to create a universal Church based upon the fundamentals of the gospel. He sought to cut away the bonds of customs and liberate men from their blind obedience to the past. He wanted to help men free themselves from sin and learn to grow in wisdom and love as free Christian men and women. And he believed that the millennial age was about to dawn in the United States of America.

It is true that Finney never took the stump for Andrew Jackson. His antislavery convictions were sufficient to prevent this. Moreover, like

Emerson, he preferred to vote against the party that shared his broad principles because he was convinced the other side had the more honest men. His pietistic evangelicalism made him see politics through moralistic eyes, and he cast his vote in terms of particular moral issues rather than in terms of party politics.

The clue to Finney's Jacksonian temper lies not in his attitude toward politics but in his attitude toward Calvinism. The first thing that strikes the reader of the *Lectures on Revivals* is the virulence of Finney's hostility toward traditional Calvinism and all it stood for. He denounced its doctrinal dogmas (which, as embodied in the Westminster Confession of Faith, he referred to elsewhere as "this wonderful theological fiction"); he rejected its concept of nature and the structure of the universe (especially its exaltation of the sovereign and miraculous power of God in regard to conversions and the promotion of revivals); he scorned its pessimistic attitude toward human nature and progress (particularly in regard to the freedom of the will); and he thoroughly deplored its hierarchical and legalistic polity (as embodied in the ecclesiastical system of the Presbyterian Church). Or to put it more succinctly, John Calvin's philosophy was theocentric and organic; Charles Finney's was anthropocentric and individualistic. It is little wonder that Finney was considered a renegade, a radical, and a "revolutionary" by so many of his strait-laced church brethren throughout his career. As one prominent Calvinist editor wrote in 1838 of Finney's revivals, "Who is not aware that the Church has been almost revolutionized within four or five years by means of such excitements?"

But this volume is more than a destructive attack upon "the traditions of the elders," as Finney scornfully referred to the old Calvinistic doctrines. It is a positive, ringing statement of the new religious, social, and intellectual philosophy that came to dominate popular American thought until well into the twentieth century—a philosophy that, however inconsistently, blended reason and faith, science and revelation, self-reliance and divine guidance, pragmatism and intuition, head and heart, moral self-denial and spiritual freedom, social reform and rugged individualism, humanitarianism and piety in a form perfectly adapted to the needs of the expanding and prospering American society. Within the broader frame of western civilization, Finney's faith, like that of the Jacksonians, was part and parcel of Thomas Reid's "Scottish Common Sense School" of philosophy, Jeremy Bentham's "philosophical radicalism," John Stuart Mills' "utilitarianism," Adam Smith's "laissez faire," plus that spongey modification of Jonathan Edwards' Calvinism in terms of John Wesley's Arminianism that is commonly called "evangelicalism." The one element that produced the tensile strength of this miscellaneous compound, and the strongest note in Finney's preaching, was the pietistic sectarianism he got from his separatist Pilgrim forebears.

Finney struck the keynote of the intellectual revolution for which this volume speaks in the very first lecture, when he stated it as axiomatic that a revival of religion "is not a miracle or dependent on a miracle. It is a purely philosophical result of the right use of the constituted means." This was obviously a direct contradiction of the theocentric cosmology of John Calvin and especially of the doctrines of God's arbitrary grace and inscrutable sovereignty that John Cotton and Jonathan Edwards had so vigorously upheld in America. Jonathan Edwards had described the famous revival in Northampton, Massachusetts, in 1734 as "a marvelous work of God," a "shower of divine blessing," which, like a shower of rain in a parched land, came miraculously through the divine hand of Providence. Finney, writing one hundred years later, insisted that the revivals with which he was so prominently connected in the years 1825–1835 were simply the result of cause and effect in which the revival preacher was the principal agent: "The connection between the right use of means for a revival and a revival is as philosophically sure as between the right use of means to raise grain and a crop of wheat." And as Finney went on to claim, the physical, psychological, and physiological laws of nature were now so well known (as perhaps they were not in Edwards' day) that it was clearly God's intention that men should make use of them to evangelize the world. Therefore, for the better advancement of God's kingdom, Finney designed the *Lectures on Revivals* to be a handbook, a how-to-do-it book for ministers interested (as all ministers should be) in promoting revivals and winning souls. . . .

If the essence of Finney's Jacksonian temper lies in his attitude toward progress, this in turn is closely connected with his doctrines of millennialism, disinterested benevolence, and perfectionism. Progress Finney defined as the working out of God's will, and since God was by definition benevolent, His ultimate aim was to produce the great[est] possible happiness in the universe. Because Finney no longer accepted the Calvinist view of God's inscrutable sovereignty and of man's ineradicable depravity and because he did not believe that the Bible justified the view that only a few predestined elect were eligible for salvation, he saw no reason why the whole world might not someday be made up of converted Christians living in brotherly love. Nor did he doubt that as the world became increasingly Christian through the conversion of more and more individuals it would become increasingly happy and prosperous. Men, especially regenerated men, would grow in wisdom, learn all the laws of science, and someday create a perfect utopia which would start the millennium of God's kingdom on earth. When he accepted the post as professor of theology at Oberlin early in 1835 (while still in the midst of writing his lectures on revivalism), he expressly did so in order to help educate "a new race of revival ministers," who would constitue the advance guard of the world-wide evangelistic movement.

Finney was sufficiently patriotic to believe that the United States was to be the first nation in which the whole population would be completely converted. Unlike those theocratically inclined Calvinists (Old School and New School) who saw an inevitable conflict between democracy and religion, Finney believed that democracy was the form of government most approved by God. There is an illuminating chapter on "Human Government" in his *Systematic Theology* (a book based upon his lectures at Oberlin and first published in 1846). In this chapter he stated explicitly that a republic is a "less pure form of self-government" than a democracy, and "a democracy is in many respects the most desirable form of government." In 1776 God, who controls the outcome of all revolutions (as John Locke said), permitted Americans to establish a republican form of government instead of continuing as subjects of a monarchy, because "God always allows his children as much liberty as they are prepared to enjoy" and "the intelligence and virtue of our Puritan forefathers rendered a monarchy an unnecessary burden." Consequently, if Americans continued to grow still more intelligent and virtuous, it was probable that God, in his benevolence, would someday grant them a democratic form of complete self-government that would be tantamount to a withering away of the state. Finney of course recognized the possibility of a nation's backsliding in virtue and hence slipping into a monarchy or a despotism, but he did not think this would happen in the United States where revivals were flourishing, education was expanding, and social reform was overcoming one evil after another.

Finney clearly did not share the view of Dwight L. Moody and most other revivalists of the post-Civil War period that only the cataclysm of Christ's Second Coming could bring about the millennium. However, this premillennial pessimism was advanced in Finney's day by William Miller, the Baptist preacher who predicted the return of Christ and the end of the world in the year 1843. Finney flatly rejected Miller's views. "I have examined Mr. Miller's theory," Finney wrote, "and am persuaded that what he expects to come after the judgment will come before it. Read the sixty-fifth chapter of Isaiah. The Prophet there speaks of the advancement to be made as the creation of a new heaven and a new earth." Scattered throughout the *Lectures on Revivals* there are continual references to the millennial hope. Perhaps the most striking of these, and one that doubtless astonished the less optimistic Albert Dod, was Finney's statement in Lecture XV that "if the church will do her duty the millennium may come in this country in three years."

Probably Finney did not believe that the Church would or could do its duty until all ministers were New School "revival ministers" and all Christians were dedicated to the doctrines of disinterested benevolence and perfectionism. In some ways it is odd that Finney should have preached the doctrine of disinterested benevolence, for it was originally put forth by Jonathan Edwards and his pupil, Samuel Hopkins, as a complement to the doctrine of God's absolute sovereignty. Samuel Hopkins was a hero of the Old School Calvinists of New England, many of whom referred to themselves as "Hopkinsians." And Finney devoted much of his time to attacking "Hopkinsianism" as a particularly malevolent form of "hyper-Calvinism." It is probable that Finney adopted the doctrine of disinterested benevolence without realizing who its authors were.

Hopkins set forth the doctrine in 1773 in his book *An Inquiry into the Nature of True Holiness* (a gloss upon Edwards' book on *The Nature of True Virtue*). The key to the doctrine is Hopkins' statement that true holiness is "disinterested benevolent affection" toward "God and our neighbor" and "true benevolence always seeks the greatest good of the whole." Hopkins meant by this to define virtue or holiness in terms of cosmic altruism. But Finney transformed the doctrine into cosmic ultilitarianism. He defined benevolence in terms of the greatest happiness of the greatest number and spoke of "the utility of benevolence" as the fact that benevolent actions increased both the happiness of our neighbors, of God, and of the universe in general. Hence, in his *Lectures on Revivals* he insisted that all young converts "should set out with a determination to aim at being useful in the highest degree" and "if they can see an opportunity where they can do more good, they must embrace it whatever may be the sacrifice to themselves." This is the heart and core of nineteenth-century evangelical activism, and as Finney's comments on the various social issues of the day indicate in these lectures, he and his converts embraced the great reform movements of the day with the passion of crusaders. It is not surprising that in his *Systematic Theology* he said of all true Christians that "their spirit is necessarily that of the reformer. To the universal reformation of the world they stand committed."

Among the many reforms of the day in which Finney expressed interest in his *Lectures on Revivals* were abolition, temperance, dietary regulations (especially the disuse of all stimulants, including tea and coffee), education, gambling, dueling, and hygiene (see his remarks in Lecture III[1] on the evils of "that filthy poison, tobacco"). In addition he attacked the sins of fashionable display, luxury, idleness, novel-reading,

---

[1] EDITOR'S NOTE: This and subsequent numbers refer to lectures in Finney's book, recently edited by McLoughlin, which interested students may want to consult.

theater-going, card-playing, dancing, and gluttony. There is a close relationship between Finney's moral code and Victorian prudery. Although the twentieth century mislabeled this evangelical moralizing "puritanism," most of it was simply lower-middle-class pietism reacting against what Finney called "the starch and flattery of high life." An historically inclined sociologist could discover much about the class structure and the social code of the 1830's by reading these lectures. The general reader will doubtless find these passages among the most amusing, especially his remarks about the evils of tightly laced corsets.

But it is important to note that Finney's attitude toward social reform, like his attitude toward politics and economics, was a distinctly moralistic one. That is, he believed that personal moral reform rather than political or legislative action was the surest and fastest way to improve the social order. The first step toward the millennium was to convert men to Christ; the rest would follow automatically from this. And herein lies the conservative side of Finney's preaching. For there is an inevitable tendency among pietistic evangelicals to limit their horizon entirely to the regeneration of individuals and to deny or ignore the complexities of custom, prejudice, and sectional or class conflict that lie at the root of so much social injustice. Pessimistic, premillennial revivalists since the Civil War have usually opposed efforts toward social reform on a broad scale, because they maintain that nothing but the return of Christ can possibly solve the major problems of this world. But Finney erred on the optimistic side. He believed that revivals could produce such sweeping results, could reform so many individuals so completely and rapidly, that legislative attempts at reform paled in comparison. In any case, his words spoke louder than his actions on the crucial reform movements of his day. Finney's stand on the question of slavery, for example, on which issue he was more radical than most Jacksonian democrats but not nearly so radical as an extreme pietist like William Lloyd Garrison, typifies this conservative element in his outlook.

As he states in Lecture XV in this volume, Finney firmly believed in 1835 that slavery was not only a sin which all Christians should oppose but that it was a problem with which the churches also must be concerned. As a pastor he refused to admit anyone to membership in his church who owned or trafficked in slaves. And yet Finney showed the prevailing prejudice of his day about social equality between Negroes and whites. He segregated Negro members from whites in his New York church, and he wished the Negro students at Oberlin to sit separately from whites. When his friend Lewis Tappan expostulated with him concerning this lack of Christian charity, Finney gave the standard answer that social equality was not a Christian duty, and he asked Tappan whether he would want his daughter to marry a Negro.

But more important in this regard was Finney's cautious attitude toward carrying antislavery agitation too far and too fast—especially in terms of legislative activity. When mobs in New York City attacked the home of his friend Arthur Tappan in July 1834, Finney began to retreat from his outspoken endorsement of the movement. He wrote to his wife that fall, "I don't believe that it would do to say too much about abolition here in publick." And in his revival lectures delivered that winter he repeatedly urged his abolitionist friends "to avoid a censorious spirit," to "consider it calmly," and to "act judiciously." Perhaps the most active and effective leader of the abolition movement in the 1830's was the brilliant and energetic young Theodore Weld, who had been converted by Finney in Utica in 1826. Weld always looked up to Finney as his "father in Christ," but when Weld tried to persuade the students at Oberlin to become abolitionist lecturers, Finney took the students aside and urged them not to do it. As one student wrote to Weld in August 1836: Finney "poured out his soul before us in agony in view of our continuing in the abolition field" and said that "the only hope of the country, the church, the oppressor, and the slave was in *wide spread* revivals." And Finney himself wrote to Weld about this time to try to persuade him that the whole slavery problem could be solved "in 2 years" if only "the publick mind can be engrossed with the subject of salvation and make abolition an appendage [of revivals] just as we made temperance an appendage of revival in Rochester." To an ardent social reformer such an attitude smacks of blind escapism, but to a pietist like Finney it is simply reliance upon God.

Much the same attitude exhibited itself in Finney's statements about politics. As he wrote in Lecture XV in this volume, it did not seem to him important whether a political candidate was for or against Andrew Jackson, whether he favored the National Bank or not, whether he was a Whig or a Democrat. The only important question was whether he was a Christian and an honest man or not. And in the field of economics, Finney, like most revivalists ever since, expressed more concern over the evils of indebtedness and the spiritual welfare of factory workers than over whether the incipient industrial revolution in the United States placed new social responsibilities upon Christian businessmen and upon the churches. Finney was so far from understanding the whole system of laissez faire capitalism that he condemned the practice of doing business on credit and echoed the old Puritan demand for a just price and a just wage.

There is a close connection between this pietistic attitude toward reform and Finney's doctrine of perfectionism. His emphasis upon personal regeneration as the only basis for social reform, his belief in progress, and his doctrine that "obligation and ability are commensurate" all combined to push him to the conclusion that the most desperate need of the age was a higher degree of consecration among professing Christians. For a perfect society must consist of perfect men. Finney did not evolve the view that came to be known as "Oberlin Perfectionism" (but which he preferred to call "entire consecration" or "sanctification") until after the *Lectures on Revivals* was completed. His *Lectures to Professing Christians,* published in 1837, was the first clear-cut statement of this doctrine—a doctrine that at once caused almost all of his New School colleagues to disown him. But there are several passages in the *Lectures on Revivals* that clearly indicate that this point of view had always been implicit in his preaching. For example, he states in Lecture XIX, all converts "should aim at being holy and not rest satisfied till they are as perfect as God." If this statement is taken in conjunction with his theory that God never commands any action with which man is not capable of complying, then the conclusion follows that all Christians can become perfect, for Christ declared, "Be ye therefore perfect even as your Father which is in heaven is perfect." Albert Dod saw this, perhaps even before Finney, and pointed it out in his review of the *Lectures on Revivals.* But Dod assumed that Finney's perfectionism (which was to him but the proof of the absurdity of New School Pelagianism) was precisely the same as that of John Humphrey Noyes and various other New England and western New York perfectionists in these years. It is necessary to point out that Finney expressly repudiated what he called the "antinomian perfectionism" of Noyes, because its purpose was to release the inhibitions and permit the perfected Christian complete freedom. To Noyes one of the most important freedoms for the perfected was sexual freedom and in the communistic community which he founded at Oneida, New York, Noyes and his associates practised a form of free love called "complex marriage," which thoroughly shocked Finney. Finney's perfectionism was based upon precisely the opposite approach to behavior. He believed that an entirely consecrated or sanctified Christian would become more perfect as he learned how to practice self-denial and to avoid self-indulgence. Declaring that "a self-indulgent Christian is a contradiction," Finney spoke of attaining "perfect obedience to the law of God." And of course the law of God implied conformity to the entire code of Victorian prudery and small-town morality that played so prominent a part in his exhortatory preaching. To Finney a Christian who gave up drinking tea and coffee was on the road to perfection, while one who took up "complex marriage" was on the primrose path to hell. But at least he and Noyes agreed that men were perfectible and that a perfect social order was well within the realm of possibility for Americans who were alive in the year 1835.

In the light of Finney's theology and social philosophy it is of some interest to compare briefly his views with those of a typical Jacksonian spokesman like John L. O'Sullivan in order to see how much they had in common. O'Sullivan, who was the part-owner and editor of the *United States Magazine and Democratic Review* is generally acknowledged to have been a particularly articulate and representative spokesman of the Jacksonian spirit. In the first number of his newspaper, in October 1837, he issued a statement of his political and social philosophy that is often quoted as a manifesto of the age. Among the beliefs that O'Sullivan here espoused were "the principle of democratic republicanism," "an abiding confidence in the virtue, intelligence, and full capacity for self-government of the great mass of our people," and a deep-seated dislike for those "aristocratic interests" or "better classes" who claim a "more enlightened wisdom" than the average man and therefore a greater right to govern. Finney would have agreed with all of these beliefs. O'Sullivan then went on to advocate "the general diffusion of knowledge" among all classes, to acknowledge "the moral elements implanted by its Creator in human society," and to profess "a true and living faith in the existence and attributes of that Creator." Finney used more theological and Scriptural terminology, but he would have endorsed all of this. In his argument for the view that that government is best which governs least, O'Sullivan, like Finney, saw "the democratic principle walking hand in hand with the sister spirit of Christianity" down through time until "our theory and practice of government shall be sifted and analyzed down to the lowest point of simplicity consistent with the preservation of some degree of national organization." O'Sullivan attacked men, like Beecher and Dod, who "cast the weight of their social influence against the cause of democracy under the false prejudice of an affinity between it and infidelity." The cause of Democracy "is the cause of Christianity" he asserted. And just as Finney attacked the dead hand of Calvinism for trying to preserve the outmoded "traditions of the elders," so O'Sullivan argued that progress depended upon avoiding "that specious sophistry by which old evils always struggle to perpetuate themselves by appealing to our veneration for the wisdom of our fathers." Like Finney, O'Sullivan praised the great step forward made by those who led the American Revolution and declared that Americans were "a chosen people" with a "glorious destiny," which would be guided by the unseen hand of Providence. The whole of this manifesto breathes the optimistic faith in God, in man, in America, and in the future that underlies Finney's fervent pietism. Both men saw God as a benevolent Creator who has endowed human kind with moral principles and who requires of all men the abandonment of selfish desires and a devotion to the reformation of the world. There is even in O'Sullivan something of Finney's distrust of the wealth and social pretensions of the *nouveaux riches* of the wicked cities. O'Sullivan deprecates the rising "cities, where wealth accumulates, where luxury gradually unfolds its corrupting tendencies, where aristocratic habits and social classifications form and strengthen themselves, where the congregation of men stimulates and exaggerates all ideas."

There is no denying, of course, that there was a strong tinge of rationalism, free thought, and anticlericalism in the Jacksonian spirit, which runs directly counter to Finney's evangelical temper. And, too, the Jacksonian politicians were opposed to such moral reforms as temperance, Sabbath legislation, and abolition, just as Finney was uninterested in the political and economic reforms of the party platform. Finney probably shared the view of his close friend—Lewis Tappan regarding Andrew Jackson. Tappan stated that the General was "a very unfit man to be at the head of the government." But there were many reasons why a pietist might dislike Jackson without disliking the principles of Jacksonian democracy. And it can be said that Finney and Jackson, each in his own way, were striving for much the same kind of free, individualistic, and egalitarian society.

Religious Groups and
Political Parties

LEE BENSON

If the evangelism of Finney and his abolitionist converts can be seen as a branch of Jacksonian democracy, it is still necessary to distinguish such reformers from the Americans who equated progress with a laissez-faire state in which everyone minds his own business. The very concept of "Jacksonian democracy" has become so general and ambiguous that Lee Benson (1922–   ), a professor of history at the University of Pennsylvania, has questioned its usefulness. Applying the techniques and principles of modern political and behavioral science, Benson has sought to discover who supported and who opposed the evangelical reformers. In an intensive study of politics in New York State, he has concluded that political behavior reflected moral attitudes and ways of life that were deeply embedded in the social structure. While the results of his analysis are admittedly tentative, they suggest that a predisposition toward reform was not simply the product of a New England heritage or economic interest.

T HE WHIGS CLAIMED NOT ONLY THAT THEY WERE THE PARTY OF "all the religion," but also that "decency" and "respectability" marched to the polls armed with their ballots. Writing a letter of condolence to Henry Clay after the latter's defeat in 1844, Philip Hone, the prominent New York merchant, observed that "nine tenths of 'our respectable citizens,' the merchants, the professional men, the mechanics and workingmen, those who went to church on Sunday," voted Whig. And a correspondent from Pittsburgh struck the same consoling note: "You had

Lee Benson, *The Concept of Jacksonian Democracy: New York as a Test Case,* 1961, pp. 198–207, 209–213. Reprinted without footnotes and with minor deletions by permission of Princeton University Press. Copyright © 1961 by Princeton University Press.

nine-tenths of the virtue, intelligence, and respectability of the nation on our side." There is little doubt that Clay's correspondents took their theme from Horace Greeley. So overwhelmed by grief and disappointment that he literally broke into tears, Greeley had abandoned all restraint and charged that the Democratic victory resulted largely from successful demagogic appeals to the dissolute and the ignorant:

"Loafers around the grog-shops of our Manufacturing villages! subsisting on the earnings of your wives and children in the factories—give an extra glass and an extra yell for Polk and Dallas, and down with Cooney Clay! The time will come when you can no longer riot thus on the wages of your families; therefore make the most of the present, in venting curses on those who have earned and saved while you have idled and squandered, rejoicing in the hope that your victory will soon bring all to a common level of bankruptcy. What if there be sadness and despair among the thrifty, the thoughtful, the industrious—is there not illumination, revelry and extra blue ruin at the Five Points [notorious slum and vice district] and in nine-tenths of the three thousand drunkard-manufactories of our city? Does not ignorance and vice exult, if only to see Intelligence and Virtue perplexed and afflicted? Let Universal Rowdyism strain its throat on one more execration of Clay, and three cheers for *Polk* and Dallas!"

Accused by the editor of the *Eastern Argus* (Maine) of slandering the Democrats, Greeley renewed the attack several weeks later: "The Argus is right in supposing that we believe that there is a great moral difference between the two parties, and that we quoted the vote of the Five Points and Corlear's Hook [another 'den of vice'] to show it . . . It was by . . . ['incendiary appeals to Poverty to array itself against Wealth'] that nine-tenths of those broken down by dissipation and degraded by their own profligacy were combined in a solid and powerful phalanx against the Whigs. Upon those Working Men who stick to their business, hope to improve their circumstances by honest industry, *and go on Sundays to church rather than the grog-shop* [italics added] the appeals of Loco-Focoism[1] fell comparatively harmless; while the opposite class were rallied with unprecedented unanimity against us."

Were such outbursts designed to conceal the real cause of the Whig defeat? Did they inadvertently support Democratic charges that the Whigs were the party of the classes and had scarcely disguised contempt for the masses? I do not believe so. Instead of indicating differences in the class composition of parties, Greeley's editorials indicated party differences in *moral attitudes and ways of life.*

[1] EDITOR'S NOTE: Loco-Foco was a nickname applied to the reformist, equal-rights faction of the Democratic Party.

Stripped of their more extravagant features, scaled down and reformulated, Greeley's tirades are consistent with the impressionistic evidence reported in the historical literature. To recognize the existence of *something like* "a great moral difference between the two parties" does not, of course, require literal acceptance of his description of "intelligence and virtue" at war with "universal rowdyism." In effect, Greeley asserted that differences in men's attitudes and opinions concerning moral issues cut across class and ethnocultural lines and formed a significant basis for party divisions. This does not seem surprising when we recall that the Antimasons translated Reverend Ely's dream of "a Christian Party in Politics" into reality. Among other things, Ely demanded "the application of Christian principles to the exercise of the suffrage, viz. 'never wittingly to support for any public office' anyone possessing a 'bad moral character,' which includes not only 'confirmed sots and persons judicially convicted of high crimes,' but also 'all profane swearers, notorious Sabbath-breakers, seducers, slanderers, prodigals, and riotous persons, as well as the advocates of duelling.' "

No one has yet studied the subject systematically, but it seems that on all class levels—particulary the "lower-class"—and among all ethnocultural groups, Whigs were more likely than Democrats to share puritanical attitudes and to disdain the antipuritanical qualities that were esteemed on the American frontier and among urban "lower-class radicals." As conceived here, puritanical attitudes are independent of theological creed. They connote a related set of definitions and values—piety, sobriety, propriety, thrift, "steady habits," and "book-learning." (No implication is intended that all people who valued book-learning were puritans by any definition, nor that approval of book-learning implied approval of free inquiry.)

"Great personal courage, unusual physical powers, the ability to drink a quart of whiskey or to lose the whole of one's capital on the turn of a card and without the quiver of a muscle"—these hell-of-a-fellow, individualistic characteristics suggest the qualities most likely to be valued in American frontier or frontier-like regions. (Indeed, the frontier displayed a strong tendency to insist that all men possess those qualities.) My impressionistic estimate is that in most localities, more Democrats than Whigs valued or possessed those qualities or their *urban equivalents and manifestations*. The spirit of the "Protestant Ethic" may have contributed to capitalist development in long-settled areas. But in a relatively undeveloped, rapidly expanding economy that presented many opportunities to the bold and the adventurous, individualistic, antisocial frontier qualities might frequently have been more economically functional than puritanical qualities which stressed responsibility to the community and conformity to "respectable" values. Antipuritans, therefore, might well have flourished on upper class levels and found Democrats more congenial company than Whigs.

Frederick Jackson Turner's equation of Jacksonian Democracy with an idealized concept of frontier democracy no doubt pushed oversimplification beyond reasonable bounds. But at least he appreciated that Jacksonians flavored their rhetoric to the taste of the frontier and the back country. Although both parties depicted themselves as anti-aristocratic and pro-producer, until the Whigs went out of character and infringed on the Democratic patent in the 1840 Log Cabin campaign, the Democrats held a near monopoly on the rhetoric designed to conjure up a muscular, horny-handed image of their party.

Drawing distinctions between "producers" and "parasites" was not original with Americans. What did make the Jacksonian rhetoric relatively original was its imaginative merger of the theme of the virtuous producer with that of the lusty Western pioneer. If we could hold other factors constant, we would find that the Democrats tended to have their greatest success among voters who bragged about their fondness for hard liquor, fast women and horses, and strong, racy language. By this conjecture we need not grant the Antimasons and Whigs anything like their claimed monopoly on all the decency, respectability, and religion. It is even debatable whether such a study of Democratic voters could be made. But we can adduce some support for the conjecture by again contrasting the political and "moral" characteristics of two towns in the same county.

The town of Burke in Franklin County was settled "mostly from Vermont." Other places with a higher proportion of non-British immigrants supported the Democrats more strongly, but Burke gave them 60.2 per cent of its vote, although the county's median unit registered only 45.4 per cent. During the pre-Civil War period, it clearly was a "poor" lumbering and tanning town. Significantly, after it paid the standard tributes to the sterling qualities of its settlers, the local county history described them in unusual terms for a work of that genre. Along with good citizens, "bad ones came also or developed there, and at one period the hamlet of Burke, known also as the 'Hollow' and for a time as Andrusville, was exceedingly tough."

That period must have included July 4, 1861, for it was described as one of the "two days of great excitement" in the town annals. The first was in 1856 when the great tornado struck: "The other day in question [Fourth of July, 1861] was when Hiram Cartwright and other secession sympathizers raised a secession flag at the Hollow. The flag had been painted by William Hollenbeck. The time was when the Hollow was deemed one of the hardest places in the county, and the day was doubtless the wildest that Burke ever knew. It is said that there were two hundred men drunk there on that day, and drunk in no ordinary degree, but raving so. The men who were back of the flag raising armed themselves, assembled at the foot of the pole, and declared that they would shoot any one who should attempt to haul down the flag. Word of the affair reached Malone, and a company of sober men, quite as thoroughly in earnest as the rabble at Burke, was recruited, largely from the railroad machine shops, to go to Burke for the purpose of tearing down the rag."

But just as the train reached Burke, frantic admonitions by the county's leading Democratic editor prevailed, the secession flag was lowered, and the rumble never came off.

From the description by the same historian elsewhere in the volume, it can be inferred that the phrase "company of sober men" is a good indicator of Malone's moral climate. According to one nostalgic inhabitant, in 1824 it had been "the most perfect representation of the ideal puritanical village." Malone probably had retained much of that character, for the outcome of local option referendums in 1846 and 1847 made it a nominally "dry" town. Like Burke, nearly all its settlers came from Vermont, but they "were mostly of the Puritan type and of what Deacon Jehiel Berry used to call the 'white oak' strain, and of whom generally Gail Hamilton strikingly wrote: 'Every church, every school house, every town house from the Atlantic to the Pacific has Plymouth Rock for its foundation. Where ever Freedom aims a musket, or plants a standard, or nerves an arm, or sings a song, or makes a protest, or murmurs a prayer, there is Plymouth Rock.' "

Mostly of puritan type, they were also mostly of the Whig Party. In 1844 the prosperous farming town of Malone was the lowest ranking Democratic unit (36.0 per cent) in Franklin County. In 1834, before sizeable numbers of Irish Catholics and French-Canadians arrived, the Whigs had received 69.3 per cent, the Democrats 30.7 per cent, of its vote.

Like Phelps and West Bloomfield, the contrast between politics and piety in Burke and Malone supports the impressionistic finding that there were significant differences in Whig and Democratic moral attitudes. Fortunately, that finding is also supported by systematic data. But the inferences drawn from those data rest on certain assumptions that should be made explicit.

The key assumption here is that men engaged primarily in farming tended to have a different set of values, beliefs, and attitudes from those engaged primarily in lumbering and its allied pursuits (for example, tanning, charcoal-burning, shingle-making). By their nature, it is assumed, the two occupations retained or developed or attracted men who differed in psychological makeup. Other considerations aside, the environment in which they were carried out and the personal qualities necessary to their successful pursuit made belief in the value of education, religion, and temperance more functional and more likely to flourish in farming than in lumbering areas.

Except for certain specialized crops, farming was a slow process of growing things that sharply restricted men to their home boundaries and reserved its rewards for men capable of planning, self-discipline, and long adherence to a daily routine that varied little over the years. In contrast, lumbering required quick spurts of great exertion during which men destroyed things under conditions of constant physical danger, followed by long periods in which they were free to act as the spirit moved them and the spirits flowed. Moreover, it tended to bring quicker returns with more fluctuation than did farming, giving it something of the allure and excitement of gambling. Rafting logs down the Delaware, the Susquehanna, or the Allegheny in high-water season was a world away from the dull routine of hoeing weeds in home cornfields. Whatever the reasons for the difference in attitudes, if we hold ethnocultural group constant, I make the assumption that a much larger proportion of farmers than lumbermen shared puritanical views and possessed "intelligence and virtue," as defined in Greeley's and Hone's lexicon.

If the assumption is granted, the systematic data presently available indicate the existence of heavy Democratic majorities in 1844 among rural "nonpuritan" voters. One set of statistics makes the point. Twenty lumbering towns constituted the *highest-ranking* Democratic units in their counties, but lumbering towns fell into the *lowest-ranking* Democratic category in only seven counties. (Half the top towns registered Democratic tallies of 71.2 per cent or better, only one under 60.0 per cent). The strong positive relationship between lumbering and heavy Democratic majorities is not spurious, for it persists when other variables are considered and held constant. For example, despite the Yankee tendency as a group to vote Whig, they were either the numerically overwhelming or the dominant element in 15 of the 20 highest Democratic lumbering towns. In fact, partisan sympathies were so pronounced in lumbering towns that an estimate of 75 per cent Democratic appears reasonable for members of that occupational group. Since I can think of no "economic" reason why men engaged in lumbering should prefer one party to the other, I relate their voting to moral attitudes and values commonly held by lumbermen. In this respect, the argument differs radically from traditional occupational group interpretations of politics, and discredits rather than supports economic determinism.

Additional support for the finding that puritans tended more than nonpuritans to vote Whig can be inferred from the opposing views of the two parties concerning the proper role of the state in the Good Society. Committed to the doctrine of the negative state, the dominant wing of the Democratic Party in New York drew the logical conclusions and took a clear-cut liberal position on religious and moral issues. (In this context, "liberal" refers to the word's literal meaning and is free from value connotations.) As noted earlier, its official creed held that in a republic, "A great regulator of business occupations, or *consciences of men* [italics added], not only is not required, but should not be tolerated."

In 1844, the Whig Party had not yet officially gone on record as favoring legislation to regulate the consciences of men or to improve their minds and refine their society. Nevertheless, semiofficial organs of the party, as different from each other as the *New York Express* and the *New York Tribune,* in effect proudly confirmed Democratic charges that the Whigs were dedicated to what has been called the puritanical Yankees' "holy enterprise of minding other people's business." In a sense, that witticism is slanderous, for as the *Tribune* viewed the social order, no such thing existed as other people's business.

According to the assumption underlying the *Tribune's* doctrine, the righteous had no choice but to save the world from evil, and evildoers from themselves. Contrary to the Democratic position that men should be left free to make individual choices on religious and moral issues, the *Tribune* essentially argued that the state was a proper instrument for the regulation of every "evil" in society—as its editor and other "righteous" men defined evil. That doctrine was consonant with populistic doctrine and with the Antimasonic-Whig position on the positive state—but not, by any reasonable definition, with a liberal State. In respect to issues of this type, therefore, the Whig Party can accurately be described at best as "conservative" and at worst as "reactionary."

Perhaps the best way to illustrate concretely the real differences between Democratic "liberalism" and Whig "conservatism" is to cite the *Tribune's* analysis of a Democratic pamphlet entitled, *Loco-Focoism Displayed, or Government for the People; in a Dialogue between a Whig and a Loco-Foco.* Why analyze this particular pamphlet? Because it is significant index of how Locofocoism is propagated and of "the considerations which . . . [won] men to its support." Substitute "Whiggism" for "Loco-Focoism" and the *Tribune's* analysis serves precisely the same function—although the primary concern here is to identify the kinds of men won to the support of the two parties, rather than to understand their motives. "The leading idea of the writer is that popularly expressed by the current Loco-Foco axioms, 'The world is governed too much'; 'The best government is that which governs least'; etc. There is nothing new in these doctrines, and we have found them more ably set forth by Bentham, Hazlitt, and some of the modern Political Economists than by our 'Loco-Foco.' . . . Our 'Loco-Foco' of course contends that Governments have no rights and duties beyond the prevention and punishment of palpable invasions of one man's rights by another—that, consequently, all laws against Gambling, Grogselling, Debauchery, Bigamy, Brothelkeeping, etc., etc., are gross usurpations. . . . The fallacy here, as in all similar arguments against the punishment of Seduction and Licentiousness in general, lies in the assumption that the perpetrators 'injure nobody but themselves.' They do injure others; they bring scandal and reproach to their relatives; they are morally certain to prove unfaithful to their duties as parents, children, etc., and they corrupt and demoralize those around them. . . . The general doctrine of this 'Loco-Foco' is more precisely set forth in another passage:

" 'W.[hig]. Then I suppose of course you think that all legislation for morality alone is useless.

" 'L.[oc]. Not only that, but that *all legislation* having any other object but the protection of rights is not only injurious to morality, but is in itself immoral and wicked.' "

Even if we knew nothing except the two parties' conflicting views about the state's role as a regulator of the "consciences of men," we could reasonably infer that, other factors held constant, puritans would be more likely to vote Whig, nonpuritans to vote Democratic. No implication is intended, of course, that all or an overwhelming majority of Whigs and Democrats were puritans and nonpuritans, respectively. The inference refers to central tendencies, not to perfect or near perfect relationships. To draw that inference in no way denies that attitudes and opinions related to other issues, interests, loyalties, and antagonisms exerted cross-pressures upon voters. Nor is it denied that some men who might be classified as puritans opposed the Whigs on the ground that the state had neither the right nor the ability to legislate morality. But, together with the other evidence cited above, the contrasting attitudes of the two parties on such issues support the finding that puritan and nonpuritan divisions strongly corresponded to Whig and Democratic divisions. . . .

To my knowledge, no one has yet made a systematic, detailed study of the social composition of the Liberty Party in any state. The available data, however, appear to warrant several generalizations about New York.

That political abolitionism was overwhelmingly a rural movement is clear from the voting statistics. Except for Utica, no city in New York gave the Liberty Party as much as five per cent of its total vote. In every other city it received less than the state average (3.1 per cent), and in most, far less. The inverse relationship between political abolitionism and "urbanity" particularly shows up in the almost nonexistent Liberty Party vote in larger eastern cities, such as New York (0.2 per cent), Brooklyn (0.6 per cent), and Albany (1.0 per cent).

Although abolitionism was overwhelmingly a rural movement, its appeal was actually limited to *certain types* of rural areas. A prominent abolitionist, Henry Stanton, later noted that "for many years an influence on behalf of the slave radiated from the central counties of New York which was felt beyond the borders of the state. . . ." But analysis of voting statistics and other data show that political abolitionists' hammer blows struck responsive chords in central, western, and northern New York communities containing few Negro inhabitants, or in cities serving those communities—and in those areas almost exclusively. Considerable numbers of free Negroes lived in eastern and southeastern New York, areas which expressed intense hostility to antislavery "agitators" and to antislavery "agitation." Like the eastern cities, many rural counties, such as Ulster, Rockland, Dutchess, Suffolk, and Orange, registered either no Liberty votes or less than one per cent of the total cast.

Locating the towns that gave 15 per cent or more of their votes to the Liberty Party supports Stanton's observation that antislavery influence radiated out from central New York. Significantly, Smithfield in Madison County gave the highest Liberty vote (48.5 per cent) of any town in the state. The town had been founded and named by Gerrit Smith's father, and served as his family seat. Together with the energy and money concentrated upon the work in Madison County, Smith's personal influence probably accounted for its position as the strongest Liberty county (15.4 per cent). In addition to Smithfield, five other Madison towns cast more than 15 per cent of their votes "on behalf of the slave." Just across the county border, Plainfield, in Otsego, ranked as the second highest Liberty town, with 32.3 per cent. Altogether, a 50 mile radius drawn from the Smithfield center would encompass 17 of the party's top 35 towns.

Whether located near or far from the geographic center of Liberty influence, the top antislavery towns strikingly resembled each other in socioeconomic and ethnocultural composition. With few exceptions, they were small, moderately prosperous, Yankee farming communities. And impressionistic evidence suggests that the men who voted the Liberty ticket tended to have considerable standing in their communities and much better than average education. Study of county histories suggests that the following description of Erie County abolitionists might be applied generally: "The slimness of the Abolitionist vote [in 1844] could not be blamed altogether upon political inexperience. In the Anti-Slavery societies of both city [Buffalo] and county the reformers had organizations to support their efforts. Certain of the members to be sure were unworldly idealists little used to the hustings and the rough and tumble of political contest. Among them was a merchant's clerk named Douglas Williams; a former schoolmaster in East Aurora, a Dartmouth man, named George W. Johnson; a New School Presbyterian Deacon, Abner W. Bryant; a few ministers like the Reverend Mr. Parmalee of Griffin's Mills and the Reverend Calvin Grey of Wales. More were substantial farmers or men of affairs in rural towns and to that number belonged Joseph Plumb of Collins; Elihu Rice of Sardinia; Gideon Barker of Wales; Dwight Needham and Archibald Griffith of Concord. Here and there the roster of membership bore the name of a prominent professional man like Dr. Caleb Austen of Buffalo. Of these men very few were politicians; yet politicians there were who played conspicuous parts in the movement. Of this description were Isaac Phelps of Griffin's Mills, in whose bailiwick the Erie County Anti-Slavery Society had been organized; Joseph Freeman of Alden, William Mills of Clarence, and Colonel Asa Warren of Eden. These gentlemen, sometimes supervisors, magistrates, or members of the legislature, understood politics from long experience. So did the ex-Congressman and prominent member of the Buffalo bar, Thomas C. Love."

Though we must again rely on impressionistic evidence, it seems reasonable to say that most Liberty voters shared a common set of "radical religious beliefs." During the 1830's and 1840's, those beliefs inspired numerous related reform and benevolent movements, and political abolitionism represented only one manifestation of religious ultraism. "The ultraist state of mind," according to Whitney Cross, "rose from an implicit, even occasionally an explicit, reliance upon the direct guidance of the Holy Ghost." Ultraists assumed and acted on the assumption that God directly intervened in human affairs by revealing the truth to certain souls. Once it had been revealed to them, once they saw "the inner light," men had no choice but to reveal God's will to others and thus bring about the ultimate perfection of mankind in this world. A victory over slavery might launch the millennium, these optimistic Calvinists believed—a belief likely to give great energy and sense of mission to men caught up in the antislavery crusade.

Ultraists dedicated to antislavery carried the Yankee "holy enterprise of minding other people's business" to its logical extreme. No doubt they appeared intolerably self-righteous to contemporaries less convinced than they that eradicating the "sin of slavery" was God's will, or that abolitionists were His chosen instruments. And twentieth century psychologists and psychiatrists might see guilt and hyperactive superegos where ultraists saw "the spirit [that] has power to arouse the conscience and make it pierce like an arrow. . . ." However we account for them, antislavery ultraists clearly acted as righteous men compelled to follow God's inner light, wherever it led them and whatever personal vicissitudes they encountered along the way.

Read literally, rather than as a blatant expression of self-righteousness, this rhetorical question catches the ultraist essence: "For why should a good man stop," asked one minister in all innocence, "who knows certainly that he is right exactly, and that all men are wrong in proportion as they differ from him?" Whether abolitionists really were "right exactly" could not be more irrelevant here; what is relevant here is to identify the kind of men who voted for the Liberty Party, not to assess the "rightness" of their doctrines.

All political abolitionists were not religious ultraists, but it seems reasonably certain that few, if any, were not intensely religious. True, antislavery appeals were sometimes phrased in economic terms. Those were arguments, not reasons. Economic arguments for abolition actually were most relevant in areas that rejected abolitionism most fiercely and ejected abolitionists most forcibly. Given the nature and program of the Liberty Party, it is hardly surprising that its strongest support came from areas most likely to respond to the doctrines preached by New York rural evangelical sects. During the early forties, Baptists apparently led the antislavery hosts; Presbyterians and Methodists followed closely. That ranking is strictly relative, because at best only a very small minority of any major denomination cast Liberty ballots.

For our purposes, the most illuminating aspect of the Liberty Party's composition is what it reveals about the Whig and Democratic parties. As suggested earlier, Whigs tended to respond more favorably than Democrats to the "church and state" concept. Moreover, the Whig political philosophy postulated an activist, positive state, responsible for improving the material and moral well-being of society and capable of wielding broad national powers. In contrast, the Democratic philosophy postulated a negative, passive state in general, and a restricted, passive federal government in particular. Since abolitionists belonged to economic and ethnocultural groups which did not vote strongly Whig, it is significant that the overwhelming majority of Liberty voters were ex-Whigs. From these two sets of facts, the deduction seems logical that they had been originally attracted to the Whig Party, in part at least, because its activist political doctrines closely corresponded to their activist religious doctrines; that is, they believed that the state must act to purge society of moral evils. This line of reasoning can be pushed further.

Antislavery ultraists "believed progress to be attainable, by human effort and practically inevitable; but they derived from their Calvinist traditions an equally powerful suspicion that the natural tendency, *unaided by willful diligence* [italics added], was toward degeneracy." Translated into nonreligious terms, this suspicion corresponds to the belief that egoistic individual action must fail to produce the beneficial results envisioned by *laissez faire* political economists. That abolitionists almost invariably had Whig histories lends support, therefore, to a conclusion developed further in succeeding chapters: Whatever the source of their inspiration, other things being equal, men convinced that organized, collective action contributed to human progress tended more to vote Whig than Democrat. Deliberately oversimplified to make the point, Whigs tended toward collectivism, Democrats toward individualism.

FROM SOCIAL CONTROL
TO MORAL
REGENERATION

Temperance, Status Control, and Mobility, 1826–60

JOSEPH R. GUSFIELD

Turning now to a detailed analysis of a specific reform movement, we can understand how a mode of social behavior, in this case the consumption of alcoholic beverages, became a symbol of social status and of a style of life that threatened the established order. Joseph R. Gusfield (1923–   ), a sociologist at the University of Illinois, draws on the suggestions of Clifford Griffin and David Donald, and portrays the early temperance movement as an instrument of social control in the hands of an endangered or displaced elite. His analysis of the social function of temperance would seem to reinforce Lee Benson's theory of political cleavage according to moral attitudes and ways of life. But

Joseph R. Gusfield, *Symbolic Crusade: Status Politics and the American Temperance Movement,* 1963, pp. 36–57, 59–60. Reprinted without footnotes and with minor deletions by permission of the University of Illinois Press. Copyright © 1963 by the Board of Trustees of the University of Illinois.

Gusfield also points to a second phase of temperance reform which has more in common with McLoughlin's description of Finney's populistic revivalism. When abstinence from alcohol became a symbol of social respectability, temperance became associated with liberation and upward mobility.

IN DESCRIPTIONS OF AMERICAN TEMPERANCE, ABSTINENCE IS OFTEN attributed to the effects of Puritan doctrine. This view is contradicted by the facts of history. Puritan and other colonial leaders did not advocate total abstinence. They stood for the moderate and regulated use of alcohol, not its eradication. The development of Temperance doctrine and organization is best understood in the context of the social and cultural changes of the pre-Civil War period. It was especially influenced by the decline of Federalist aristocracy and the rise to social and political importance of the "common man" in the United States.

TEMPERANCE AND SOCIAL CONTROL

There are two phases to the development of the American Temperance movement in the period 1826–60. Although these phases overlap, each is connected with the status aspirations of a different social class. In the first phase, described in this section, Temperance represents the reaction of the old Federalist aristocracy to loss of political, social, and religious dominance in American society. It is an effort to re-establish control over the increasingly powerful middle classes making up the American "common man." In the second phase Temperance represents the efforts of urban, native Americans to consolidate their middle-class respectability through a sharpened distinction between the native, middle-class life styles and those of the immigrant and the marginal laborer or farmer.

THE BREAKDOWN OF THE COLONIAL SOCIAL ORDER

The use of alcohol in colonial America was governed by legal and moral sanctions which maintained a norm of moderate drinking. Taverns were licensed, not to deter their use but to regulate inns for the benefit of the traveler. Moderate use of alcohol was approved. Taverns were social centers and innkeepers respected members of the community. Although drunkenness occurred and was punished, it was seldom frequent. The controlled drinking of the American colonies was largely a result of a social order in which an elite of religious, economic, and political leadership was able to develop codes of conduct which were influential at most levels of the society. The American colonial society was rigidly divided into discrete classes and status levels. ". . . democracy was new; men were still described as gentlemen and simplemen . . . disparities of rank were still sustained by those of property." Political and social power were in the hands of an aristocracy of wealth, based on the commercial capitalism of the East and the plantation ownership of the South.

The power of the colonial aristocracy cut across the institutions of the society. The same families and social groups were represented in the holders of leadership in the courts, in the governments, and in the churches. The power of the clergy as arbiters of morality was enhanced by the direct relationship between Federalist aristocracy and church leadership. The clergy, like the judiciary, were stablizing influences in the social order. The codes of moderated drinking which were enunciated by them were reasonably well followed. Even after the development of towns and port cities, drinking in America, before the Revolution, was not a problem to which great attention was paid. Compared to the drunkenness of British cities at the same time and to the post-Revolutionary period, it was a remarkably sober era. ". . . against the dark background of conditions in England . . . town life in America stands out as a model of orderliness and sobriety."

The breakdown of the old order of town life was manifested in the decline of Calvinist church leadership and aristocratic political power after the Revolution and in the first two decades of the nineteenth century. The American Revolution was a great solvent working to dissolve the rigid class and status structure of colonial society. The period of post-Revolutionary ferment was also one of religious dissent, decline, and irreverence. In the process of change the established institutions of church power lost a great deal of their dominance in matters of moral behavior:

The trying years of the Revolution were critical for New England orthodoxy. It was an unsettled period filled with demoralizing tendencies. The use of intoxicants was well-nigh universal. Sabbath violations were winked at by the authorities; swearing, profanity and night-walking passed all but unnoticed. Depreciated money encouraged speculation and avarice. . . . Men were becoming materialistic. The minister was fast losing his autocratic sway in the parish. Congregationalism was seriously weakened. The Church of England was all but destroyed. . . . Hence one is not surprised at the inroads "nothingarianism" made into the established order.

Perhaps nothing illustrates the tolerance of excessive drinking in the late eighteenth century as much as the heavy use of whiskey at ministerial ordinations, where considerable drinking and frequent drunkenness became customary. This was so much a feature of ministerial conduct that those who tried to apply the earlier norms of moderation were liable to criticism by superiors. Rev. John Marsh, Secretary of the American Temperance Society in the 1840's, recalled the fate of a minister who had scolded his colleagues for their intemperance. His superiors in the church called him a "pest" and a "blackguard" for his excessive moralism.

By the end of the eighteenth and early nineteenth century a "drinking problem" had developed in many American states. The old norms of moderation were less effective as the Cavinist clergy lost its political and social position as an elite. The increase in transient populations, especially in the seaport cities, added to the familiar complex of urban crime, poverty, and drinking. Alcoholic beverages were more potent than they had been before the Revolution. The separation from England deprived the Americans of access to good maltsters and high-quality beer, leading drinkers to use the distilled spirits, especially rum. Whiskey became an important part of the economy. Distilling spirits from grain and then shipping the distilled product was a convenient and profitable way to market the crop. Its use as a medium of exchange made liquor an important adjunct to the slave trade. All these factors, plus the impact of war on traditional moralities, help explain the decline of controlled drinking and the increased frequency of drinking and drunkenness in the post-Revolutionary period. Excessive drinking had become the custom at weddings, funerals, and christenings. A great many people considered drinking essential to health. No doctrine of abstinence or even temperance had yet emerged.

TEMPERANCE AND THE FEDERALIST RESPONSE

The period in which Temperance doctrine and organization emerged was also the period of Jeffersonian and Jacksonian victories in politics. The Revolution and the developing frontier life spelled eventual defeat for the aristocrat at the hands of egalitarian forces. In politics, as well as religion, the dominance of the rich, the well-educated, and the wellborn of the Eastern seaboard was coming to an end. An uncultured and uneducated mass of farmers and mechanics was grasping the reins of supremacy and throwing off the controls of Federalist power. To the old aristocracy these developments were understandably frightening. If the Whiskey Rebellion and the acts of state legislatures had thown them into panic, the election of Jefferson was a deathblow and the threatened presidency of Andy Jackson the nail in the coffin.

Increased drinking was symbolic of decline in the power and prestige of the old aristocracy in the new social order. Both in the settled areas and on the frontier, the independent farmer and the artisan no longer looked to the Federalist clergy for guides to their conduct, as they no longer followed the doctrines of Federalist politics. If their role as dominant economic class was at an end, the Federalists could attempt to hold on to the prestige of the old order by a bid for their disappearing moral leadership. The manners and morals of the "common man" now had consequences for their political actions. Accordingly it was necessary to reform the citizen so that he might follow the moral convictions set by the old aristocracy. The seeming capriciousness and indecorousness of popular government was symbolized in the figure of the drunken voter. To make him respond to the moral ideals of the old order was both a way of maintaining the prestige of the old aristocracy and an attempt to control the character of the political electorate. It is in this sense that we can speak of the early stages of Temperance as a means by which a declining status group attempted to maintain social control. "If the rule of the country by the rich, the well-born and the able was ended, at least the United States might have the government of the moral, the virtuous and the sanctified."

We are aware that the political contest between the Federalists and the Jeffersonians-Jacksonians was far from a simple one between democratic virtue and aristocratic vice or a struggle between the "common man" and the forces of anti-egalitarianism. Recent historical research has shown much similarity in the economic and political views of both sides. This makes simple dichotomies unacceptable. Nevertheless, it was true that the Federalists still formed a cohesive and distinctive social stratum. As such, they did see their social and political domination waning in American society.

In his study of the Abolitionist movement, David Donald has given a every similar picture of Federalist response to declining social status. Examining biographical data on Abolitionist leaders, Donald found that almost all of them were born between 1790 and 1810, were New Englanders, and were children of steadfast Federalists. Through Abolitionism and other reforms they tried to regain their lost positions of leadership. They were men who felt the demise of the traditional values of their social class and, in trying to restore those values, attempted to recoup their dwindled status. They were out of place in a society beginning to be led by a commercial middle class. "Too distinguished a family, too gentle an education, too nice a morality were handicaps in a bustling world of business. Expecting to lead, these young people found no followers. They were an elite without function, a displaced class in American society."

The dominance of the old elite of Federalists-Calvinists in the early

Temperance movement is evident in the leadership of Temperance organizations and other groups devoted to moral improvement. As was true of other movements of religious benevolence in the early nineteenth century, the major efforts to reform American drinking habits were first led by the Calvinist ministry of New England. These were not spontaneous uprisings of self-reform among the poor, the sinful, or the drunkards. The Connecticut Society for the Reformation of Morals and the Massachusetts Society for the Suppression of Intemperance (both founded in 1813) were formed and led by clergymen and laymen of wealth, prominence, and Federalist politics. The first national Temperance association, the American Temperance Society (founded in 1826), was led by Congregationalist and nonevangelical Presbyterian ministers of Federalist commitment, such as Jedidiah Morse. They turned to the Whigs for legislative support. Despite commitment to Temperance as a doctrine, the Methodists of western Massachusetts, who were staunch Jacksonians, advised their adherents against contributing to the society.

The aims and doctrine of the early movement reveal its function as an attempt to control the newly powerful electorate, both in the cities and on the frontier. In aiming to reform the "common man," the movement attempted to re-establish prestige by "lifting" the rude mass to styles of life enunciated by an aristocratic moral authority. The movement was not viewed primarily as self-reform but as the reform of others below the status and economic level of the organizational adherents. Temperance supporters were men of religious conviction and moral righteousness whose own codes of moderate drinking were made models for the lives of the poor souls who had not yet achieved perfection.

This relationship between the early Temperance movement and status discontents is apparent in the writings of its leading spokesman Lyman Beecher, the New England minister. Beecher was the inheritor of Cavinist and Federalist church leadership and the leading opponent of revivalist methods. By 1810 he had become a leading critic of contemporary drinking habits and a supporter of abstinence from whiskey, beer, and other spirits. Under his leadership the Connecticut Society for the Reformation of Morals was established. Most moral reform movements of the 1810's and 1820's included him among their prominent officials. For Beecher, reform was clearly part of the defense of the old order against republican political sentiment and religious infidelity. In 1812 he voiced his fear at the growing power of the masses and his dismay at the decline of ecclesiastical control:

Our institutions, civil and religious, have outlived that domestic discipline and official vigilance in magistrates which rendered obedience easy and habitual. The laws are now beginning to operate extensively upon necks unaccustomed to their yoke, and when they shall become irksome to the majority, their execution will become impracticable. . . . To this situation we are already reduced in some districts of the land. Drunkards reel through the streets day after day . . . with entire impunity. Profane swearing is heard.

For Beecher the Temperance movement was an effort to reform the masses. He saw drinking in its political consequences. Reiterating the Federalist image of an ordered society in which the church was a powerful arbiter of morals, Beecher viewed intemperance as politically dangerous. In *Six Sermons on Intemperance* (1826), the leading statement of Temperance doctrine in the period, he wrote that intemperance fostered irreligion and, by undermining the church, endangered the political health of the nation. His writings displayed the classic fear the creditor has of the debtor, the propertied of the propertyless, and the dominant of the subordinate—the fear of disobedience, renunciation, and rebellion:

When the laboring classes are contaminated, the right of suffrage becomes the engine of destruction. . . . Such is the influence of interest and ambition, fear and indolence that one violent partisan, with a handful of disciplined troops, may overrule the influence of five hundred temperate men who are without concert. Already is the disposition to temporize, to tolerate, and even to court the intemperate too apparent on account of the apprehended retribution of their perverted suffrage. . . . As intemperance increases, the power of taxation will come more and more into the hands of men of intemperate habits and desperate fortunes; of course the laws will gradually become subservient to the debtor and less efficacious in protecting the rights of property.

Temperance doctrine also made an appeal as a means for controlling subordinates. Even in the colonial social order, there were two qualifications to the permissive attitude toward alcohol use. The American Indian was "out of bounds" to liquor sales, both on grounds of moral welfare and because the colonists feared rebellion as a result of intoxication. The American Negro was similarly restricted, as were apprentices and servants in many states, "lest the time of the master be spent in dissolute idleness." In some states there were legal limits to the amount of credit obtainable at liquor stores. In this fashion the poor, having less cash, were less able than the rich to purchase large quantities of alcohol. In the two earliest known local Temperance societies improvement of employee efficiency was a major argument for Temperance reform. Both groups made pleas to employers for the discontinuance of the custom by which employers provided alcoholic refreshment as part of wages or as an accompaniment to farm labor.

In the 1820's, when the Temperance movement began its organization and initiated its doctrine, the drive toward abstinence from distilled spirits (beer, wine, and cider were still permitted) functioned as a means to restore a superior position to the declining Federalist elite. As decline in moral behavior symbolized the sad facts of a waning social power, the old aristocracy sought to retain their prestige and power by upholding the standards by which the nation might then live. It was not an effort to reform the habits and behavior of those who made up its membership. The lowly, the small farmer, the wage earner, the craftsman—these were the objects of reform. This is not to maintain that there was no conviction of sin among the responsible citizens who made up the Temperance associations. What it implies is that such associations sought to disseminate and strengthen the norms of life which were part of the style of the old elite.

TEMPERANCE AND SOCIAL MOBILITY

The Temperance movement became a major social and political force in American life only as it was freed of the symbols of aristocratic dominance and converted into a popular movement to achieve self-perfection among the middle and lower classes of the nation. In the second phase of the movement Temperance became a sign of middle-class respectability and a symbol of egalitarianism.

REVIVALISM AND "BOURGEOISIFICATION"

The great waves of religious revivalism occurring during the first third of the nineteenth century destroyed whatever leadership the old aristocracy had over American religion. Paradoxically, they made possible the moral reforms which that aristocracy had tried to bring about. As the revivalist waves of Methodism, Baptism, and the "new Presbyterianism" rolled up adherents and dried the pools of religious indifference, America underwent an intense change in moral climate. The dissolute and secular nature of the post-Revolutionary period was replaced by the condemnation of moral infidelity. Abstinence became a part of necessary moral action rather than a matter of personal choice. Intemperance became sinful and the sober, nondrinking man a model of community respectability.

The relation between Temperance and the status system was influenced by revivalist activities. Embracing religion meant that the "convert" was now subject to the strict moral codes of evangelical Protestantism. Indulgence and idleness were among the major vices which the religious man swore to avoid. Chief among these was the vice of insobriety.

Religion and individual perfectionism went hand in hand. To be saved was evidenced through a change in habits. The man of spiritual conviction could be known by his style of living. If frontier life emphasized the roughness, liberty, and dissoluteness of a society without settled institutions, then there was all the more reason to stress the need for moral rigidity and an enthusiastic response to perfectionist standards. The organizers and directors of the major benevolent societies of the frontiers believed that moral and religious reform would make the convert a less radical voter and a more trustworthy credit risk.

The assumption was quite clear. Sanctified men make better borrowers, better workers, better citizens. The corollary of this was not a glorification of the humble poor, obediently carrying out the dictates of the lordly. Rather, the corollary was the doctrine of self-improvement through the Lord. In the thick of Methodist development, John Wesley had been concerned with this consequence of the religious movement. As men became more industrious, sober, thrifty, methodical, and responsible they also improved their income through work. Pure religion might decay, "for the Methodists in every place grow diligent and frugal; consequently they increase in goods."

It is in this sense that the revivalist movements of the 1820's and 1830's contributed to Temperance and to the function of abstinence as a mark of the man bent on improving his conditions of income and his status in the community. As an aspect of religious revivalism, Temperance was enjoined as a moral virtue. As a matter of self-improvement it designated the man of middle-class habits and aspirations In this sense revivalism was part of the process of "bourgeoisification," a process in which the worker or the farmer takes on a middle-class (bourgeois) mode of life.

TEMPERANCE AND SELF-IMPROVEMENT

That Temperance was one part of improving status was evident in several changes in the movement during the 1830's and 1840's. In this period it changed from one in which the rich aimed at reforming the poor into one in which members aimed at their own reformation.

During the 1830's, and especially in the 1840's, Temperance organizations and doctrine began to appear more often among groups not previously touched by the movement. Organized Temperance units emerged without the auspices of churches or ministers. A popular literature developed which used an emotional and dramatic quality of music, drama, and fiction. Even the form of the Temperance meeting was borrowed from revivalist experiences—hymn singing, vernacular speech, open-air meetings, and personal confession, all characteristics of the American revival, were put to use in eradicating Demon Rum.

The self-improvement motif is clearly observable in the Washingtonian movement and in its subsequent results. The Washingtonians began in 1840, with a small group of reformed drunkards. Like the current Alcoholics Anonymous, the movement was addressed to people who were, or were close to becoming, alcoholics. In their pledge the Washingtonians displayed the growing importance of Temperance as a sign of middle-class status: "We, whose names are annexed, desirous of forming a society for our mutual benefit, and to safeguard against a pernicious practice injurious to our health, *standing* [italics added] and families, do pledge ourselves as gentlemen, that we will not drink any spirituous or malt liquours, wine or cider."

The success of the Washingtonians in establishing a large number of units and followers among reformed drinkers and drunkards was an important element in the development of that most typical American self-improvement institution—the fraternal lodge. Even with the demise of the Washingtonians after the spread of internal conflict in the major Temperance societies, Temperance found an important source in the development of such organizations as the Good Templars, the Rechabites, and, most prominently, the Sons of Temperance. Like the Washingtonians, these groups were efforts to effect temperate habits among those who joined. In seeking to reform their own members these organizations differ sharply in attitude from the earlier Temperance societies of the 1820's. An excerpt from the 1842 report of the New York division of the Sons of Temperance is illustrative of the self-oriented tone of these societies:

The Order of the Sons of Temperance has three distinct objects. . . . To shield us from the evils of intemperance, to afford mutual assistance in cases of sickness and to elevate our characters as men.

We find the necessity of closer union . . . to be cemented by the ties of closer alliance and mutual benefit; to keep up and fully maintain an unrelaxed spirit of perseverance. . . .

The Order of the Sons of Temperance is merely intended as another link in the chain . . . to bind those who may have been so unfortunate as to acquire the insatiable thirst for alcoholic drinks more securely to the paths of rectitude and honor.

Membership was both a sign of commitment to middle-class values and a step in the process of changing a life style. Like the Washingtonians these groups often consisted of many former drinkers and drunkards and were led by laymen rather than ministers. Like the fraternal lodges of today, of which they were forerunners, the Temperance brotherhoods were also mutual societies which conferred insurance and other economic benefits on members. They became so popular that the leading organization, the Sons of Temperance, had grown in six years from a single unit to one of 6,000 units and 200,000 paying members all pledged to total abstinence.

THE DECLINE OF ARISTOCRATIC DOMINANCE

Evangelical Protestantism recruited large numbers of soldiers for the Temperance army. Converted to a more sober behavior, they pushed aside the traditional leadership of orthodox ministers in the Temperance organizations and replace them with a lay leadership drawn from far lower social ranks than the earlier organizations had encompassed. Revivalism had flourished among the churches of the common people where emotional expression was customary. When Temperance began to reflect the methods of the revivalist it acquired an appeal that had been lacking in the colder attempts of an Eastern, upper-class clergy to convert the poor to the life of righteousness. The original movement had developed in the East and its leadership remained Eastern until the late 1830's. By 1831 the American Temperance Society had 2,200 local societies with a reported membership of 170,000. Although one-sixth of the population lived in the six states northeast of the Hudson River, the area contained one-third of the Temperance organizations and one-third of the national membership. The center of Temperance was in the East, with all that this symbolized socially and politically to a nation whose political axis had begun to move westward.

As the small property holder and the propertyless were drawn to the movement, they brought to it a higher level of self-demand than had been true of the earlier movement. Concerned with self-improvement, they could not compromise with evil as those more righteously trained could have done. The entry of the West into Temperance organizations was followed by ultraist doctrines. The new Temperance adherents were not content with moral suasion alone. In its beginnings, the American Temperance Society had declared for total abstinence from all spirits, but it drew the line at beer, wines, and cider. "This," said one member, "was impolitic and carrying the thing too far." The Western units pushed for a wider conception of total abstinence, in the tradition since known as "teetotaling." In at least one Eastern state, New York, demand for total abstinence resulted in the loss of wealthy supporters. By the late 1830's, however, internal conflicts were resolved in favor of the ultraists. Total abstinence from all alcoholic beverages was the primary doctrine of Temperance organizations everywhere in the United States. There would be no compromise with Evil in any of its forms.

Another result of the decline in aristocratic leadership and the conversion of the movement into one of "common man" identification was the rise of lay leadership. The Washingtonian movement was disapproved by the good people who had formed the Temperance organizations of the 1820's and early 1830's. "Many of the leaders were uneducated and their addresses were not always of an elevating character." There was much criticism of the informal character of meetings, in which people arose from the audience to narrate their experiences with King Alcohol. Men who emerged as leaders of this movement often gained great fame as orators. These men, such as John Gough and John H. W. Hawkins, had little background in public speaking and little education. They had no connection with organized religion and they based their appeal for sobriety and temperance on grounds of personal welfare rather than religion alone. In their evangelical techniques, indifference to theology, and vulgar identification with the manners and language of the masses, they were anathema to the more conservative and sedate leaders of the earlier movement.

The Washingtonians, and the newer Temperance associations of the 1840's, brought a common touch to the movement. After that Temperance activities were couched in a more popular vein. An emotional and dramatic quality appeared in Temperance ceremony, music, drama, and fiction. Parades became a standard form of persuasion, and banners, flags, and outdoor meetings were typical parts of the program. Temperance songs were written and children enlisted in the cause. Perhaps the most vivid instance of this appeal to the emotional sensitivities of mass response is seen in the development of a children's group, the Cold Water Army. With songs, parades, and demonstrations by children the virtues of water and the iniquities of drink were dramatized to the public.

ABSTINENCE AS STATUS SYMBOL

The quest for self-improvement implies a gap between those who remain dissolute and those who have achieved respectability. By the 1850's, sobriety and abstinence were no longer rare examples of unique fidelity to saintly virtues. Drinking was at best tolerated and sobriety had become a necessary aspect of respectable, middle-class status. If not universally good, Americans were becoming, in this respect at least, somewhat better. Abstinence and sobriety had become public virtues. For reputation, if for nothing else, it was not expedient to be thought to be anything more than a moderate drinker. Atstinence had become part of the national religious faith. "Sunday morning all the land is still. Broadway is a quiet stream, looking, sober, even dull."

Temperance fiction was probably the most effective media of mass persuasion in the Temperance cause. It often played on the theme of drinking as an indication of outcast or low social position and abstinence as a symbol of middle-class life. In Temperance tales the drinker is not only an immoral and sinful man in his alcoholic vice. He is also about to be ruined. With drink comes economic deprivation. The drinker loses his industrious devotion to work. He loses his reputation for reliability. Finally he is without any employment at all. Retribution is possible. Reform, sobriety, and the pledge to abstain are rewarded by the return of economic virtues and the reappearance of economic reward.

Along with the vision of the drinker as the ruined man went the belief that the solution to poverty lay along the road to Temperance. The benefits of reformation and improvement were not pictured in terms of what they could do for the employer but for the employee. In one of his most famous stories, "Wild Dick and Good Little Robin," L. M. Sargent described the basic contrast of character between drinkers and abstainers. Dick, having reformed his drinking ways, "continued to grow in favor with God and man. He gave farmer Little complete satisfaction, by his obedience, industry and sobriety. He was permitted to cultivate a small patch of ground, on his own account."

The significance of abstinence as a symbol of respectability was enhanced when large numbers of Irish and German immigrants entered the United States and made up the unskilled labor forces of the growing urban centers during the 1840's and 1850's. In the culture of the Irish and the Germans, use of whiskey or beer was customary and often a staple part of the diet. Both groups were at the bottom of the class and status structure in American society. In the evolution of status symbols, the groups at the lowest rungs of the ladder affect the behavior of those above by a process of depletion in which those traits originally shared by both groups become progressively deprized among the more prestigeful. The incoming group thus widens the status gap between it and the natives. If the lowly Irish and Germans were the drinkers and the drunkards of the community, it was more necessary than ever that the aspirant to middle-class membership not risk the possibility that he might be classed with the immigrants. He must hew more closely to the norms which provided cultural distinctiveness. As the narrator of *Ten Nights in a Barroom* phrased it, "Between quiet, thrifty, substantial farmers and drinking bar-room loungers there are many degrees of comparison."

TEMPERANCE AS A POLITICAL SYMBOL

The Temperance movement began as one solely of moral suasion. By the 1840's it had become a significant part of American politics, capable of affecting local and state elections. As Temperance doctrine reached larger segments of the population, demands arose to limit the sale and use of intoxicants by legislation. Both the enforcement of existing laws and the passage of new, restrictive measures became important issues in many states. The drive to restrict liquor and beer consumption reached its heights in the state prohibition drive of the 1850's. By 1856, eight states had passed some form of Prohibition legislation.

As the sale and use of alcoholic beverages became a political issue, consumption and abstinence took on every greater meaning as symbols of group loyalty and differentiation. Political opposition reinforced the already evident contrasts of culture in which the daily fare of one group was the dangerous poison of the other. The supporter of anti-alcohol legislation was not simply someone who issued a moral condemnation of drinking. He was trying to make it more difficult for the drinker to follow his customary habits.

There was another way in which the emergence of Temperance in politics deepened group conflicts. It linked Temperance and anti-Temperance adherence to other class, cultural, and sectional conflicts on which it was superimposed. The supporter of legislation encouraging Temperance was also likely to be a supporter of religious benevolence movements, of Abolition, and of nativist measures. His opponents were likely to oppose these measures as well.

FEDERALIST CONSERVATISM AND EARLY TEMPERANCE

The heavily Eastern and upper-class support of the American Temperance Society was one aspect of the identification of the early movement with anti-Jacksonianism. In Beecher and in the officials of the leading Temperance associations, the commitment to the struggle against Jackson was evident. Although the Temperance movement did not seek legislative results until the 1840's, earlier it had a political tone which made it suspect by the Jacksonian, who was also likely to be a Westerner and religiously evangelical. In Congress, for example, Senator Theodore Frelinghuysen was the outstanding exponent of Temperance and the other goals of benevolent societies. He was one of Jackson's major opponents. Like Beecher, he was explicit in viewing moral benevolence and religion as a way of controlling the sources of Jacksonian support in the West.

In terms of practical party politics this meant that Temperance supporters tended to find allies among the Whigs during the 1820's and 1830's. This relation between political conservatism and Temperance appears in the career of one of the leading Temperance agitators of the pre-Civil War period, Neal Dow. Dow was sympathetic to the Federalists. In 1824 he voted for John Quincy Adams, whose protectionist policy he favored. He was always an intense foe of Jackson. In 1832 he found political refuge within the anti-Masonic movement. He supported Harrison in 1840 though he bitterly disliked the "log cabin" appeal to the average man.

Until 1838 the American Temperance movement did not attempt direct political action. In that year the Massachusetts legislature passed the first major Temperance bill, the Fifteen-Gallon law, which prohibited purchase of liquor in quantities of less than 15 gallons. Since cash was scarcest among the poorer sections of the state, the law restricted drinking among the poor more than among the rich. It was repealed two years later but the precedent of seeking Temperance through law was established. It was the first wave in a campaign to outlaw taverns and to limit the sale of alcoholic beverages.

As the movement gained adherents in the West, Temperance organizations increasingly saw legislation as a mechanism through which reform could be accomplished. During this period (1840's) neither the Whigs nor the Democrats were clearly pro- or anti-Temperance, although it was still among the Whigs that most support might be found. The remnant of Jacksonian issues was still strong enough so that Horace Greeley characterized the Whigs as pro-Temperance and the Loco-Focos as anti-Temperance in the New York No-License campaign of 1845.

THE REFORMIST MOVEMENT AND TEMPERANCE

Party splits were overshadowed by the growing relationship between Temperance and other political issues of the late 1840's and the 1850's. The activities of church groups had made Temperance one aspect of movements to improve the country's religious adherence. Sabbatarianism, the home missionary movements, Bible tract societies, and the move to abolish drink, as we have seen, had affinities for those who feared the common man as the new source of power. The issues of the pre-Civil War era, however, involved conflicts of economic interest and cultural differences to a vaster extent than the narrower moral problems of the churches.

The period from 1830 to 1860 has been referred to by some historians as "the era of reform" because there were so many organizations and movements devoted to improving mankind, changing social conditions, and reforming the character of human beings. These movements were seldom separate affairs. Indeed, the same people were often involved in a great many of the movements. People like Gerrit Smith, Theodore Weld, and Arthur Tappan were found in the moral benevolence societies, the Abolitionists', and the Temperance societies, as well as less flamboyant movements such as peace and the abolition of Sunday mail. Among these, only the antislavery movement surpassed Temperance in the intensity of its support and the influence of its political power.

As American politics underwent a reformulation on the eve of the Civil War, Temperance and Abolitionism went hand in hand. Neal Dow is again an illustration of the process. Although a Whig during most of his life, Dow became a Free Soiler in 1848 and a Republican in 1856. His antislavery feeling was deep and had existed since his youth, when his home was a stop on the Underground Railroad. He had an immense admiration for Lincoln and an intense hatred of the South. In Dow's successful Temperance campaigns for statewide Prohibition in Maine, the Liberty Party and the Free Soilers were his strongest supporters. "The one group in the state on which the Prohibitionists could count was the anti-slavery element." Temperance and antislavery were united in the Massachusetts victory of the Know-Nothings as they were in similar victories in the United States.

Temperance emerged in the 1850's in political association with forces which were breaking away from the old parties. Perhaps there were ideological similarities between Abolition and Temperance. They were both highly moralistic and perfectionist. Perhaps it was the occurrence of both in the same parts of the society—the native American independent farmer of the Midwest and East. The identification with antislavery was strong enough to stifle completely the organization of the Temperance movement in the South. Although Temperance agitation had developed in Southern states during the 1820's, by the late 1830's Temperance was unable to gain any strength in the South. Temperance was emerging as a point of union between segments of politics splitting off from the major parties. "While Whigs and Democrats split over anti-slaveryism and other matters, former partisans of both groups became Know-Nothings. These politicians also became Prohibitionists, and out of such ingredients came the potpourri of Republicanism."

TEMPERANCE AND NATIVISM

The association of the Irish and Germans with opposition to Temperance programs added a significant meaning to Temperance in the political arena. It widened the cultural gap between native and immigrant by placing each as opponent to the other's way of life. The American Protestant and immigrant Catholic were not simply two people of somewhat different cultures. When Temperance sought legislative ends, each group became the impediment to the other's victories. The alliance between Temperance and the anti-alien movement of the Know-Nothings completed a polarization process in which political defeat was tantamount to a loss of status and power for the cultural group that bore the loss.

The relation between the native American and the immigrant populations of the cities added a third orientation—a welfare orientation—to the two already described as major sources of Temperance doctrine and sentiment. The upper-class, displaced power-elite of the Eastern seaboard attempted to shore up a fading control through the moral regeneration of the new electorate. The "common man" sought his own self-improvement through the Temperance societies. Both sought to assimilate the immigrant to American society and to solve the problems of urban poverty through Temperance. They viewed the immigrant as an object of benevolence; someone they would help to achieve the morally sanctified habits of the native American, of which abstinence had become so cardinal a virtue. Here, as in the antislavery movement, Temperance was again an effort of those who practiced virtue to make their style of life a universal one.

That the immigrant was an object for the commiseration and concern of native Protestants was logical enough if one examined his standards of welfare, as well as morality. During the 1840's and 1850's the American labor force began to develop significant industrial characteristics as the American economy became larger, more urbanized, and more composed of unskilled labor. The Irish and German immigrants were the backbone of that industrial expansion. Wherever cities developed, so did the complex of criminality, intemperance, poverty, and ill-health. It was more typical of the Irish than of the Germans but it was an apparent problem in German Ohio as well as Irish Massashusetts. During the 1840's the cost of intemperance to the society was one important theme in Temperance literature. One of the leading tracts of the late 1840's was Samuel Chipman's "Temperance Lecturer: being facts gathered from a personal examination of all the jails and poor-houses in the State of New York, showing the effects of intoxicating drinks in producing Taxes, Pauperism, and Crime." The subtitle of this work was typical of this genre in its stress on Temperance as a solution to a perplexing public problem of both moral and financial dimensions. In Boston and other parts of Massachusetts, rural areas resented the large state tax bill, resulting in part from the high rates of pauperism among the Irish immigrants.

Benevolence and hostility . . . are dual ways of responding to the existence of a different culture in our midst. We can feel sorry for the poor, ignorant heathen who know no better, and try to lift them to our standards. We also can see them as immoral creatures who threaten our safety and institutions and who must be stopped and restrained. In the 1840's and 1850's the Temperance movement engaged in both moral benevolence and nativistic hostility. The hostility was evidenced in the political affinities between Prohibition and anti-alienism, as well as anti-slavery.

The Know-Nothings and the Free Soilers made considerable headway through the combination of Abolitionism, Temperance, and an appeal to nativism. The Know-Nothings, and the other new parties of the 1850's, can justly be called "a collection of men looking for new political homes." There was a pronounced affinity between the three elements of opposition to immigration, drink, and slavery. The same people were not always found in each other's company but the tendency was considerable.

The political confrontation between native and immigrant was a real one, based on real cultural differences. Temperance, to the Irish Catholic and the German Lutheran, was a tyranny over their ways of life and not a move to uplift the society. The "grogshop" and beer stein were accepted parts of Irish and German group life. There was no experience with revivalism nor any tradition of moderate drinking to be revived. When the Temperance reform swept the Americans, heavy drinking was a falling off from a once-accepted moral standard. This was not the case among the immigrants, where drinking patterns were not viewed as a severe problem.

Politically, the immigrant populations were the most powerful opponents of the Temperance forces. The fear of losing immigrant support was a major source of political compromise on Prohibition issues in the 1850's, as it was to be in the twentieth century. In 1854 the Republicans had been outspokenly for Prohibition. As they became a national party, this was a liability which they dropped when immigrant opposition proved strong enough to cost state elections.

Out of the political conflicts of the 1840's and 1850's nondrinking had become more and more a symbol of middle-class, native American respectability. The urban, immigrant, lower class had emerged as both the counterimage to the Temperance hero and a political opponent of significant concern.

We are not asserting that Temperance adherents during the 1840's were not deeply moved by the emotional appeals of religious revivals, that they did not "feel" benevolent toward those who were not abstinent, that they were not motivated by ideas and ideals. When we maintain that drinking had become a status symbol, we do not imply that religious reasons were merely cloaks for status interests. We mean that as a consequence of revivals, parts of the population that had been drinkers now were abstinent; that where drinking had been legitimate for middle-class people, now it was disapproved and sanctions placed against it. A function of Temperance activities was to enhance the symbolic proper-ties of liquor and abstinence as marks of status. This is not an assertion that this was its only function nor is it an assertion about motives. It is merely pointing out that as a consequence of such activities, abstinence became symbolic of a status level.

A similar logic underlies our analysis of Temperance as a system of social control in the 1820's. When we assert that the Federalist elite sought to control the newly powerful democratic electorate through Temperance we are not "debunking" the movement nor reducing it to political motives. We are maintaining that the lost position of power and prestige which the old elite had suffered made them sensitive to the moral failings of the formerly subservient classes. It represented a problem which had not existed in the past. Their conviction of the righteousness of their way of life rested on religious ideas, but to "feel" the need to help those not sharing it meant that the victims of intemperance were being "bettered" by the moral values of the old elite, which implies that those values were becoming dominant.

Such functions of actions are generally latent rather than manifest. At times, as in Beecher's statements, they become explicit. Such times often help the sociologist to see the significance for the structure of the actions performed.

Let us bring this section to a close with an illustration taken from a historian's analysis of the Social Gospel:

> The discovery that the doctrine of sanctification and the methods of mass evangelism played an increasingly important role in the program of the churches after 1842 compels a revaluation of their impact on every facet of the contemporary religious scene . . . whatever may have been the role of other factors, the quest for perfection joined with compassion for poor and needy sinners and a rebirth of millennial expectation to make popular Prot-estantism a mighty social force. . . .

The sociologist is not denying the existence of a quest for perfection or compassion for the poor as factors in a social situation. He wants to know the groups within the social structure in which they arise and why they arose in that part. He wants to know how and why the vision of perfection of one group is the standard upheld for others to follow. Such questions are not reductions of one set of factors to another set. They are bridges through which the sociologist attempts to develop general schemes of analysis of structure by looking for the functions which a given set of ideas performs and the conditions within which they arise. The ideas have an independent existence but not an existence *in vacuo*. [Max] Weber wrote that although religious forces were an essential element in the development of modern capitalism, one could not deduce the economic institution from the Reformation. No more are we attempting to deduce Temperance from status structure or reduce one to the other.

The Emergence of Immediatism in British and American Antislavery Thought

DAVID BRION DAVIS

There can be no doubt that temperance and antislavery were the two leading reform movements of the ante-bellum era. Most discussions of the abolitionist crusade have been limited to the United States and have concentrated on the period from 1831 to the Civil War. The purposes of this essay were to show the importance of the preceding decades for an understanding of antislavery thought, to trace parallel developments in England and America, and to relate the key doctrine of abolitionism to a fundamental shift in social attitudes and values, which can be described as a movement from rational expedi-

David Brion Davis, "The Emergence of Immediatism in British and American Antislavery Thought," in *Mississippi Valley Historical Review*, Vol. XLIX, September 1962, pp. 209–230. Reprinted without footnotes by permission of the Managing Editor of the *Journal of American History*. Copyright © 1962 by the Organization of American Historians.

ency and moderation toward a romantic and evangelical frame of mind. Like the selection by Frank Thistlethwaite, this essay points to an Atlantic community of reform. When placed beside Joseph Gusfield's analysis of social structure, the approach of intellectual history offers an alternative but complementary method for investigating reform.

IN THE HISTORY OF REFORM FEW SLOGANS HAVE BROUGHT FORTH such confusion and controversy as "immediate emancipation." To the general public in the 1830's the phrase meant simply the abolition of Negro slavery without delay or preparation. But the word "immediate" may denote something other than a closeness in time; to many abolitionists it signified a rejection of intermediate agencies or conditions, a directness or forthrightness in action or decision. In this sense immediatism suggested a repudiation of the various media, such as colonization or apprenticeship, that had been advocated as remedies for the evils of slavery. To some reformers the phrase seemed mainly to imply a direct, intuitive consciousness of the sinfulness of slavery, and a sincere personal commitment to work for its abolition. In this subjective sense the word "immediate" was charged with religious overtones and referred more to the moral disposition of the reformer than to a particular plan for emancipation. Thus some reformers confused immediate abolition with an immediate personal decision to abstain from consuming slave-grown produce; and a man might be considered an immediatist if he were genuinely convinced that slavery should be abolished absolutely and without compromise, though not necessarily without honest preparation. Such a range of meanings led unavoidably to misunderstanding, and the antislavery cause may have suffered from so ambiguous a slogan. The ambiguity, however, was something more than semantic confusion or the unfortunate result of a misleading watchword. The doctrine of immediacy, in the form it took in the 1830's, was at once a logical culmination of the antislavery movement and a token of a major shift in intellectual history.

A belief in the slave's right to immediate freedom was at least implicit in much of the antislavery writing of the eighteenth century. If Negro slavery were unjust, unnatural, illegal, corrupting, and detrimental to the national interest, as innumerable eighteenth-century writers claimed, there could be no excuse for its perpetuation. Several of the *philosophes* held that since masters relied on physical force to impose their illegal demands, slave revolts would be just; Louis de Jaucourt went so far as to argue that slaves, never having lost their inherent liberty, should be immediately declared free. Anthony Benezet advanced a similar argument, asking what course a man should follow if he discovered that an inherited estate was really the property of another: "Would you not give it up immediately to the lawful owner? The voice of all mankind would mark him for a villian, who would refuse to comply with this demand of justice. And is not keeping a slave after you are convinced of the unlawfulness of it—a crime of the same nature?"

In England, Granville Sharp denounced slavery as a flagrant violation of the common law, the law of reason, and the law of God. After exhorting Lord North to do something about the plight of the slaves, he warned: "I say immediate redress, because, *to be in power,* and to neglect . . . even a day in endeavoring to put a stop to such monstrous injustice and abandoned wickedness, must necessarily endanger a man's *eternal* welfare, be he ever so great in *temporal* dignity or office." Sharp, who argued that "No Legislature on Earth . . . can alter the Nature of Things, or make that to be lawful, which is contrary to the Law of God," secured a judicial decision outlawing slavery in England. Americans like James Otis, Nathaniel Appleton, and Isaac Skillman took a similarly uncompromising stand before the Revolution; by the 1780's the doctrine of natural rights had made the illegality of slavery an established fact in Vermont and Massachusetts.

But the natural rights philosophy was not the only source of immediatism. Officially, the Society of Friends showed extreme caution in encouraging emancipation, but from the time of George Keith a latent impulse of moral perfectionism rose to the surface in the radical testimony of individual Quakers, who judged slavery in the uncompromising light of the Golden Rule. For such reformers, slavery was not a social or economic institution, but rather an embodiment of worldly sin that corrupted the souls of both master and slave; emancipation was not an objective matter of social or political expediency, but a subjective act of purification and a casting off of sin.

Immediatism, in the sense of an immediate consciousness of the guilt of slaveholding and an ardent desire to escape moral contamination, is similarly evident in the writings of men who differed widely in their views of religion and political economy. John Wesley's combined attack on the opposite poles of Calvinism and natural religion could also be directed against slavery, which some defended by arguments similar to those that justified seeming injustice or worldly evils as part of God's master plan or nature's economy. In 1784 Wesley's antislavery beliefs were developed into a kind of immediatism in the rules of American Methodists: "We . . . think it our most bounden duty to take immediately some effectual method to extirpate this abomination from among us." A related source of immediatism can be traced in the development of the romantic sensibility and the cult of the "man of feeling," which merged with Rousseau and the French Enlightenment in the writings of such men as Thomas Day and William Fox.

In the light of this evidence we may well ask why immediatism appeared so new and dangerously radical in the 1830's. The later abolitionists charged that slavery was a sin against God and a crime against nature; they demanded an immediate beginning of direct action that would eventuate in general emancipation. Yet all of this had been said at least a half-century before, and we might conclude that immediatism was merely a recurring element in antislavery history.

But if immediatism was at least latent in early antislavery thought, the dominant frame of mind of the eighteenth century was overwhelmingly disposed to gradualism. Gradualism, in the sense of a reliance on indirect and slow-working means to achieve a desired social objective, was the logical consequence of fundamental attitudes toward progress, natural law, property, and individual rights.

We cannot understand the force of gradualism in antislavery thought unless we abandon the conventional distinction between Enlightenment liberalism and evangelical reaction. It is significant that British opponents of abolition made little use of religion, appealing instead to the need for calm rationality and an expedient regard for the national interest. Quoting Hume, Lord Kames, and even Montesquieu to support their moral relativism, they showed that principles of the Enlightenment could be easily turned to the defense of slavery. A belief in progress and natural rights might lead, of course, to antislavery convictions; but if history seemed to be on the side of liberty, slavery had attained a certain prescriptive sanction as a nearly universal expression of human nature. Men who had acquired an increasing respect for property and for the intricate workings of natural and social laws could not view as an unmitigated evil an institution that had developed through the centuries.

Though evangelicals attacked natural religion and an acceptance of the world as a divinely contrived mechanism in which evils like slavery served a legitimate function, they nevertheless absorbed many of the assumptions of conservative rationalists and tended to express a middle-class fear of sudden social change. Despite the sharp difference between evangelicals and rationalists, they shared confidence, for the most part, in the slow unfolding of a divine or natural plan of historical progress. The mild and almost imperceptible diffusion of reason, benevolence, or Christianity had made slavery—a vestige of barbarism—anachronistic. But while eighteenth-century abolitionists might delight in furthering God's or nature's plan for earthly salvation, they tended to assume a detached, contemplative view of history, and showed considerable fear of sudden changes or precipitous action that might break the delicate balance of natural and historial forces.

There was therefore a wide gap between the abstract proposition that slavery was wrong, or even criminal, and the cautious formulation of antislavery policy. It was an uncomfortable fact that slavery and the slave trade were tied closely to the rights of private property, the political freedom of colonies and states, and the economic rewards of international competition. Yet from the 1790's to the 1820's British and American reformers were confident that they understood the basic principles of society and could thus work toward the desired goal indirectly and without infringing on legitimate rights or interests. Frequently they seemed to think of slavery as a kind of unfortunate weed or fungus that had spread through the Lord's garden in a moment of divine inattention. As expert horticulturalists they imagined they could gradually kill the blight without injuring the plants. The British reformers focused their attention on the slave trade, assuming that if the supply of African Negroes were shut off planters would be forced to take better care of their existing slaves and would ultimately discover that free labor was more profitable. In America, reform energies were increasingly directed toward removing the free Negroes, who were thought to be the principal barrier to voluntary manumission. Both schemes were attempts at rather complex social engineering, and in both instances the desired reform was to come from the slaveowners themselves. Antislavery theorists assumed that they could predict the cumulative effects and consequences of their limited programs, and since they never doubted the goodness or effectiveness of natural laws, they sought only to set in motion a chain of forces that would lead irresistibly to freedom.

This gradualist mentality dominated antislavery thought from the late eighteenth century to the 1820's. Though French thinkers had been among the first to denounce slavery as a crime, the emancipation scheme which they pioneered was one of slow transformation of the slave into a free laborer. Even the *Amis des Noirs* feared immediate emancipation; and the French decree abolishing slavery in 1794, which was the result of political and military crisis in the West Indies, seemed to verify the ominous warnings of gradualists in all countries. The years of bloodshed and anarchy in Haiti became an international symbol for the dangers of reckless and unplanned emancipation.

British abolitionists were particularly cautious in defining their objectives and moving indirectly, one step at a time. When outlawing the slave trade did not have the desired effect on colonial slavery, they then sought to bring the institution within the regulatory powers of the central government by limiting the extension of slavery in newly acquired islands and by using the crown colonies as models for gradual melioration; and when these efforts failed they urged a general registration of slaves, which would not only interpose imperial authority in the colonies but provide a mechanism for protecting the Negroes' rights. By 1822 these methods had proved inadequate and the British reformers began agitating for direct parliamentary intervention. Even then, however, and for the following eight years, British antislavery leaders limited their aims to melioration and emancipation by slow degrees.

Between British and American antislavery men there was a bond of understanding and a common interest in suppressing the international slave trade and finding a home in Haiti or western Africa for free Negroes. But in America the antislavery movement was given a distinctive color by the discouraging obstacles that stood in the way of even gradual emancipation. While states like New York and Pennsylvania provided tangible examples of gradual manumission, they also showed the harsh and ugly consequences of racial prejudice. Americans, far more than the British, were concerned with the problem of the emancipated slave. Even some of the most radical and outspoken abolitionists were convinced that colonization was the inescapable prerequisite to reform. Others stressed the importance of education and moral training as the first steps toward eventual freedom.

In America the gradualist frame of mind was also related to the weakness and limitations of political institutions. British abolitionists could work to enlist the unlimited power of a central Parliament against colonies that were suffering acute economic decline. But slavery in America was not only expanding but was protected by a sectional balance of power embodied in nearly every national institution. A brooding fear of disunion and anarchy damped down the aspirations of most American abolitionists and turned energies to such local questions as the education and legal protection of individual Negroes. Antislavery societies might call for the government to outlaw slavery in the District of Columbia or even to abolish the interstate slave trade, but in the end they had to rely on public opinion and individual conscience in the slave states. While British abolitionists moved with the circumspection of conservative pragmatists, their American counterparts acted with the caution of men surrounded by high explosives. For many, the only prudent solution was to remove the explosives to a distant country.

But if British and American abolitionists were gradualists in their policies and expectations, they did not necessarily regard slavery as simply one of many social evils that should be mitigated and eventually destroyed. The policy of gradualism was related to certain eighteenth-century assumptions about historical progress, the nature of man, and the principles of social change; but we have also noted a subjective, moral aspect to antislavery thought that was often revealed as an immediate consciousness of guilt and a fear of divine punishment. During the British slave trade controversy of the 1790's the entire system of slavery and slave trade became identified with sin, and reform with true virtue. Though antislavery leaders adopted the gradualist policy of choosing the slave trade as their primary target, they bitterly fought every attempt to meliorate or gradually destroy the African trade. It was the determined opponents of the slave trade who first gave popular currency to the slogan, "immediate abolition," which became in the early 1790's a badge of moral sincerity. When uncompromising hostility to the slave trade became a sign of personal virtue and practical Christianity, the rhetoric of statesmen acquired the strident, indignant tone that we associate with later American abolitionists. Charles James Fox made scathing attacks on those who pled for moderation; he even said that if the plantations could not be cultivated without being supplied with African slaves, it would be far better for England to rid herself of the islands. "How shall we hope," asked William Pitt, "to obtain, if it is possible, forgiveness from Heaven for those enormous evils we have committed, if we refuse to make use of those means which the mercy of Providence hath still reserved to us for wiping away the guilt and shame with which we are now covered?"

This sense of moral urgency and fear of divine retribution persisted in British antislavery thought and was held in check only by a faith in the certain and predictable consequences of indirect action. Whenever the faith was shaken by unforeseen obstacles or a sense of crisis, there were voices that condemned gradualism as a compromise with sin. Granville Sharp, who interpreted hurricanes in the West Indies as supernatural agencies "to blast the *enemies* of *law* and *righteousness*," called in 1806 for direct emancipation by act of Parliament, and warned that continued toleration of slavery in the colonies "must finally draw down the Divine vengeance upon our state and nation!" When William Allen, Zachary Macaulay, and James Cropper became disillusioned over the failure to secure an effective registration scheme and international suppression of the slave trade, they pressed for direct though gradual emancipation by the British government. The British Anti-Slavery Society remained officially gradualist until 1831, but individual abolitionists, particularly in the provinces, became increasingly impatient over the diffidence of the government and the intransigence of colonial legislatures. From 1823 to 1832 the British Caribbean planters violently attacked the government's efforts to meliorate slavery. They not only devised schemes to nullify effective reform but threatened to secede from the empire and seek protection from the United States. Though the evils of West Indian slavery were probably mitigated in the 1820's, the planters' resistance convinced many abolitionists that gradual improvement was impossible.

The most eloquent early plea for immediate emancipation was made in 1824 by a Quaker named Elizabeth Heyrick, who looked to the women of Great Britain as a source of invincible moral power, and who preached a massive consumer's crusade against West Indian produce. The central theme in Mrs. Heyrick's pamphlet, *Immediate, Not Gradual Abolition,* was the supremacy of individual conscience over social and political institutions. Since antislavery was a *"holy war"* against "the very powers of darkness," there was no ground for compromise or for a polite consideration of slaveholders. Like the later American immediatists, she excoriated gradualism as a satanic plot to induce gradual indifference. It was a delusion to think that slavery could be gradually improved, for "as well might you say to a poor wretch, gasping and languishing in a pest house, 'here will I keep you, till I have given you a capacity for the enjoyment of pure air.'" For Mrs. Heyrick the issue was simple and clearcut: sin and vice should be immediately exterminated by individual action in accordance with conscience and the will of God.

In 1824 such views were too strong for British antislavery leaders, who still looked to direct government action modeled on the precedent of the Canning Resolutions, which had proposed measures for ameliorating the condition of West Indian slaves as a step toward ultimate emancipation. Abolitionists in Parliament continued to shape their strategy in the light of political realities, but by 1830 several prominent reformers had adopted the uncompromising stand of Elizabeth Heyrick. The shift from gradualism to immediatism is most dramatically seen in James Stephen, who possessed a mind of great clarity and precision and who, having practiced law in the West Indies, had acquired direct experience with slavery as an institution. For a time Stephen adhered to the principle of gradualism, transferring his hopes from the slave registration scheme to a "digested plan" of abolition by stages, beginning with domestic servants. By 1830, however, he was convinced that debate over alternative plans merely inhibited action and obscured what was essentially a question of principle and simple moral duty. It would be a tragic mistake, he felt, for the abolitionists to propose any measure short of "a general, entire, immediate restitution of the freedom wrongfully withheld." Lashing out at the moral lethargy of the government, he denounced the principle of compensation to slaveowners and rejected all specific gradualist measures such as the liberation of Negro women or the emancipation of infants born after a certain date. Stephen's immediatism was based ultimately on a fear of divine vengeance and an overwhelming sense of national guilt. "We sin remorselessly," he said, "because our fathers sinned, and because multitudes of our own generation sin, in the same way without [public] discredit."

On October 19, 1830, the Reverend Andrew Thomson, of St. George's Church in Edinburgh, delivered a fire-and-brimstone speech that provided ideology for George Thompson and the later Agency Committee. Beginning with the premise that slavery is a crime and sin, Thomson dismissed all consideration of economic and political questions. When the issue was reduced to what individual men should do as mortal and accountable beings, there was no possibility of compromise or even controversy. The British public should "compel" Parliament to order total and immediate emancipation. With Calvinistic intensity he exhorted the public to cut down and burn the "pestiferous tree," root and branch: "You must annihilate it,—annihilate it now,—and annihilate it forever." Since Thomson considered every hour that men were kept in bondage a repetition of the original sin of man-stealing, he did not shrink from violence: "If there must be violence, . . . let it come and rage its little hour, since it is to be succeeded by lasting freedom, and prosperity, and happiness."

Taking its cue from men like Stephen, Thomson, and Joseph Sturge, the Anti-Slavery Society reorganized itself for more effective action and focused its energies on raising petitions and arousing public feeling against slavery. While Thomas Fowell Buxton sought to make the fullest use of public opinion to support his campaign in Parliament, he found himself under mounting pressure from abolitionists who refused to defer to his judgment. People's principles, he told his daughter, were the greatest nuisance in life. When the government finally revealed its plan for gradual and compensated emancipation, the Anti-Slavery Society committed itself to vigorous and aggressive opposition. But once the law had been passed, the antislavery leaders concluded that they had done as well as possible and that their defeat had actually been a spectacular victory. They had achieved their primary object, which was to induce the people to support a tangible act that could be interpreted as purging the nation of collective guilt and proving the moral power of individual conscience.

In America the developing pattern was somewhat similar. Despite the conservatism of most antislavery societies, a number of radical abolitionists branded slaveholding as a heinous sin, which, if not immediately abandoned, would bring down the wrath of the Lord. A few early reformers like Theodore Dwight, David Rice, Charles Osborn, and John Rankin, were well in advance of British antislavery writers in their sense of moral urgency and their mistrust of gradualist programs. As early as 1808, David Barrow, although he denied favoring immediate abolition, anticipated the later doctrine of the American Anti-Slavery Society by refusing to recognize the lawfulness of slavery or the justice of compensation. Holding that slavery was the crying sin of America, he urged a prompt beginning of manumission in order to avert the retribution of God. Three years earlier Thomas Branagan, who opposed "instantaneous emancipation" if the freed Negroes were to remain within the United States, contended that his plan for colonization in the West would bring a speedy end to slavery and avert the divine judgment of an apocalyptic racial war. In 1817 John Kenrick showed that colonization could be combined with a kind of immediatism, for though he proposed settlement of free Negroes in the West, he went so far as to suggest that the powers of the central government should be enlarged, if necessary, in order to abolish slavery. "If slavery is 'a violation of the divine laws,'" Kenrick asked, "is it not absurd to talk about a gradual emancipation? We might as well talk of gradually leaving off piracy—murder—adultery, or drunkenness."

The religious character of this radical abolitionism can best be seen in the writings of George Bourne, an English immigrant who was to have a deep influence on William Lloyd Garrison. In 1815 Bourne condemned professed Christians who upheld the crime of slavery. "The system is so entirely corrupt," he wrote, "that it admits of no cure, but by a total and immediate, abolition. For a gradual emancipation is a virtual recognition of the right, and establishes the rectitude of the practice." But while Bourne associated slavery with the very essence of human sin, his main concern was not the plight of Negroes but the corruption of the Christian church:

Had this compound of all corruption no connection with the church of Christ; however deleterious are the effects of it in political society, however necessary is its immediate and total abolition, and however pregnant with danger to the *Union,* is the prolongation of the system; to Legislators and Civilians, the redress of the evil would have been committed. But *Slavery* is the *golden Calf,* which has been elevated among the Tribes, and before it, the Priests and the Elders and the *nominal* sons of Israel, *eat, drink, rise up to play, worship and sacrifice.*

Thus for Bourne "immediatism" meant an immediate recognition of the sin of slavery and an immediate decision on the part of Christians to purge their churches of all contamination. He was far more interested in the purification of religion than in slavery as an institution.

In 1825 the Boston *Recorder and Telegraph* published a long correspondence that further clarified the origins of immediatism. After arguing that slavery was unlawful and suggesting that slaves might have a right to revolt, "Vigornius" [Samuel M. Worcester] asserted that *"the slave-holding system must be abolished;* and in order to the accomplishment of this end, immediate, determined measures must be adopted for the ultimate emancipation of every slave within our territories." This was the position of the later Kentucky and New York abolitionists, but Vigornius combined it with strong faith in the American Colonization Society. He was bitterly attacked by "A Carolinian," who accused him of believing in "an entire and immediate abolition of slavery." ."Philo," the next contributor, said he opposed immediate emancipation on grounds of expediency, but recognized the right of slaves to immediate freedom; he advocated, therefore, "immediate and powerful remedies," since "We are convinced, and if our Southern brethren are not convinced, we wish to convince them, and think with a little discussion we could convince them, that to postpone these prospective measures a day, is a great crime . . . and moreover, we wish to state directly, that this postponement is that, in which we consider the guilt of slavery, so far as the present proprietors are concerned, to consist."

A Southerner, who called himself "Hieronymus," defended Vigornius and tried to avoid the ambiguities that were later to cloud discussions of immediate abolition. Vigornius, he wrote,

> pleads, it is true, for *speedy* emancipation, and immediate preparatory steps. But immediate and speedy are not synonimous [*sic*] expressions. One is an absolute, the other a relative or comparative term. An event may in one view of it be regarded as very speedy, which in another might be pronounced very gradual. If slavery should be entirely abolished from the United States in 30, 40, or even 50 years, many . . . will readily admit, that it would be a speedy abolition; while every one must perceive, that it would be far, very far, from an immediate abolition. In a certain sense abolition may be immediate; in another, speedy; and in both, practicable and safe. There are not a few blacks now at the South, qualified for immediate emancipation, if Legislatures would permit, and owners would confer it.

Hieronymus, who had read and been impressed by Elizabeth Heyrick's pamphlet, agreed with Vigornius that colonization was the only practicable solution to the nation's most critical problem.

These ardent colonizationists believed that slavery was a sin that would increase in magnitude and danger unless effective measures were adopted without delay. Yet by 1821 Benjamin Lundy and other abolitionists had come to the opinion that the American Colonization Society was founded on racial prejudice and offered no real promise of undermining slavery. Lundy thought that slavery could not be eradicated until his fellow Americans in both North and South were willing to accept the free Negro as an equal citizen. But in the meantime the institution was expanding into the Southwest and even threatening to spread to such states as Illinois. In the face of such an imposing problem, Lundy called for the swift and decisive use of political power by a convention of representatives from the various states, who might devise and implement a comprehensive plan for emancipation.

The American antislavery organizations absorbed some of this sense of urgency and mistrust of palliatives. The Pennsylvania Society for the Abolition of Slavery was cautious in its approach to the national problem, but in 1819 it approved a declaration that "the practice of holding and selling human beings as property . . . ought to be *immediately* abandoned." In 1825 the Acting Committee of the American Convention for Promoting the Abolition of Slavery advocated the "speedy and entire" emancipation of slaves, a phrase later used by the British Society. The Convention showed little confidence in any of the specific proposals for gradual abolition but at the same time rejected direct emancipation by act of Congress as an impossibility. Alert always to the need for conciliating the South and remaining within the prescribed bounds of the Constitution, the Convention considered every conceivable plan in a rationalistic and eclectic spirit. In the South, however, there was an increasing tendency to see the most conservative antislavery proposals as immediatism in disguise. By 1829 the gradualist approach of the American Convention had reached a dead end.

It is a striking coincidence that both the British and American antislavery movements had come to a crucial turning point by 1830. In both countries the decline of faith in gradualism had been marked in the mid-1820's by enthusiasm for a boycott of slave produce, a movement which promised to give a cutting edge to the moral testimony of individuals. In both countries the truculence and stubborn opposition of slaveholders to even gradualist reforms brought a sense of despair and indignation to the antislavery public. To some degree immediatism was the creation of the British and American slaveholders themselves. By accusing the most moderate critics of radical designs and by blocking the path to many attempted reforms they helped to discredit the gradualist mentality that had balanced and compromised a subjective conviction that slavery was sin. The sense of crisis between 1829 and 1831 was also accentuated by an increasing militancy of Negroes, both slave and free. In 1829 David Walker hinted ominously of slave revenge; groups of free Negroes openly repudiated the colonization movement; and in 1831 bloody revolts erupted in Virginia and Jamaica. In that year a new generation of American reformers adopted the principle of immediatism, which had recently acquired the sanction of eminent British philanthropists. But while American abolitionists modeled their new societies and techniques on British examples, the principle of immediatism had had a long and parallel development in both countries.

In one sense immediatism was simply a shift in strategy brought on by the failure of less direct plans for abolition. Earlier plans and programs had evoked little popular excitement compared with parliamentary reform or Catholic emancipation in England, or with tariff or land policies in the United States. As a simple, emotional slogan, immediate abolition would at least arouse interest and perhaps appeal to the moral sense of the public. As a device for propaganda it had the virtue of avoiding economic and social complexities and focusing attention on a clear issue of right and wrong. If the public could once be brought to the conviction that slavery was wrong and that something must be done about it at once, then governments would be forced to take care of the details.

But immediatism was something more than a shift in strategy. It represented a shift in total outlook from a detached, rationalistic perspective on human history and progress to a personal commitment to make no compromise with sin. It marked a liberation for the reformer from the ideology of gradualism, from a toleration of evil within the social order, and from a deference to institutions that blocked the way to personal salvation. Acceptance of immediatism was the sign of an immediate transformation within the reformer himself; as such, it was seen as an expression of inner freedom, of moral sincerity and earnestness, and of victory over selfish and calculating expediency. If slaveholders received the doctrine with contempt and scathing abuse, the abolitionist was at least assured of his own freedom from guilt. He saw the emergence of immediatism as an upswelling of personal moral force which, with the aid of God, would triumph over all that was mean and selfish and worldly.

There are obvious links between immediate emancipation and a religious sense of immediate justification and presence of the divine spirit that can be traced through the early spiritual religions to the Quakers, Methodists, and evangelical revivals. The new abolitionism contained a similar pattern of intense personal anxiety, rapturous freedom, eagerness for sacrifice, and mistrust of legalism, institutions, and slow-working agencies for salvation. It was no accident that from the late seventeenth century the boldest assertions of antislavery sentiment had been made by men who were dissatisfied with the materialism and sluggish formality of institutionalized religion, and who searched for a fresh and assuring meaning of Christian doctrine in a changing world. To the extent that slavery became a concrete symbol of sin, and support of the antislavery cause a sign of Christian virtue, participation in the reform became a supplement or even alternative to traditional religion. As a kind of surrogate religion, antislavery had long show tendencies that were pietistic, millennial, and anti-institutional. By the 1830's it had clearly marked affinities with the increasingly popular doctrines of free grace, immediate conversion, and personal holiness. According to Amos A. Phelps, for example, immediatism was synonymous with immediate repentance: "All that follows is the carrying out of the new principle of action, and is to emancipation just what sanctification is to conversion."

Immediate emancipation was also related to a changing view of history and human nature. Whereas the gradualist saw man as at least partially conditioned by historical and social forces, the immediatist saw him as essentially indeterminate and unconditioned. The gradualist, having faith in the certainty of economic and social laws, and fearing the dangers of a sudden collapse of social controls, was content to wait until a legal and rational system of external discipline replaced the arbitrary power of the slaveowner. The immediatist, on the other hand, put his faith in the innate moral capacities of the individual. He felt that unless stifling and coercive influences were swept away, there could be no development of the inner controls of conscience, emulation, and self-respect, on which a free and Christian society depended. His outlook was essentially romantic, for instead of cautiously manipulating the external forces of nature, he sought to create a new epoch of history by liberating the inner moral forces of human nature.

It falls beyond the scope of the present essay to show how immediatism itself became institutionalized as a rigid test of faith, and how it served as a medium for attacking all rival institutions that limited individual freedom or defined standards of thought and conduct. It is enough to suggest that immediatism, while latent in early antislavery thought, was part of a larger reaction against a type of mind that tended to think of history in terms of linear time and logical categories, and that emphasized the importance of self-interest, expediency, moderation, and planning in accordance with economic and social laws. Immediatism shared with the romantic frame of mind a hostility to all dualisms of thought and feeling, an allegiance to both emotional sympathy and abstract principle, an assumption that mind can rise above self-interest, and a belief that ideas, when held with sufficient intensity, can be transformed into irresistible moral action. If immediate emancipation brought misunderstanding and violent hostility in regions that were charged with racial prejudice and fear of sectional conflict, it was nevertheless an appropriate doctrine for a romantic and evangelical age.

Romantic Reform in America, 1815-1865

JOHN L. THOMAS

As I have suggested in the preceding selection, the emergence of immediatism was part of a major shift in intellectual history. John L. Thomas
(1926–   ), a biographer of William Lloyd Garrison and an associate professor of history at Brown University, applies similar concepts to the entire
history of ante-bellum reform, and shows how a seemingly conservative religious revival could lead to a radical and romantic crusade to regenerate the
social order. Thomas finds the key to this transformation in the doctrine of
individual perfectibility, which was latent in a "theological revolution" fostered by the very missionaries and moralists who were originally obsessed
with the need for social control.

CONFRONTED BY THE BEWILDERING VARIETY OF PROJECTS FOR RE-
generating American society, Emerson concluded his survey of
humanitarian reform in 1844 with the observation that "the Church,
or religious party, is falling away from the Church nominal, and . . . appearing in temperance and nonresistance societies; in movements of
abolitionists and of socialists . . . of seekers, of all the soul of the soldiery
of dissent." Common to all these planners and prophets, he noted, was the
conviction of an "infinite worthiness" in man and the belief that reform
simply meant removing "impediments" to natural perfection.

Emerson was defining, both as participant and observer, a romantic
revolution which T. E. Hulme once described as "spilt religion." A
romantic faith in perfectibility, originally confined by religious institu-

John L. Thomas, "Romantic Reform in America, 1815–1865," *American Quarterly,* Vol. XVII, No. 4, Winter 1965, pp. 656–681. Reprinted without footnotes by
permission of the author and editor. Copyright © 1965 by the Trustees of the
University of Pennsylvania.

tions, overflows these barriers and spreads across the surface of society, seeping into politics and culture. Perfectibility—the essentially religious notion of the individual as a "reservoir" of possibilities—fosters a revolutionary assurance "that if you can so rearrange society by the destruction of oppressive order then these possibilities will have a chance and you will get Progress." Hulme had in mind the destructive forces of the French Revolution, but his phrase is also a particularly accurate description of the surge of social reform which swept across Emerson's America in the three decades before the Civil War. Out of a seemingly conservative religious revival there flowed a spate of perfectionist ideas for the improvement and rearrangement of American society. Rising rapidly in the years after 1830, the flood of social reform reached its crest at midcentury only to be checked by political crisis and the counterforces of the Civil War. Reform after the Civil War, though still concerned with individual perfectibility, proceeded from new and different assumptions as to the nature of individualism and its preservation in an urban industrial society. Romantic reform ended with the Civil War and an intellectual counterrevolution which discredited the concept of the irreducible self and eventually redirected reform energies.

Romantic reform in America traced its origins to a religious impulse which was both politically and socially conservative. With the consolidation of independence and the arrival of democratic politics the new nineteenth-century generation of American churchmen faced a seeming crisis. Egalitarianism and rising demands for church disestablishment suddenly appeared to threaten an inherited Christian order and along with it the preferred status of the clergy. Lyman Beecher spoke the fears of more than one of the clerical party when he warned that Americans were fast becoming "another people." When the attempted alliance between sound religion and correct politics failed to prevent disestablishment or improve waning Federalist fortunes at the polls, the evangelicals, assuming a defensive posture, organized voluntary benevolent associations to strengthen the Christian character of Americans and save the country from infidelity and ruin. Between 1815 and 1830 nearly a dozen moral reform societies were established to counter the threats to social equilibrium posed by irreligious democrats. Their intense religious concern could be read in the titles of the benevolent societies which the evangelicals founded: the American Bible Society, the American Sunday School Union, the American Home Missionary Society, the American Tract Society. By the time of the election of Andrew Jackson the benevolent associations formed a vast if loosely coordinated network of conservative reform enterprises staffed with clergy and wealthy laymen who served as self-appointed guardians of American morals.

The clerical diagnosticians had little difficulty in identifying the symptoms of democratic disease. Infidelity flourished on the frontier and licentiousness bred openly in seaboard cities; intemperance sapped the strength of American workingmen and the saving word was denied their children. Soon atheism would destroy the vital organs of the republic unless drastic moral therapy prevented. The evangelicals' prescription followed logically from their diagnosis: large doses of morality injected into the body politic under the supervision of Christian stewards. No more Sunday mails or pleasure excursions, no more grog-shops or profane pleasures, no family without a Bible and no community without a minister of the gospel. Accepting for the moment their political liabilities, the moral reformers relied on the homeopathic strategy of fighting democratic excess with democratic remedies. The Tract Society set up three separate printing presses which cranked out hundreds of thousands of pamphlets for mass distribution. The Home Missionary Society subsidized seminarians in carrying religion into the backcountry. The Temperance Union staged popular conventions; the Peace Society sponsored public debates; the Bible Society hired hundreds of agents to spread its propaganda.

The initial thrust of religious reform, then, was moral rather than social, preventive rather than curative. Nominally rejecting politics and parties, the evangelicals looked to a general reformation of the American character achieved through a revival of piety and morals in the individual. By probing his conscience, by convincing him of his sinful ways and converting him to right conduct they hoped to engineer a Christian revolution which would leave the foundations of the social order undisturbed. The realization of their dream of a nonpolitical "Christian party" in America would ensure a one-party system open to moral talent and the natural superiority of Christian leadership. Until their work was completed, the evangelicals stood ready as servants of the Lord to manage their huge reformational apparatus in behalf of order and sobriety.

But the moral reformers inherited a theological revolution which in undermining their conservative defenses completely reversed their expectations for a Christian America. The transformation of American theology in the first quarter of the nineteenth century released the very forces of romantic perfectionism that conservatives most feared. This religious revolution advanced along three major fronts: first, the concentrated antitheocratic assault of Robert Owen and his secular utopian followers, attacks purportedly atheistic and environmentalist but in reality Christian in spirit and perfectionist in method; second, the revolt of liberal theology beginning with Unitarianism and culminating in transcendentalism; third, the containment operation of the "new divinity" in adapting orthodoxy to the criticism of liberal dissent. The central fact in the romantic reorientation of American theology was the rejection of determinism. Salvation, however variously defined, lay open to everyone. Sin was voluntary: men were not helpless and depraved by nature but free agents and potential powers for good. Sin could be reduced to the selfish preferences of individuals, and social evils, in turn, to collective sins which, once acknowleged, could be rooted out. Perfectionism spread rapidly across the whole spectrum of American Protestantism as different denominations and sects elaborated their own versions of salvation. If man was a truly free agent, then his improvement became a matter of immediate consequence. The progress of the country suddenly seemed to depend upon the regeneration of the individual and the contagion of example.

As it spread, perfectionism swept across denominational barriers and penetrated even secular thought. Perfection was presented as Christian striving for holiness in the "new heart" sermons of Charles Grandison Finney and as an immediately attainable goal in the come-outer prophecies of John Humphrey Noyes. It was described as an escape from outworn dogma by Robert Owen and as the final union of the soul with nature by Emerson. The important fact for most Americans in the first half of the nineteenth century was that it was readily available. A romantic religious faith had changed an Enlightenment doctrine of progress into a dynamic principle of reform.

For the Founding Fathers' belief in perfectibility had been wholly compatible with a pessimistic appraisal of the present state of mankind. Progress, in the view of John Adams or James Madison, resulted from the planned operation of mechanical checks within the framework of government which balanced conflicting selfish interests and neutralized private passions. Thus a properly constructed governmental machine might achieve by artifact what men, left to their own devices, could not—gradual improvement of social institutions and a measure of progress. Perfectionism, on the contrary, as an optative mood demanded total commitment and immediate action. A latent revolutionary force lay in its demand for immediate reform and its promise to release the new American from the restraints of institutions and precedent. In appealing to the liberated individual, perfectionism reinforced the Jacksonian attack on institutions, whether a "Monster Bank" or a secret Masonic order, entrenched monopolies or the Catholic Church. But in emphasizing the unfettered will as the proper vehicle for reform it provided a millenarian alternative to Jacksonian politics. Since social evils were simply individual acts of selfishness compounded, and since Americans could attempt the perfect society any time they were so inclined, it followed that the duty of the true reformer consisted in educating them and making them models of good behavior. As the sum of individual sins social wrong would disappear when enough people had been converted and rededicated to right conduct. Deep and lasting reform, therefore, meant an educational crusade based on the assumption that when a sufficient number of individual Americans had seen the light, they would automatically solve the country's social problems. Thus formulated, perfectionist reform offered a program of mass conversion achieved through educational rather than political means. In the opinion of the romantic reformers the regeneration of American society began, not in legislative enactments or political manipulation, but in a calculated appeal to the American urge for individual self-improvement.

Perfectionism radically altered the moral reform movement by shattering the benevolent societies themselves. Typical of these organizations was the American Peace Society founded in 1828 as a forum for clerical discussions of the gospel of peace. Its founders, hoping to turn American attention from the pursuit of wealth to the prevention of war, debated the question of defensive war, constructed hypothetical leagues of amity, and in a general way sought to direct American foreign policy into pacific channels. Perfectionism, however, soon split the Peace Society into warring factions as radical nonresistants, led by the Christian perfectionist, Henry C. Wright, denounced all use of force and demanded the instant creation of an American society modeled on the precepts of Jesus. Not only war but all governmental coercion fell under the ban of the nonresistants who refused military service and political office along with the right to vote. After a series of skirmishes the nonresistants seceded in 1838 to form their own New England Non-Resistant Society; and by 1840 the institutional strength of the peace movement had been completely broken.

The same power of perfectionism disrupted the temperance movement. The founders of the temperance crusade had considered their reform an integral part of the program of moral stewardship and had directed their campaign against "ardent spirits" which could be banished "by a correct and efficient public sentiment." Until 1833 there was no general agreement on a pledge of total abstinence: some local societies required it, others did not. At the first national convention held in that year, however, the radical advocates of temperance, following their perfectionist proclivities, demanded a pledge of total abstinence and hurried on to denounce the liquor traffic as "morally wrong." Soon both the national society and local and state auxiliaries were split between moderates content to preach to the consumer and radicals bent on extending moral suasion to public pressure on the seller. After 1836 the national movement disintegrated into scattered local societies which attempted with no uniform program and no permanent success to establish a cold-water America.

By far the most profound change wrought by perfectionism was the sudden emergence of abolition. The American Colonization Society, founded in 1817 as another key agency in the moral reform complex, aimed at strengthening republican institutions by deporting an inferior and therefore undesirable Negro population. The cooperation of Southerners hoping to strengthen the institution of slavery gave Northern colonizationists pause, but they succeeded in repressing their doubts until a perfectionist ethic totally discredited their program. The abolitionist pioneers were former colonizationists who took sin and redemption seriously and insisted that slavery constituted a flat denial of perfectibility to both Negroes and whites. They found in immediate emancipation a perfectionist formula for casting off the guilt of slavery and bringing the Negro to Christian freedom. Destroying slavery, the abolitionists argued, depended first of all on recognizing it as sin; and to this recognition they bent their efforts. Their method was direct and intensely personal. Slaveholding they considered a deliberate flouting of the divine will for which there was no remedy but repentance. Since slavery was sustained by a system of interlocking personal sins, their task was to teach Americans to stop sinning. "We shall send forth agents to lift up the voice of remonstrance, of warning, of entreaty, and of rebuke," the Declaration of Sentiments of the American Anti-Slavery Society announced. Agents, tracts, petitions and conventions—all the techniques of the moral reformers—were brought to bear on the consciences of Americans to convince them of their sin.

From the beginning, then, the abolitionists mounted a moral crusade rather than an engine of limited reform. For seven years, from 1833 to 1840, their society functioned as a loosely coordinated enterprise—a national directory of antislavery opinion. Perfectionist individualism made effective organization difficult and often impossible. Antislavery delegates from state and local societies gathered at annual conventions to frame denunciatory resolutions, listen to endless rounds of speeches and go through the motions of electing officers. Nominal leadership but very little power was vested in a self-perpetuating executive committee. Until its disruption in 1840 the national society was riddled with controversy as moderates, disillusioned by the failure of moral suasion, gradually turned to politics, and ultras, equally disenchanted by public hostility, abandoned American institutions altogether. Faced with the resistance of Northern churches and state legislatures, the perfectionists, led by William Lloyd Garrison, deserted politics for the principle of secession. The come-outer abolitionists, who eventually took for their motto "No Union with Slaveholders," sought an alternative to politics in the command to cast off church and state for a holy fraternity which would convert the nation by the power of example. The American Anti-Slavery Society quickly succumbed to the strain of conflicting philosophies and warring personalities. In 1840 the Garrisonians seized control of the society and drove their moderate opponents out. Thereafter neither ultras nor moderates were able to maintain an effective national organization.

Thus romantic perfectionism altered the course of the reform enterprise by appealing directly to the individual conscience. Its power stemmed from a millennial expectation which proved too powerful a moral explosive for the reform agencies. In one way or another almost all of the benevolent societies felt the force of perfectionism. Moderates, attempting political solutions, scored temporary gains only to receive sharp setbacks. Local option laws passed one year were repealed the next. Despite repeated attempts the Sunday School Union failed to secure permanent adoption of its texts in the public schools. The Liberty Party succeeded only in electing a Democratic president in 1844. Generally, direct political action failed to furnish reformers with the moral leverage they believed necessary to perfect American society. The conviction spread accordingly that politicians and legislators, as Albert Brisbane put it, were engaged in "superficial controversies and quarrels, which lead to no practical results." Political results, a growing number of social reformers were convinced, would be forthcoming only when the reformation of society at large had been accomplished through education and example.

The immediate effects of perfectionism, therefore, were felt outside politics in humanitarian reforms. With its confidence in the liberated individual perfectionism tended to be anti-institutional and exclusivist; but at the same time it posited an ideal society in which this same individual could discover his power for good and exploit it. Such a society would tolerate neither poverty nor suffering; it would contain no condemned classes or deprived citizens, no criminals or forgotten men. Impressed with the necessity for saving these neglected elements of American society, the humanitarian reformers in the years after 1830 undertook a huge rescue operation.

Almost to a man the humanitarians came from moral reform backgrounds. Samuel Gridley Howe was a product of Old Colony religious zeal and a Baptist education at Brown; Thomas Gallaudet a graduate of Andover and an ordained minister; Dorothea Dix a daughter of an itinerant Methodist minister, school mistress and Sunday school teacher-turned-reformer; E. M. P. Wells, founder of the reform school, a pastor of a Congregational church in Boston. Louis Dwight, the prison reformer, had been trained for the ministry at Yale and began his reform career as a traveling agent for the American Tract Society. Robert Hartley, for thirty years the secretary of the New York Association for Improving the Condition of the Poor, started as a tract distributor and temperance lecturer. Charles Loring Brace served as a missionary on Blackwell's Island before founding the Children's Aid Society.

In each of these cases of conversion to humanitarian reform there was a dramatic disclosure of deprivation and suffering which did not tally with preconceived notions of perfectibility—Dorothea Dix's discovery of the conditions in the Charlestown reformatory, Robert Hartley's inspection of contaminated milk in New York slums, Samuel Gridley Howe's chance conversation with Dr. Fisher in Boston. Something very much like a conversion experience seems to have forged the decisions of the humanitarians to take up their causes, a kind of revelation which furnished them with a ready-made role outside politics and opened a new career with which they could become completely identified. With the sudden transference of a vague perfectionist faith in self-improvement to urgent social problems there emerged a new type of professional reformer whose whole life became identified with the reform process.

Such, for example, was the conversion of Dorothea Dix from a lonely and afflicted schoolteacher who composed meditational studies of the life of Jesus into "D. L. Dix," the militant advocate of the helpless and forgotten. In a very real sense Miss Dix's crusade for better treatment of the insane and the criminal was one long self-imposed subjection to suffering. Her reports, which recorded cases of unbelievable mistreatment, completed a kind of purgative rite in which she assumed the burden of innocent suffering and passed it on as guilt to the American people. The source of her extraordinary energy lay in just this repeated submission of herself to human misery until she felt qualified to speak out against it. Both an exhausting schedule and the almost daily renewal of scenes of suffering seemed to give her new energies for playing her romantic reform role in an effective and intensely personal way. Intense but not flexible: there was little room for exchange and growth in the mood of atonement with which she approached her work. Nor was her peculiarly personal identification with the victims of American indifference easily matched in reform circles. Where other reformers like the abolitionists often made abstract pleas for "bleeding humanity" and "suffering millions," hers was the real thing—a perfectionist fervor which strengthened her will at the cost of psychological isolation. Throughout her career she preferred to work alone, deploring the tendency to multiply reform agencies and ignoring those that existed either because she disagreed with their principles, as in the case of Louis Dwight's Boston

Prison Discipline Society, or because she chose the more direct method of personal appeal. In all her work, even the unhappy and frustrating last years as superintendent of nurses in the Union Army, she saw herself as a solitary spokesman for the deprived and personal healer of the suffering.

Another reform role supplied by perfectionism was Bronson Alcott's educator-prophet, the "true reformer" who "studied man as he is from the hand of the Creator, and not as he is made by the errors of the world." Convinced that the self sprang from divine origins in nature, Alcott naturally concluded that children were more susceptible to good than people imagined and set out to develop a method for uncovering that goodness. With the power to shape personality the teacher, Alcott was sure, held the key to illimitable progress and the eventual regeneration of the world. The teacher might literally make society over by teaching men as children to discover their own divine natures. Thus true education for Alcott consisted of the process of self-discovery guided by the educator-prophet. He sharply criticized his contemporaries for their fatal mistake of imposing partial and therefore false standards on their charges. Shades of the prison house obscured the child's search for perfection, and character was lost forever. "Instead of following it in the path pointed out by its Maker, instead of learning by observation, and guiding it in that path; we unthinkingly attempt to shape its course to our particular wishes. . . ."

To help children avoid the traps set by their elders Alcott based his whole system on the cultivation of self-awareness through self-examination. His pupils kept journals in which they scrutinized their behavior and analyzed their motives. Ethical problems were the subject of frequent and earnest debate at the Temple School as the children were urged to discover the hidden springs of perfectibility in themselves. No mechanical methods of rote learning could bring on the moment of revelation; each child was unique and would find himself in his own way. The real meaning of education as reform, Alcott realized, came with an increased social sense that resulted from individual self-discovery. As the creator of social personality Alcott's teacher was bound by no external rules of pedagogy: as the primary social reformer he had to cast off "the shackles of form, of mode, and ceremony" in order to play the required roles in the educational process.

Alcott's modernity lay principally in his concept of the interchangeability of roles—both teacher and pupils acquired self-knowledge in an exciting give-and-take. Thus defined, education became a way of life, a continuing process through which individuals learned to obey the laws of their own natures and in so doing to discover the laws of the good society. This identification of individual development with true social unity was crucial for Alcott, as for the other perfectionist communitarians, because it provided the bridge over which they passed from self to society. The keystone in Alcott's construction was supplied by the individual conscience which connected with the "common conscience" of mankind. This fundamental identity, he was convinced, could be demostrated by the learning process itself which he defined as "sympathy and imitation, the moral action of the teacher upon the children, of the children upon him, and each other." He saw in the school, therefore, a model of the good community where self-discovery led to a social exchange culminating in the recognition of universal dependency and brotherhood. The ideal society—the society he hoped to create—was one in which individuals could be totally free to follow their own natures because such pursuit would inevitably end in social harmony. For Alcott the community was the product rather than the creator of the good life.

Fruitlands, Alcott's attempt to apply the lessons of the Temple School on a larger scale, was designed to prove that perfectionist educational reform affected the "economies of life." In this realization lay the real import of Alcott's reform ideas; for education, seen as a way of life, meant the communitarian experiment as an educative model. Pushed to its limits, the perfectionist assault on institutions logically ended in the attempt to make new and better societies as examples for Americans to follow. Communitarianism, as Alcott envisioned it, was the social extension of his perfectionist belief in education as an alternative to politics.

In the case of other humanitarian reformers like Samuel Gridley Howe perfectionism determined even more precisely both the role and intellectual content of their proposals. Howe's ideal of the good society seems to have derived from his experiences in Greece where, during his last year, he promoted a communitarian plan for resettling exiles on the Gulf of Corinth. With government support he established his colony, "Washingtonia," on two thousand acres of arable land, selected the colonists himself, bought cattle and tools, managed its business affairs, and supervised a Lancastrian school. By his own admission these were the happiest days of his life: "I laboured here day & night in season & out; & was governor, legislator, clerk, constable, & everything but patriarch." When the government withdrew its support and brigands overran the colony, Howe was forced to abandon the project and return home. Still, the idea of an entire community under the care of a "patriarch" shouldering its collective burden and absorbing all its dependents in a cooperative life continued to dominate the "Doctor's" reform thinking and to determine his methods.

The ethical imperatives in Howe's philosophy of reform remained constant. "Humanity demands that every creature in human shape should command our respect; we should recognise as a brother every being upon whom God has stamped the human impress." Progress he likened to the American road. Christian individualism required that each man walk separately and at his own pace, but "the rear should not be left too far behind . . . none should be allowed to perish in their helplessness . . . the strong should help the weak, so that the whole should advance as a band of brethren." It was the duty of society itself to care for its disabled or mentally deficient members rather than to shut them up in asylums which were "offsprings of a low order of feeling." "The more I reflect upon the subject the more I see objections in principle and practice to asylums," he once wrote to a fellow-reformer. "What right have we to pack off the poor, the old, the blind into asylums? They are of us, our brothers, our sisters—they belong in families. . . ."

In Howe's ideal society, then, the handicapped, criminals and defectives would not be walled off but accepted as part of the community and perfected by constant contact with it. Two years of experimenting with education for the feeble-minded convinced him that even "idiots" could be redeemed from what he called spiritual death. "How far they can be elevated, and to what extent they may be educated, can only be shown by the experience of the future," he admitted in his report to the Massachusetts legislature but predicted confidently that "each succeeding year will show even more progress than any preceding one." He always acted on his conviction that "we shall avail ourselves of special institutions less and the common schools more" and never stopped hoping that eventually all blind children after proper training might be returned to families and public schools for their real education. He also opposed the establishment of reformatories with the argument that they only collected the refractory and vicious and made them worse. Nature mingled the defective in common families, he insisted, and any departure from her standards stunted moral growth. He took as his model for reform the Belgian town of Geel where mentally ill patients were boarded at public expense with private families and allowed maximum freedom. As soon as the building funds were available he introduced the cottage system at Perkins, a plan he also wanted to apply to reformatories. No artificial and unnatural institution could replace the family which Howe considered the primary agency in the perfection of the individual.

Howe shared his bias against institutions and a preference for the family unit with other humanitarian reformers like Robert Hartley and Charles Loring Brace. Hartley's "friendly visitors" were dispatched to New York's poor with instructions to bring the gospel of self-help home to every member of the family. Agents of the AICP dispensed advice and improving literature along with the coal and groceries. Only gradually did the organization incorporate "incidental labors"—legislative programs for housing reform, health regulations and child labor—into its system of reform. Hartley's real hope for the new urban poor lay in their removal to the country where a bootstrap operation might lift them to sufficiency and selfhood. "Escape then from the city," he told them, "—for escape is your only recourse against the terrible ills of beggary; and the further you go, the better." In Hartley's formula the perfectionist doctrine of the salvation of the individual combined with the conservative appeal of the safety-valve.

A pronounced hostility to cities also marked the program of Charles Loring Brace's Children's Aid Society, the central feature of which was the plan for relocating children of the "squalid poor" on upstate New York farms for "moral disinfection." The Society's placement service resettled thousands of slum children in the years before the Civil War in the belief that a proper family environment and a rural setting would release the naturally good tendencies in young people so that under the supervision of independent and hard-working farmers they would save themselves.

There was thus a high nostalgic content in the plans of humanitarians who emphasized pastoral virtues and the perfectionist values inherent in country living. Their celebration of the restorative powers of nature followed logically from their assumption that the perfected individual— the truly free American—could be created only by the reunification of mental and physical labor. The rural life, it was assumed, could revive and sustain the unified sensibility threatened by the city. A second assumption concerned the importance of the family as the primary unit in the reconstruction of society. As the great debate among social reformers proceeded it centered on the question of the limits to which the natural family could be extended. Could an entire society, as the more radical communitarians argued, be reorganized as one huge family? Or were there natural boundaries necessary for preserving order and morality? On the whole, the more conservative humanitarians agreed with Howe in rejecting those communal plans which, like Fourier's, stemmed from too high an estimate of "the capacity of mankind for family affections."

That intensive education held the key to illimitable progress, however, few humanitarian reformers denied. They were strengthened in their certainty by the absolutes inherited from moral reform. Thus Howe, for example, considered his work a "new field" of "practical religion." The mental defective, he was convinced, was the product of sin—both the sin of the parents and the sin of society in allowing the offspring to languish in mental and moral darkness. Yet the social evils incident to sin were not inevitable; they were not "inherent in the very constitution of man" but the "chastisements sent by a loving Father to bring his children to obedience to his beneficent laws." These laws—infinite perfectibility and social responsibility—reinforced each other in the truly progressive society. The present condition of the dependent classes in America was proof of "the immense space through which society has yet to advance before it even approaches the perfection of civilization which is attainable." Education, both the thorough training of the deprived and the larger education of American society to its obligations, would meet the moral challenge.

The perfectionist uses of education as an alternative to political reform were most thoroughly explored by Horace Mann. Mann's initial investment in public school education was dictated by his fear that American democracy, lacking institutional checks and restraints, was fast degenerating into "the spectacle of gladiatorial contests" conducted at the expense of the people. Could laws save American society? Mann thought not.

With us, the very idea of legislation is reversed. Once, the law prescribed the actions and shaped the wills of the multitude; here the wills of the multitude prescribe and shape the law. . . . now when the law is weak, the passions of the multitude have gathered irresistible strength, it is fallacious and insane to look for security in the moral force of law. Government and law . . . will here be moulded into the similitude of the public mind. . . .

In offering public school education as the only effective countervailing force in a democracy Mann seemingly was giving vent to a conservative dread of unregulated change in a society where, as he admitted, the momentum of hereditary opinion was spent. Where there was no "surgical code of laws" reason, conscience and benevolence would have to be provided by education. "The whole mass of mind must be instructed in regard to its comprehensive and enduring interests." In a republican government, however, compulsion was theoretically undesirable and practically unavailable. People could not be driven up a "dark avenue" even though it were the right one. Mann, like his evangelical predecessors, found his solution in an educational crusade.

Let the intelligent visit the ignorant, day by day, as the oculist visits the blind mind, and detaches the scales from his eyes, until the living sense leaps to light. . . . Let the love of beautiful reason, the admonitions of conscience, the sense of religious responsibility, be plied, in mingled tenderness and earnestness, until the obdurate and dark mass of avarice and ignorance and prejudice shall be dissipated by their blended light and heat.

Here in Mann's rhetorical recasting was what appeared to be the old evangelical prescription for tempering democratic excess. The chief problem admittedly was avoiding the "disturbing forces of party and sect and faction and clan." To make sure that education remained nonpartisan the common schools should teach on the *"exhibitory"* method, "by an actual exhibition of the principle we would inculcate."

Insofar as the exhibitory method operated to regulate or direct public opinion, it was conservative. But implicit in Mann's theory was a commitment to perfectionism which gradually altered his aims until in the twelfth and final report education emerges as a near-utopian device for making American politics simple, clean and, eventually, superfluous. In the Twelfth Report Mann noted that although a public school system might someday guarantee "sufficiency, comfort, competence" to every American, as yet "imperfect practice" had not matched "perfect theory." Then in an extended analysis of social trends which foreshadowed Henry George's classification he singled out "poverty" and "profusion" as the two most disturbing facts in American development. "With every generation, fortunes increase on the one hand, and some new privation is added to poverty on the other. We are verging toward those extremes of opulence and penury, each of which unhumanizes the mind." A new feudalism threatened; and unless a drastic remedy was discovered, the "hideous evils" of unequal distribution of wealth would cause class war.

Mann's alternative to class conflict proved to be nothing less than universal education based on the exhibitory model of the common school. Diffusion of education, he pointed out, meant wiping out class lines and with them the possibility of conflict. As the great equalizer of condition it would supply the balance-wheel in the society of the future. Lest his readers confuse his suggestions with the fantasies of communitarians Mann hastened to point out that education would perfect society through the individual by creating new private resources. Given full play in a democracy, education gave each man the "independence and the means by which he can resist the selfishness of other men."

Once Mann had established education as an alternative to political action, it remained to uncover its utopian possibilities. By enlarging the "cultivated class" it would widen the area of social feelings—"if this education should be universal and complete, it would do more than all things else to obliterate factitious distinctions in society." Political reformers and revolutionaries based their schemes on the false assumption that the amount of wealth in America was fixed by fraud and force, and that the few were rich because the many were poor. By demanding a redistribution of wealth by legislative fiat they overlooked the power of education to obviate political action through the creation of new and immense sources of wealth.

Thus in Mann's theory as in the programs of the other humanitarians the perfection of the individual through education guaranteed illimitable progress. The constantly expanding powers of the free individual ensured the steady improvement of society until the educative process finally achieved a harmonious, self-regulating community. "And will not the community that gains its wealth in this way . . . be a model and a pattern for nations, a type of excellence to be admired and followed by the world?" The fate of free society, Mann concluded, depended upon the conversion of individuals from puppets and automatons to thinking men who were aware of the strength of the irreducible self and determined to foster it in others.

As romantic perfectionism spread across Jacksonian society it acquired an unofficial and only partly acceptable philosophy in the "systematic subjectivism" of transcendental theory. Transcendentalism, as its official historian noted, claimed for all men what a more restrictive Christian perfectionism extended only to the redeemed. Seen in this light, self-culture—Emerson's "perfect unfolding of our individual nature" —appeared as a secular amplification of the doctrine of personal holiness. In the transcendentalist definition, true reform proceeded from the individual and worked outward through the family, the neighborhood and ultimately into the social and political life of the community. The transcendentalist, Frothingham noted in retrospect, "was less a reformer of human circumstances than a regenerator of the human spirit. . . . With movements that did not start from this primary assumption of individual dignity, and come back to that as their goal, he had nothing to do." Emerson's followers, like the moral reformers and the humanitarians, looked to individuals rather than to institutions, to "high heroic example" rather than to political programs. The Brook-Farmer John Sullivan Dwight summed up their position when he protested that "men are anterior to systems. Great doctrines are not the origins, but the product of great lives."

Accordingly the transcendentalists considered institutions—parties, churches, organizations—so many arbitrarily constructed barriers on the road to self-culture. They were lonely men, Emerson admitted, who repelled influences. "They are not good citizens; not good members of society. . . ." A longing for solitude led them out of society, Emerson to the woods where he found no Jacksonian placards on the trees, Thoreau to his reclusive leadership of a majority of one. Accepting for the most part Emerson's dictum that one man was a counterpoise to a city, the transcendentalists turned inward to examine the divine self and find there the material with which to rebuild society. They wanted to avoid at all costs the mistake of their Jacksonian contemporaries who in order to be useful accommodated themselves to institutions without realizing the resultant loss of power and integrity.

The most immediate effect of perfectionism on the transcendentalists, as on the humanitarians, was the development of a set of concepts which, in stressing reform by example, opened up new roles for the alienated intellectual. In the first place, self-culture accounted for their ambivalence toward reform politics. It was not simply Emerson's reluctance to raise the siege on his hencoop that kept him apart, but a genuine confusion as to the proper role for the reformer. If government was simply a "job" and American society the senseless competition of the marketplace, how could the transcendentalist accept either as working premises? The transcendentalist difficulty in coming to terms with democratic politics could be read in Emerson's confused remark that of the two parties contending for the presidency in 1840 one had the better principles, the other the better men. Driven by their profound distaste for manipulation and chicanery, many of Emerson's followers took on the role of a prophet standing aloof from elections, campaigns and party caucuses and dispensing wisdom (often in oblique Emersonian terminology) out of the vast private resources of the self. In this sense transcendentalism, like Christian perfectionism, represented a distinct break with the prevailing Jacksonian views of democratic leadership and the politics of compromise and adjustment.

One of the more appealing versions of the transcendental role was the hero or genius to whom everything was permitted, as Emerson said, because "genius is the character of illimitable freedom." The heroes of the world, Margaret Fuller announced, were the true theocratic kings: "The hearts of men make music at their approach; the mind of the age is like the historian of their passing; and only men of destiny like themselves shall be permitted to write their eulogies, or fill their vacancies." Margaret Fuller herself spent her transcendentalist years stalking the American hero, which she somehow confused with Emerson, before she joined the Roman Revolution in 1849 and discovered the authentic article in the mystic nationalist Mazzini.

Carlyle complained to Emerson of the "perilous altitudes" to which the transcendentalists' search for the hero led them. Despite his own penchant for hero-worship he came away from reading the *Dial* "with a kind of shudder." In their pursuit of the self-contained hero they seemed to separate themselves from "this same cotton-spinning, dollar-hunting, canting and shrieking, very wretched generation of ours." The transcendentalists, however, were not trying to escape the Jacksonian world of fact, only to find a foothold for their perfectionist individualism in it. They sought a way of implementing their ideas of self-culture without corrupting them with the false values of materialism. They saw a day coming when parties and politicians would be obsolescent. By the 1850s Walt Whitman thought that day had already arrived and that America had outgrown parties.

What right has any one political party, no matter which, to wield the American government? No right at all . . . and every American young man must have sense enough to comprehend this. I have said the old parties are defunct; but there remains of them empty flesh, putrid mouths, mumbling and speaking the tones of these conventions, the politicians standing back in shadow, telling lies, trying to delude and frighten the people. . . .

Whitman's romantic alternative was a "love of comrades" cementing an American brotherhood and upholding a redeemer president.

A somewhat similar faith in the mystical fraternity informed Theodore Parker's plan for spiritual devotion. Like the other perfectionists, Parker began by reducing society to its basic components—individuals, the "monads" or "primitive atoms" of the social order—and judged it by its tendency to promote or inhibit individualism. "Destroy the individuality of those atoms, . . . all is gone. To mar the atoms is to mar the mass. To preserve itself, therefore, society is to preserve the individuality of the individual." In Parker's theology perfectionist Christianity and transcendental method merged to form a loving brotherhood united by the capacity to apprehend primary truths directly. A shared sense of the divinity of individual man held society together; without it no true community was possible. Looking around him at ante-bellum America, Parker found only the wrong kind of individualism, the kind that said, "I am as good as you, so get out of my way." The right kind, the individualism whose motto was "You are as good as I, and let us help one another," was to be the work of Parker's spiritual revolution. He explained the method of revolution as one of *"intellectual, moral* and *religious* education—everywhere and for all men." Until universal education had done its work Parker had little hope for political stability in the United States. He called instead for a new "party" to be formed in society at large, a party built on the idea that "God still inspires men as much as ever; that he is immanent in spirit as in space." Such a party required no church, tradition or scripture. "It believes God is near the soul as matter to the sense. . . . It calls God father and mother, not king; Jesus, brother, not redeemer, heaven home, religion nature."

Parker believed that this "philosophical party in politics," as he called it, was already at work in the 1850s on a code of universal laws from which to deduce specific legislation "so that each statute in the code shall represent a fact in the universe, a point of thought in God; so . . . that legislation shall be divine in the same sense that a true system of astronomy be divine." Parker's holy band represented the full fruition of the perfectionist idea of a "Christian party" in America, a party of no strict political or sectarian definition, but a true reform movement, apostolic in its beginnings but growing with the truths it preached until it encompassed all Americans in a huge brotherhood of divine average men. Party members, unlike time-serving Whigs and Democrats, followed ideas and intuitions rather than prejudice and precedent, and these ideas led them to question authority, oppose legal injustice and tear down rotten institutions. The philosophical party was not to be bound by accepted notions of political conduct or traditional attitudes toward law. When unjust laws interpose barriers to progress, reformers must demolish them.

So Parker himself reasoned when he organized the Vigilance Committee in Boston to defeat the Fugitive Slave Law. His reasoning epitomized perfectionist logic: every man may safely trust his conscience, properly informed, because it is the repository for divine truth. When men learn to trust their consciences and act on them, they naturally encourage others to do the same with the certainty that they will reach the same conclusions. Individual conscience thus creates a social conscience and a collective will to right action. Concerted right action means moral revolution. The fact that moral revolution, in its turn, might mean political revolt was a risk Parker and his perfectionist followers were willing to take.

Both transcendentalism and perfectionist moral reform, then, were marked by an individualist fervor that was disruptive of American institutions. Both made heavy moral demands on church and state; and when neither proved equal to the task of supporting their intensely personal demands, the transcendentalists and the moral reformers became increasingly alienated. The perfectionist temperament bred a come-outer spirit. An insistence on individual moral accountability and direct appeal to the irreducible self, the faith in self-reliance and distrust of compromise, and a substitution of universal education for partial reform measures, all meant that normal political and institutional reform channels were closed to the perfectionists. Alternate routes to the millennium had to be found. One of these was discovered by a new leadership which made reform a branch of prophecy. Another was opened by the idea of a universal reawakening of the great god self. But there was a third possibility, also deeply involved with the educational process, an attempt to build the experimental community as a reform model. With an increasing number of reformers after 1840 perfectionist anti-institutionalism led to heavy investments in the communitarian movement.

The attraction that drew the perfectionists to communitarianism came from their conviction that the good society should be simple. Since

American society was both complicated and corrupt, it was necessary to come out from it; but at the same time the challenge of the simple life had to be met. Once the true principles of social life had been discovered they had to be applied, some way found to harness individual perfectibility to a social engine. This urge to form the good community, as John Humphrey Noyes experienced it himself and perceived it in other reformers, provided the connection between perfectionism and communitarianism, or, as Noyes put it, between "Revivalism" and "Socialism." Perfectionist energies directed initially against institutions were diverted to the creation of small self-contained communities as educational models. In New England two come-outer abolitionists, Adin Ballou and George Benson, founded cooperative societies at Hopedale and Northampton, while a third Garrisonian lieutenant, John Collins, settled his followers on a farm in Skaneateles, New York. Brook Farm, Fruitlands and the North American Phalanx at Redbank acquired notoriety in their own day; but equally signficant, both in terms of origins and personnel, were the experiments at Raritan Bay under the guidance of Marcus Spring, the Marlboro Association in Ohio, the Prairie Home Community of former Hicksite Quakers, and the Swedenborgian Brocton Community. In these and other experimental communities could be seen the various guises of perfectionism.

Communitarianism promised drastic social reform without violence. Artificiality and corruption could not be wiped out by partial improvements and piecemeal measures but demanded a total change which, as Robert Owen once explained, "could make an immediate, and almost instantaneous, revolution in the minds and manners of society in which it shall be introduced." Communitarians agreed in rejecting class struggle which set interest against interest instead of uniting them through association. "Whoever will examine the question of social ameliorations," Albert Brisbane argued in support of Fourier, "must be convinced that *the gradual perfecting of Civilization* is useless as a remedy for present social evils, and that the only effectual means of doing away with indigence, idleness and the dislike for labor is to do away with civilization itself, and organize Association . . . in its place." Like the redemptive moment in conversion or the experience of self-discovery in transcendentalist thought, the communitarian ideal pointed to a sharp break with existing society and a commitment to root-and-branch reform. On the other hand, the community was seen as a controlled experiment in which profound but peaceful change might be effected without disturbing the larger social order. Massive change, according to communitarian theory, could also be gradual and harmonious if determined by the model.

Perfectionist religious and moral reform shaded into communitarianism, in the case of a number of social reformers, with the recognition that the conversion of the individual was a necessary preparation for and logically required communal experimentation. Such was John Humphrey Noyes' observation that in the years after 1815 "the line of socialistic excitement lies parallel with the line of religious Revivals. . . . The Revivalists had for their one great idea the regeneration of the soul. The great idea of the Socialists was the regeneration of society, which is the soul's environment. These ideas belong together and are the complements of each other." So it seemed to Noyes' colleagues in the communitarian movement. The course from extreme individualism to communitarianism can be traced in George Ripley's decision to found Brook Farm. Trying to win Emerson to his new cause, he explained that his own personal tastes and habits would have led him away from plans and projects. "I have a passion for being independent of the world, and of every man in it. This I could do easily on the estate which is now offered. . . . I should have a city of God, on a small scale of my own. . . . But I feel bound to sacrifice this private feeling, in the hope of the great social good." That good Ripley had no difficulty in defining in perfectionist terms:

. . . to insure a more natural union between intellectual and manual labor than now exists; to combine the thinker and the worker, as far as possible, in the same individual; to guarantee the highest mental freedom, by providing all with labor, adapted to their tastes and talents, and securing to them the fruits of their industry; to do away with the necessity of menial services, by opening the benefits of education and the profits of labor to all; and thus to prepare a society of liberal, intelligent, and cultivated persons, whose relations with each other would permit a more simple and wholesome life, than can be led amidst the pressure of our competitive institutions.

However varied their actual experiences with social planning, all the communitarians echoed Ripley's call for translating perfectionism into concerted action and adapting the ethics of individualism to larger social units. Just as the moral reformers appealed to right conduct and conscience in individuals the communitarians sought to erect models of a collective conscience to educate Americans. Seen in this light, the communitarian faith in the model was simply an extension of the belief in individual perfectibility. Even the sense of urgency characterizing moral reform was carried over into the communities where a millennial expectation flourished. The time to launch their projects, the social planners believed, was the immediate present when habits and attitudes were still fluid, before entrenched institutions had hardened the American heart and closed the American mind. To wait for a full quota of useful members or an adequate supply of funds might be to miss the single chance to make the country perfect. The whole future of America seemed to them to hinge on the fate of their enterprises.

Some of the projects were joint-stock corporations betraying a middle-class origin; others were strictly communistic. Some, like the Shaker communities, were pietistic and rigid; others, like Oneida and Hopedale, open and frankly experimental. Communitarians took a lively interest in each others' projects and often joined one or another of them for a season before moving on to try utopia on their own. The division between religious and secular attempts was by no means absolute: both types of communities advertised an essentially religious brand of perfectionism. Nor was economic organization always an accurate means of distinguishing the various experiments, most of which were subjected to periodic constitutional overhauling and frequent readjustment, now in the direction of social controls and now toward relaxation of those controls in favor of individual initiative.

The most striking characteristic of the communitarian movement was not its apparent diversity but the fundamental similarity of educational purpose. The common denominator or "main idea" Noyes correctly identified as *"the enlargement of home—the extension of family union beyond the little man-and-wife circle to large corporations."* Communities as different as Fruitlands and Hopedale, Brook Farm and Northampton, Owenite villages and Fourier phalanstaeries were all, in one way or another, attempting to expand and apply self-culture to groups. Thus the problem for radical communitarians was to solve the conflict between the family and society. In commenting on the failure of the Brook Farmers to achieve a real community, Charles Lane, Alcott's associate at Fruitlands, identified what he considered the basic social question of the day—"whether the existence of the marital family is compatible with that of the universal family, which the term 'Community' signifies." A few of the communitarians, recognizing this conflict, attempted to solve it by changing or destroying the institution of marriage. For the most part, the perfectionist communitarians shied away from any such radical alteration of the family structure and instead sought a law of association by which the apparently antagonistic claims of private and universal love could be harmonized. Once this law was known and explained, they believed, then the perfect society was possible—a self-adjusting mechanism constructed in accordance with their recently discovered law of human nature.

Inevitably communitarianism developed a "science of society," either the elaborate social mathematics of Fourier or the constitutional mechanics of native American perfectionists. The appeal of the blueprint grew overwhelming: in one way or another almost all the communitarians succumbed to the myth of the mathematically precise arrangement, searching for the perfect number or the exact size, plotting the precise disposition of working forces and living space, and combining these estimates in a formula which would ensure perfect concord. The appeal of Fourierism stemmed from its promise to reconcile productive industry with "passional attractions." "Could this be done," John Sullivan Dwight announced, "the word 'necessity' would acquire an altogether new and pleasanter meaning; the outward necessity and the inward prompting for every human being would be one and identical, and his life a living harmony." Association fostered true individuality which, in turn, guaranteed collective accord. In an intricate calculation involving ascending and descending wings and a central point of social balance where attractions equalled destinies the converts to Fourierism contrived a utopian alternative to politics. The phalanx represented a self-perpetuating system for neutralizing conflict and ensuring perfection. The power factor—politics—had been dropped out; attraction alone provided the stimulants necessary to production and progress. Here in the mathematical model was the culmination of the "peaceful revolution" which was to transform America.

The communitarian experiments in effect were anti-institutional institutions. In abandoning political and religious institutions the communitarians were driven to create perfect societies of their own which conformed to their perfectionist definition of the free individual. Their communities veered erratically between the poles of anarchism and collectivism as they hunted feverishly for a way of eliminating friction without employing coercion, sure that once they had found it, they could apply it in a federation of model societies throughout the country. In a limited sense, perhaps, their plans constituted an escape from urban complexity and the loneliness of alienation. But beneath the nostalgia there lay a vital reform impulse and a driving determination to make American society over through the power of education.

The immediate causes of the collapse of the communities ranged from loss of funds and mismanagement to declining interest and disillusionment with imperfect human material. Behind these apparent reasons, however, stood the real cause in the person of the perfectionist self, Margaret Fuller's "mountainous me," that proved too powerful a disruptive force for even the anti-institutional institutions it had created. It was the perfectionist ego which allowed the communitarian reformers to be almost wholly nonselective in recruiting their membership and to put their trust in the operation of an atomistic general will. Constitution-making and paper bonds, as it turned out, were not enough to unite divine egoists in a satisfactory system for the free expression of the personality. Perfectionist individualism did not make the consociate family. The result by the 1850s was a profound disillusionment with the principle of association which, significantly, coincided with the political crisis over slavery. Adin Ballou, his experiment at Hopedale in shambles, summarized the perfectionist mood of despair when he added that "few people are near enough right in heart, head and habits to live in close social intimacy." Another way would have to be found to carry divine principles into social arrangements, one that took proper account of the individual.

The collapse of the communitarian movement in the 1850s left a vacuum in social reform which was filled by the slavery crisis. At first their failure to consolidate alternative social and educational institutions threw the reformers back on their old perfectionist individualism for support. It was hardly fortuitous that Garrison, Mann, Thoreau, Howe, Parker, Channing, Ripley and Emerson himself responded to John Brown's raid with a defense of the liberated conscience. But slavery, as a denial of freedom and individual responsibility, had to be destroyed by institutional forces which could be made to sustain these values. The antislavery cause during the secession crisis and throughout the Civil War offered reformers an escape from alienation by providing a new identity with the very political institutions which they had so vigorously assailed.

The effects of the Civil War as an intellectual counterrevolution were felt both in a revival of institutions and a renewal of an organic theory of society. The war brought with it a widespread reaction against the seeming sentimentality and illusions of perfectionism. It saw the establishment of new organizations like the Sanitary and the Christian Commissions run on principles of efficiency and professionalism totally alien to perfectionist methods. Accompanying the wartime revival of institutions was a theological reorientation directed by Horace Bushnell and other conservative churchmen whose longstanding opposition to perfectionism seemed justified by the war. The extreme individualism of the ante-bellum reformers was swallowed up in a Northern war effort that made private conscience less important than saving the Union. Some of the abolitionists actually substituted national unity for freedom for the slave as the primary war aim. Those reformers who contributed to the war effort through the Sanitary Commission or the Christian Commission found a new sense of order and efficiency indispensable. Older perfectionists, like Dorothea Dix, unable to adjust to new demands, found their usefulness drastically confined. Young Emersonians returned from combat convinced that professionalism, discipline and subordination, dubious virtues by perfectionist standards, were essential in a healthy society. A new emphasis on leadership and performance was replacing the benevolent amateurism of the perfectionists.

Popular education and ethical agitation continued to hold the post-war stage, but the setting for them had changed. The three principal theorists of social reform in post-war industrial America—Henry George, Henry Demarest Lloyd and Edward Bellamy—denounced class conflict, mini-mized the importance of purely political reform, and, like their perfec-tionist precursors, called for moral revolution. The moral revolution which they demanded, however, was not the work of individuals in whom social responsibility developed as a by-product of· self-discovery but the ethical revival of an entire society made possible by the natural development of social forces. Their organic view of society required new theories of personality and new concepts of role-playing, definitions which appeared variously in George's law of integration, Lloyd's religion of love, and Bellamy's economy of happiness. And whereas Nemesis in the perfectionist imagination had assumed the shape of personal guilt and estrangement from a pre-established divine order, for the post-war reformers it took on the social dimensions of a terrifying relapse into barbarism. Finally, the attitudes of the reformers toward individualism itself began to change as Darwinism with the aid of a false analogy twisted the prewar doctrine of self-reliance into a weapon against reform. It was to protest against a Darwinian psychology of individual isolation that Lloyd wrote his final chapter of *Wealth Against Commonwealth,* declaring that the regeneration of the individual was only a half-truth and that "the reorganization of the society which he makes and which makes him is the other half."

We can become individual only by submitting to be bound to others. We extend our freedom only by finding new laws to obey. . . . The isolated man is a mere rudiment of an individual. But he who has become citizen, neighbor, friend, brother, son, husband, father, fellow-member, in one is just so many times individualized.

Lloyd's plea for a new individualism could also be read as an obituary for perfectionist romantic reform.

SELECTIVE
BIBLIOGRAPHY

The literature on ante-bellum reform is so vast that only a few of the most useful and important titles can be listed here, to supplement the more general interpretations mentioned in the Introduction. The most recent and thorough bibliography of ante-bellum reform can be found in Louis Filler, *The Crusade Against Slavery, 1830–1860* (1960; paperback*). A nearly exhaustive list of printed primary sources on antislavery is Dwight L. Dumond, *Antislavery Bibliography* (1961).

Students interested in the religious and ideological background of social consciousness would do well to begin with such classic works as Karl Mannheim, *Ideology and Utopia* (1936; paperback); Ernst Troeltsch, *The Social Teaching of the Christian Churches* (2 vols., 1931; paperback), as well as more recent studies such as Norman Cohn, *The Pursuit of the Millennium* (1957; paperback) and David Owen, *English Philanthropy, 1660–1960* (1964).

Since Protestant perfectionism, revivalism, and millennialism are so cru-

* Dates in parentheses are original publication dates. The word "paperback" indicates that the work is now available in paperback. If only the word "paperback" appears after the work cited, its original publication was in paper.

cial for an understanding of American reform, it is enlightening to examine the origins of Quaker benevolence in Sydney V. James, *A People Among Peoples: Quaker Benevolence in Eighteenth-Century America* (1963); the meanings of millennialism in H. Richard Niebuhr, *The Kingdom of God in America* (1937; paperback), and in Charles L. Sanford, *The Quest for Paradise: Europe and the American Moral Imagination* (1961); and the character of evangelical revivalism in Perry Miller, *The Life of the Mind in America from the Revolution to the Civil War* (1965), in William G. McLoughlin, *Modern Revivalism* (1959), and in Timothy L. Smith, *Revivalism and Social Reform in Mid-19th Century America* (1957).

The emergence of the missionary spirit and the religious response to various social issues are well covered by Oliver W. Elsbree, *The Rise of the Missionary Spirit in America* (1928); Clifford S. Griffin, *Their Brothers' Keepers: Moral Stewardship in the United States, 1800–1865* (1960); Charles I. Foster, *An Errand of Mercy: The Evangelical United Front, 1790–1837* (1960); Charles C. Cole, Jr., *The Social Ideas of the Northern Evangelists* (1954); and John R. Bodo, *The Protestant Clergy and Public Issues, 1812–1848* (1954).

Unfortunately, there is no satisfactory study of secular radicalism in ante-bellum America. Significant information may be gleaned from Albert Post, *Popular Free Thought in America, 1825–1850* (1943); Arthur M. Schlesinger, Jr., *The Age of Jackson* (1945; paperback); L. L. and J. Bernard, *The Origins of American Sociology* (1943); David M. Ludlum, *Social Ferment in Vermont, 1791–1850* (1939); John R. Commons, *History of Labour in the United States, Vol. I* (1918); and from the anthologies, *Social Theories of Jacksonian Democracy*, ed. Joseph L. Blau (1947; paperback), and *Patterns of Anarchy*, eds. Leonard I. Krimerman and Lewis Perry (paperback).

A helpful guide to names, concepts, and movements is Louis Filler, *Dictionary of American Social Reform* (1963). Although no serious student should rely on secondary sources alone, few primary sources have been collected or reprinted. A brief but valuable selection may be found in *The Era of Reform, 1830–1860*, ed. Henry Steele Commager (paperback). For a wider coverage of abolitionist writings one may turn to *The Abolitionists*, ed. Louis Ruchames (1963) and *The Antislavery Argument*, eds. William H. Pease and Jane Pease (paperback). The *Letters of Theodore Dwight Weld, Angelina Grimké Weld, and Sarah Grimké, 1822–1844*, eds. Gilbert H. Barnes and Dwight L. Dumond (2 vols., 1934, reprinted

1965), are indispensable for serious study of abolitionism and reveal much about related reforms. This is also true of the *Letters of James Gillespie Birney, 1831–1857*, ed. Dwight L. Dumond (2 vols., 1938). The *Autobiography of Lyman Beecher*, ed. Barbara M. Cross (2 vols., 1961) sheds much light on the religious sources of temperance and other reforms. Timothy S. Arthur's classic temperance drama, *Ten Nights in a Bar-Room* (1964) is now fortunately available in a modern edition.

The standard and comprehensive work on the temperance movement is still John A. Krout, *The Origins of Prohibition* (1925). The most imaginative study of penal reform is W. David Lewis, *From Newgate to Dannemora: the Rise of the Penitentiary in New York, 1796–1848* (1965). A more general treatment of the subject is Orlando F. Lewis, *The Development of American Prisons and Prison Customs, 1776–1845* (1922). A survey of a related reform movement is David Brion Davis, "The Movement to Abolish Capital Punishment in America, 1787–1860," *American Historical Review* (1957).

The best introduction to educational reform is Rush Welter, *Popular Education and Democratic Thought* (1962). The problem of poverty is explored in Robert H. Bremner, *From the Depths: the Discovery of Poverty in the United States* (1956); Bremner, *American Philanthropy* (1960; paperback); Roy Lubove, "The New York Association for Improving the Condition of the Poor: the Formative Years," *New York Historical Society Quarterly* (1959); and Blanche D. Coll, "The Baltimore Society for the Prevention of Pauperism, 1820–1860," *American Historical Review* (1955). Eleanor Flexner, *A Century of Struggle: the Woman's Rights Movement in the United States* (1959), is a good general survey of the woman's rights movement, although it is still necessary to turn for detail to Elizabeth Cady Stanton, *et. al., History of Woman Suffrage* (1881). The best introduction to utopianism and communitarianism are the essays in *Socialism and American Life*, eds. Donald Egbert and Stow Persons (1952). The Owenite phase of communitarianism is imaginatively dealt with by Arthur Bestor, *Backwoods Utopias* (1950). A more recent study is William Wilson, *The Angel and the Serpent* (1964). John Humphrey Noyes, *History of American Socialisms* (1870) is still valuable for its perceptive insights. Noyes himself is studied in Robert Parker, *A Yankee Saint: John Humphrey Noyes and the Oneida Community* (1935). The standard work on early American pacifism is Merle Curti, *The American Peace Crusade* (1929).

No reform movement has drawn so much attention or aroused so much controversy as the abolitionist crusade. The sources of antislavery thought have been analyzed in David Brion Davis, *The Problem of Slavery in Western Culture* (1966). Two modern and comprehensive surveys of the American antislavery movement are Dwight L. Dumond, *Antislavery* (1961), and Louis Filler, *The Crusade Against Slavery, 1830–1860* (1960; paperback). New departures for studying the subject are suggested by the essays in *The Antislavery Vanguard,* ed. Martin Duberman (1965), and by such recent monographs as Larry Gara, *The Liberty Line: the Legend of the Underground Railroad* (1961); Donald G. Mathews, *Slavery and Methodism: a Chapter in American Morality, 1780–1845* (1965); and James M. McPherson, *The Struggle for Equality: Abolitionists and the Negro in the Civil War and Reconstruction* (1964).

Some of the most valuable material on ante-bellum reform is to be found in biographies of reformers. Among the most useful are John L. Thomas, *The Liberator: William Lloyd Garrison* (1963); Walter M. Merrill, *Against Wind and Tide: a Biography of William Lloyd Garrison* (1963); Harold Schwartz, *Samuel Gridley Howe* (1956); Otelia Cromwell, *Lucretia Mott* (1958); Frank Otto Gatell, *John Gorham Palfrey and the New England Conscience* (1963); Martin Duberman, *Charles Francis Adams* (1962); Betty Fladeland, *James Gillespie Birney* (1955); Ralph V. Harlow, *Gerrit Smith, Philanthropist and Reformer* (1939); Henry Steele Commager, *Theodore Parker* (1936; paperback); William R. Waterman, *Frances Wright* (1924); Benjamin Quarles, *Frederick Douglass* (1948); Irving H. Bartlett, *Wendell Phillips: Brahmin Rebel* (1961); and Helen E. Marshall, *Dorothea Dix, Forgotten Samaritan* (1937).